MW00569003

The Complete AMA Guide to Management Development

The Complete
AMA Guide
to Management
Development

TRAINING
EDUCATION
DEVELOPMENT

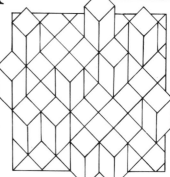

William J. Rothwell & H.C. Kazanas

amacom

American Management Association

New York • Atlanta • Boston • Chicago • Kansas City • San Francisco • Washington, D.C.
Brussels • Toronto • Mexico City

*This publication is designed to provide accurate and authoritative
information in regard to the subject matter covered. It is sold with
the understanding that the publisher is not engaged in rendering
legal, accounting, or other professional service. If legal advice or
other expert assistance is required, the services of a competent
professional person should be sought.*

Library of Congress Cataloging-in-Publication Data

Rothwell, William J., 1951–
    The complete AMA guide to management development:
training, education, development / William J. Rothwell,
H. C. Kazanas.
        p. cm.
    Includes bibliographical references and index.
    ISBN 0-8144-5079-2
    1. Executives—Training of—United States. 2. Supervisors
—Training of—United States. 3. Management—Study and
teaching—United States. 4. Supervision of employees—Study
and teaching—United States. I. Kazanas, H. C. II. Title.
HD30.42.U5R68 1993
658.4'07124—dc20   92-42962
                                                                              CIP

Printing number

10 9 8 7 6 5 4 3 2 1

To
Marcelina Rothwell
and
Nuria Kazanas

Contents

List of Exhibits

Preface

Doomsayers claim that the United States is in big economic trouble. Several trends are commonly cited to back up this claim: swelling government deficits, increasing foreign competition, declining investments in research and development, falling rates of labor productivity growth, and pervasive layoffs. Some believe that these and other trends are evidence that the United States is losing its world-class standing in comparison to nations of the Pacific Rim and the European Economic Community.

It is popular in the United States to hunt for scapegoats for these problems. Unions and government are frequently criticized for contributing to the problems. Much blame is also placed on American management. While few observers fix sole responsibility for the problems on management alone, management does stand accused of numerous sins. For example:

- A short-term focus
- Inattention to operations, quality, and human factors
- Excessive analysis
- Excessive attention to legal affairs
- Resistance to change and to risk taking
- Excessive executive compensation
- Insufficient training

Foreign observers claim that U.S. managers devote too much time to planning layoffs and searching for quick fixes and too little time to developing new products, marketing new services, improving customer service, cultivating quality improvement, or making long-term investments in their people or businesses.

If there is any merit to these charges, the response should be corrective action rather than personal defensiveness or national protectionism. One such step is to improve ways by which management employees are trained, educated, and developed in organizational settings. This book is intended to be a tool for that purpose.

The Crucial Importance of Management's Role

Management plays the key leadership role in planning and deploying organizational assets. Management decisions dramatically affect the lives of other people. Indeed, management employees make strategic decisions about layoffs, mergers, acquisitions, expansions, union negotiations, and bankruptcy filings. They also make tactical decisions about work-group structure and individual pay increases, promotions, demotions, dismissals, and transfers. Present trends point toward less arbitrary management decision making in an effort to improve productivity and product or service quality through increased employee involvement. Nonetheless, management continues to play a key leadership role, whether efforts are focused on authoritatively directing the work of others or on participatively guiding it.

The Purpose of This Book

Many people we know have been asked to establish, maintain, renew, or evaluate a Management Development (MD) program. Rarely do they know where to turn for help. They invent their own job descriptions and struggle to satisfy the (sometimes conflicting) preferences of executives, managers, and supervisors who see the need for a planned MD program but do not know how to establish and operate one successfully.

Many books and articles have been written about MD. Among the best for future reference:

> Bittel, Lester. *The Complete Guide to Supervisory Training and Development*. Reading, Mass.: Addison-Wesley, 1987.

> London, Manuel. *Developing Managers: A Guide to Motivating and Preparing People for Successful Managerial Careers*. San Francisco: Jossey-Bass, 1985.

> Margerison, Charles. *Making Management Development Work: Achieving Success in the Nineties*. London: McGraw-Hill, 1991.

> Nilsson, William. *Achieving Strategic Goals Through Executive Development*. Reading, Mass.: Addison-Wesley, 1987.

Another immensely helpful tool is *The Bibliography of Management Development Literature*, by Ann Brooks, Judith Ottoson, and Sally Vernon (Alexandria, Va.: The American Society for Training and Development, 1992).

However, few books provide practical guidance for those starting up or renewing a planned MD program. We wrote this book to serve as a practical, how-to-do-it manual for establishing and administering a planned MD program geared to addressing the training, education, and development needs of supervisors, managers, and executives. Its purpose is to slake the growing thirst for information about successful MD programs.

You may have heard already that many large organizations have enjoyed immense success with planned MD programs. Small organizations have also benefited from them, although their triumphs are usually less widely publicized. Many of you may have already worked in or visited high-performing organizations in which MD programs, while not highly visible, play important roles in strategic and tactical decisions and actions.

Whatever your interests, this book is intended to give you useful information on how to plan, establish, manage, operate, and evaluate a planned MD program in an organizational setting.

Sources of Information

As we took up the task of writing this book, we decided that it was important to base it on state-of-the-art practices. To that end, we consulted several major sources of information:

1. *MD professionals.* As an initial step in researching this book, we surveyed MD professionals in early 1992 about practices in their organizations. The survey results are published in this book for the first time.
2. *Surveys.* We have also included in this book selected results from several surveys on MD previously published by others, as well as the results of earlier surveys we have conducted.
3. *Literature.* We conducted an exhaustive literature search on MD. We provide key references throughout the book so that you can delve further into issues of special interest to you.
4. *Firsthand experience.* The first author is an experienced MD professional. The fruits of his experience are reflected in this book.

The Organization of This Book

The Complete AMA Guide to Management Development is written primarily for MD specialists, human resources development (HRD) specialists, and human resources managers. But the book also contains valuable information for chief executive officers, chief operating officers, general managers, university faculty members who do consulting on MD, and other people who bear responsibilities for developing management talent.

The book is divided into four major parts. *Part I*, consisting of only one chapter, serves as the book's prologue. In it we provide background information about MD. Specifically, we define a planned MD program, distinguish between training, education, and development, explain the purposes of a planned MD program, describe the scope of MD activities in the United States, distinguish between planned and unplanned MD efforts, summarize major barriers to a planned MD program, and explain ways to overcome those major barriers.

Part II, consisting of chapters 2 through 5, focuses on planning and designing MD programs.

Chapter 2 describes the initial steps in the start-up of most planned MD programs. These include:

› Setting up a committee
› Determining the purpose of a planned MD program
› Establishing program goals and objectives
› Targeting groups to be served
› Preparing a program policy and philosophy
› Preparing a flexible action plan to guide program start-up
› Establishing a regular schedule to review program results

In Chapter 3 we turn to identifying MD needs. This chapter is important because MD is carried out to meet individual, group, and organizational learning needs and is designed to improve individual, group, and organizational performance. We distinguish between learning and nonlearning needs and explain when corrective actions other than training, education, or development are warranted. The most important part of this chapter focuses on methods for collecting and analyzing information about MD learning needs.

In Chapter 4 we describe how to establish a long-term learning plan to meet predictable learning needs. We call such a plan a *curriculum*. In the chapter we explain how a comprehensive MD curriculum is designed and summarize different ways to design an MD curriculum.

Chapter 5 poses the following questions:

› Where should the MD function be positioned in the organization's reporting structure?
› What rewards or incentives should be offered to management to encourage members to accept responsibility for developing themselves and those reporting to them?

‣ What kind of leader should direct the planned MD program?
‣ How should the program leader be recruited, selected, and oriented?
‣ How should internal staff members and external vendors be selected, oriented, and trained?
‣ How should planned MD activities be scheduled?
‣ How should budgeting be handled?
‣ What records of MD activities should be kept?
‣ How should MD program activities be publicized?

Part III, consisting of chapters 6 through 9, describes formal, informal, and special MD methods. We use the term *method* to mean an organized way by which to meet learning needs and thus to bring about individual or group change through learning. *Formal methods* are planned, and are usually focused on meeting group learning needs. *Informal methods* are not planned, and are usually used spontaneously to meet individual needs. *Special methods* are on the cutting edge of practice, and sometimes can be controversial.

Chapter 6 provides two models to help select appropriate MD methods to meet identified needs.

Chapter 7 focuses on planning and using formal MD methods. These methods include succession planning programs, management career planning programs, internal group training programs, external group training programs, external education programs, job rotation programs, and position assignment programs.

Chapter 8 discusses planning and using informal MD methods, such as on-the-job management training, on-the-job management coaching, management mentoring or sponsorship, management self-development, and management self-study.

Chapter 9 focuses on planning and using special MD methods, including adventure learning, New Age Training (NAT), and action learning.

Part IV consists of Chapter 10 only. In this chapter we define evaluation. We also describe different types of evaluation, key obstacles to evaluation, methods for overcoming those obstacles, and a step-by-step approach for conducting a program evaluation.

Finally, the Epilogue focuses on three special issues affecting MD: globalism, downsizing, and team-based management. Our aim in this final chapter is not to address these issues exhaustively but rather to explain the issues and provide general guidance about reviewing and revamping MD programs in light of the recent, pervasive influence of these issues.

Acknowledgments

No book is the work of a single person. This book is no different. While the authors must accept complete responsibility for the final product, we do appreciate the comments made by those who looked over an earlier draft of the manuscript. The authors therefore express thanks to the following people (in alphabetical order):

Bill Bartley, Associate, Education and Development, Human Resource Division, Growmark Inc., Bloomington, Illinois.

Constance Holmes, Director of Management Development and Practice Management and Practice Services, The Arthur Andersen Worldwide Organization, St. Charles, Illinois.

John Ryan, former Director, Human Resource Development and Human Resource Planning, Country Companies, Bloomington, Illinois.

Jerry Wright, Manager, Caterpillar Training Institute, Caterpillar Inc., Peoria, Illinois.

Part I

Management Development: Background Issues

INTRODUCTION TO PART I

Part I provides background information about Management Development (MD). We introduce Chapter 1 with a realistic case study. Planned MD programs often originate from efforts to handle an isolated crisis like the one dramatized in the case study. In Chapter 1 we also:

- Define a planned MD program.
- Distinguish between management training, education, and development.
- Explain the reasons for a planned MD program.
- Describe the scope of MD activities in the United States.
- Distinguish between planned and unplanned MD efforts.
- Summarize major barriers to a planned MD program.
- Explain ways to overcome those barriers.

Chapter 1

Defining Management Development

Josephine Irons is worried. As executive in charge of a large division in a prominent, well-known, and financially stable bank, she has just received word that Leah Smith, one of her most experienced supervisors, will retire in three months. Leah, a twenty-three-year bank veteran, supervises a critically important work unit of thirty employees.

The announcement of Leah's retirement does not come as a complete surprise to Josephine, since the bank recently extended a generous early retirement offer to long-service employees. Josephine has known for six months that Leah would qualify, but Leah did not indicate until recently that she would accept the offer. Amid painful cost-cutting and downsizing efforts, Josephine's division has become so shorthanded that she feels lucky to be getting the work out at all. In some areas her employees have been working 600 hours of overtime annually to hold down staffing needs and employee benefit expenses.

Leah is not the only supervisor Josephine will be losing to retirement. But Leah's departure poses the greatest problem because Josephine has not prepared anyone to assume Leah's important, technically oriented, and tough-to-master position.

Josephine can fill the vacancy created by Leah's retirement in several ways.

One way is to promote from within, gambling that someone from Leah's work unit can master the job in a reasonable time. Should she take this approach, she knows she can always ask Leah about which employees have the best potential for success in the job. Promotion from within is the bank's time-honored method of filling supervisory openings; in fact, many employees expect a new supervisor to be promoted from within the work unit, and some would be upset if the vacancy were filled in any other way. Unfortunately, Josephine is not convinced that anyone in the work unit is capable of mastering Leah's duties.

Josephine has other ways to fill the vacancy. She can ask other executives in the bank to nominate employees with management potential from their departments. If chosen, such a candidate would be promoted or would receive a lateral transfer to Leah's position. But Josephine knows that moving a worker from another area would touch off moves all over the bank as a replacement was sought for each vacated position, a problem complicated by the early retirement offer. Nor would it be an easy task to convince other managers to give up a trained worker—even for a promotion. During downsizing, some managers hoard workers so that they need not justify replacements or take precious time to train newcomers. To make matters worse, the bank has no centralized skill or staffing inventory and has temporarily suspended job posting for supervisory positions. Josephine's efforts to recruit a qualified candidate inside the bank would thus be complicated by lack of information, and the process could prove to be time-consuming and difficult.

Josephine is also aware that she could hire a supervisor from outside the bank. That option, Josephine worries, is a minefield of potentially explosive problems because outsiders have no established track record inside the bank. In any case, Josephine would clearly want someone with banking industry experience, preferably someone who has worked at another bank in a position similar to Leah's. Although such people exist, they are rare. Recruiting one would not be easy. Even if a suitable candidate could be located and hired, he or she would lack job- and organization-specific knowledge about *this* bank's unique procedures and culture. A new hire, no matter how experienced, would also lack a social support network to ease the transition from outside. Unexpected turnover in Leah's position is an unpleasant prospect for Josephine. But the bank does not have a good record of retaining those hired from outside to fill supervisory positions.

A fourth way to deal with the vacancy, Josephine knows, is to restructure the division to eliminate the need for Leah's position. If that move resulted in reduced staffing, it would undoubtedly please the CEO, Josephine's boss, because it would reduce the bank's operating expenses. But Leah's duties would still have to be shifted somewhere—probably to other supervisors—and Josephine feels that they have already been saddled with too much work. Through their facial expressions and occasional comments, they show evidence that stress and overtime are taking their toll. Josephine is reluctant to push them any harder for fear that several might quit. That would only intensify her staffing problems.

A fifth way to deal with the vacancy is to eliminate the need for any supervisor by making Leah's unit a self-directed work group. If Josephine were to choose that option, she would redistribute Leah's work to unit employees. Josephine would like to experiment with this promising, popular new approach designed to increase employee involvement. But she realizes that employees must first be trained in supervising themselves. Three months is not long enough to introduce such a radical change to the work unit's culture, which (like that of the bank) has long been accustomed to a top-down approach to decision making. The workers, Josephine knows, are presently ill prepared to accept such a radical shift of responsibility. (However, Josephine will bear this idea in mind for the future and perhaps introduce it at a later time.)

Despite all these possibilities—and Josephine can think of others as well—she remains unsure of what to do about the pending vacancy in Leah's position. But she knows she is not alone in facing a problem of this kind. The early retirement offer affects many other people and positions. Perhaps it is time, Josephine reasons, to suggest that the bank introduce a planned Management Development (MD) program. While starting such a program now will not help solve the immediate problem created by Leah's early retirement, it may help avoid similar staffing problems in the future. Moreover, Josephine remembers she was not all that happy about the "sink-or-swim" approach she experienced when she entered management. She feels that there must be better ways to train, educate, and develop people—and she resolves to find out what they are.

Defining a Planned MD Program

As defined in this book, a *planned Management Development (MD) program* means "a systematic effort to train, educate, and develop individuals who aspire to—or are already functioning in—the management ranks. It is conducted on the job or off the job to meet individual, group, and organizational learning needs and to improve individual, group, and organizational performance."

A planned MD program thus serves many purposes. One is to help individuals perform effectively and efficiently in their current jobs, since good performance in the current job is usually a prerequisite to advancement to other jobs. At least one other purpose is to prepare to meet predictable replacement needs for an organization's management talent, an issue dramatically illustrated by the case study introducing this chapter.

In this definition, *planned* means that MD should be thought out ahead of time. *Management Development,* in an often cited but controversial* definition, is "an attempt to improve managerial effectiveness through a planned and deliberate learning process."[1]

Systematic means that a planned MD program should be:

- Based on a careful review of management learning needs
- Designed and delivered to meet those needs
- Evaluated for results

One way to meet learning needs is to train individuals so that their knowledge and skills will match current or future management job requirements and organizational needs. In this sense, *training* means "learning, provided by employers to employees, that is related to employees' current jobs."[2] Management training narrows or closes the gap between what individuals already know or do and what they must know or do to perform competently.

A second way to meet learning needs is to educate individuals to prepare them for eventual advancement or increased responsibility.

*Controversial because management employees may be developed using unplanned as well as planned methods.

Education means "learning focused on a future job."[3] Management education narrows or closes the gap between what individuals already know or do and what they must know or do to qualify for higher-level, or more technical, responsibilities.

A third way to meet learning needs is to develop people. *Development* means "offering learning experiences, provided by employer to employees, that are not job-related"[4] or "changing attitudes or values."[5] In this narrow sense, development refers to opportunities offered to individuals so they can come up with new ideas. Development is just one way to meet learning needs and should not be confused with Management Development, which encompasses management training, education, and development.

Individuals are often the primary targets for change in a planned MD program. In one sense, all development is self-development. But because management employees exert profound influence over others, their individual development greatly influences group or organization performance. For this reason, then, a planned MD program is one way in which to effect culture change in an organization, division, department, work group, or team.

By *on-* or *off-the-job*, we mean that management employees can be developed in more than one setting. Off-the-job MD experiences usually afford opportunities to interact with others; on-the-job MD furnishes opportunities to learn while doing.

By *aspire to—or are already functioning in—the management ranks*, we mean that a planned MD program can effect change in individuals already shouldering management responsibilities, those who would like to qualify for management positions, and those who may exercise management responsibilities during the course of their everyday activities but whose jobs are not otherwise considered part of management.

By *conducted to meet individual, group, or organizational learning needs*, we mean that a planned MD program can serve many purposes. It benefits the following categories of people:

- *Individuals*, by helping them master job requirements
- *Groups*, by helping management employees learn how to exert effective leadership skills and to build teamwork
- *Organizations*, by giving management employees the skills they need to lead their organizations through a fiercely competitive business environment

For these reasons, a planned MD program is viewed by some supporters as a tool for changing culture, the unspoken roles and norms that guide people's behavior in organizational settings.

By *improve individual, group, and organizational performance*, we mean that important outcomes sought from a planned MD program are increased efficiency (*doing things right*) and increased effectiveness (*doing the right things*).

Reasons for a Planned MD Program

Why do organizations sponsor planned MD programs? What are the chief reasons that they exist?

To answer these questions, we mailed a questionnaire to 500 randomly selected MD specialists in January 1992. All survey respondents were members of the Management Development Professional Practice Area of the American Society for Training and Development (ASTD). In all, eighty-eight MD specialists responded. That made the survey response rate 17.6 percent—respectable for a twenty-page survey. Exhibit 1-1 presents demographic information about the respondents' industries; Exhibit 1-2 presents demographic information about the size of the respondents' organizations; Exhibit 1-3 presents information about the respondents' jobs within their organizations; and, Exhibit 1-4 lists the chief reasons for an organization to sponsor a planned MD program. An explanation of each reason is described in the following paragraphs.

Reason 1: Building Skills in People Management

Our survey respondents indicated that the single most important reason for sponsoring a planned MD program is "to build skills in 'people management' for individuals who have never received formal instruction on supervision or management." That reason underscores the increasingly critical nature of interpersonal, or "people," skills for achieving organizational success.

After all, people are the primary assets in an information society. Financial assets can be acquired through borrowing or through mergers, acquisitions, or takeovers. Technological assets can be purchased. But the skills of people must usually be cultivated over time.

Reason 2: Developing Individuals for More Responsibility

It is a fundamental fact that the education and experience necessary for individuals to qualify for entry-level jobs are not identical to those necessary for advancement. In many technical specialties—such as engineering, accounting, and data processing—people are hired at

Exhibit 1-1. Demographic information from 1992 survey on management development: industries.

	Organizations With a Planned MD Program (total respondents N = 63)		Organizations Without a Planned MD Program (total respondents N = 23)*	
	Frequencies	Percentages	Frequencies	Percentages
Manufacturing	16	25.40	4	17.39
Transportation/ communication/ electric/gas	9	14.29	2	8.69
Retail trade	7	11.11	0	0
Finance/insurance/real estate	13	20.63	5	21.75
Health care	11	17.46	2	8.69
Government/armed forces	2	3.17	4	17.39
Other services	1	1.59	0	0
Other industries**	3	4.76	6	26.09
No response	1	1.73	0	0

*Not all respondents chose to answer this question.
**Other industries included hospitality, commercial printing, a nonprofit youth agency, a nonprofit service organization, a family planning organization, and a nonprofit homeless shelter.
Source: William J. Rothwell and H. C. Kazanas, "Results of a 1992 Survey on Management Development Practices in the U.S." (Urbana, Ill.: Department of Vocational and Technical Education, 1992, unpublished).

entry level for their technical education and experience. But technical success does not necessarily lead to management success, and advancement beyond entry level often requires management skills. Technical specialists must learn to work with and through others to achieve results, a lesson complicated by their early training in doing work tasks by themselves and on their own initiative. Nor can they acquire the ability to work with others quickly or easily by taking one or two college courses on management or a few training courses. Courses, whether offered by a college or by a training department, serve an important purpose by providing a valuable foundation of theory, but they are seldom sufficiently organization-specific or job-specific to give participants opportunities to *observe* a principle in action, *practice* it, or *reflect* on it. More focused, structured, practical and long-term developmental experiences are often necessary to build management skills. These experiences can be provided by a planned MD program.

Exhibit 1-2. Demographic information from 1992 survey on management development: size of organizations.

Number of Employees	Organizations With a Planned MD Program (total respondents N = 63)*		Organizations Without a Planned MD Program (total respondents N = 23)*	
	Frequencies	Percentages	Frequencies	Percentages
0–99	1	1.59	3	13.04
100–249	2	3.17	3	13.04
250–499	4	6.35	6	26.09
500–1,999	16	27.40	5	21.75
2,000–4,999	15	23.81	4	17.39
5,000 or more	24	38.09	2	8.69
No response	1	1.59	0	0

*Not all respondents chose to answer this question.
Source: William J. Rothwell and H. C. Kazanas, "Results of a 1992 Survey on Management Development Practices in the U.S." (Urbana, Ill.: Department of Vocational and Technical Education, 1992, unpublished).

Reason 3: Increasing Management Productivity

Management productivity is an elusive concept. In its simplest sense, of course, it is defined and measured in precisely the same way as any employee productivity: It is a ratio of inputs to outputs or of resources used to results achieved.

The trouble with this definition is that management productivity is often only indirectly measurable. Management employees achieve their results only by working with and through others, rather than by individual effort. Hence, *management* productivity is measured by *organizational* productivity.

Accountants have long accepted this principle. They apply well-known methods of financial analysis to balance sheet and income statement information and credit or blame the organization's management for the results. They assume management is responsible for an organization's survival, success, or failure.

Another problem with the input/output method of assessing management productivity is that management does not produce unique, tangible work products. Indeed, regardless of industry, management is inherently service-oriented, focusing on customer needs and creating the environment in which employees perform their jobs. A planned MD program contributes to this service orientation by equipping manage-

Exhibit 1-3. Job titles of survey respondents.

Job Function	Organizations With a Planned MD Program (total respondents N = 63)*		Organizations Without a Planned MD Program (total respondents N = 23)*	
	Frequencies	Percentages	Frequencies	Percentages
Trainer with no supervisory responsibility	12	19.05	8	34.78
Trainer with supervisory responsibility	29	46.03	11	47.83
Other	20	31.75	4	17.39
No response	2	3.17	0	0

*Not all respondents chose to answer this question.
Source: William J. Rothwell and H. C. Kazanas, "Results of a 1992 Survey on Management Development Practices in the U.S." (Urbana, Ill.: Department of Vocational and Technical Education, 1992, unpublished).

ment employees with the knowledge and skills they need to offer these services.

Reason 4: Implementing Strategic Plans

Strategic planning is the means by which organizations prepare for competing in the present and in the future. Central to strategic success is positioning the right leaders with the right skills in the right places at the right times to achieve desired competitive results. It is this need to match the right leader to the right task that makes a planned MD program particularly interesting to top managers, who are chiefly responsible for formulating and implementing strategic plans. MD can become a means by which to identify and supply the competitive skills necessary for the survival or success of an organization.

Reason 5: Responding to Environmental Change

Organizations are open systems that depend on the external environment—suppliers, distributing wholesalers, customers, competitors, government regulators, and other stakeholders. Organizations succeed or fail depending on their ability to satisfy external stakeholders and to anticipate or react swiftly to dynamic external conditions.

A planned MD program can be a tool to supply management

Exhibit 1-4. Reasons for offering MD programs.

Order of Importance Ranked by Mean	Reasons for Sponsoring a Management Development Program	Frequency	Mean*
1	Builds skills in "people management" for individuals who have never received formal instruction on supervision or management.	63	4.33
2	Develops individuals for increased responsibility.	62	4.18
3	Increases the productivity of management employees.	63	4.11
4	Contributes to implementing the organization's strategic plan.	62	3.74
5	Improves the organization's ability to respond to environmental change.	63	3.70
6	Increases the pool of promotable management employees.	63	3.62
7	Provides general training to individuals inside the organization.	63	3.46
8	Contributes to implementing the organization's succession plans.	62	3.31
9	Improves morale of management employees.	63	3.29
10	Improves the organization's ability to respond to technological change.	61	3.28
11	Provides increased opportunities for "high-potential" workers.	63	3.24
12	Helps individuals realize their career plans within the organization.	61	3.20
13	Provides increased opportunities for women.	63	2.62
14	Provides increased opportunities for minorities.	62	2.61

Other Reason(s)
—Develops a common language in one organization.
—Meets industry-specific needs better than outside programs.
—Promotes common culture among diverse groups.
—Reduces turnover.
—Helps the organization accomplish its mission.
—Builds desired culture with identified values.
—Promotes interdepartment relations.

*1 = not at all important; 5 = very important.
Source: William J. Rothwell and H. C. Kazanas, "Results of a 1992 Survey on Management Development Practices in the U.S." (Urbana, Ill.: Department of Vocational and Technical Education, 1992, unpublished).

employees with the knowledge and skills they need to scan the environment for issues affecting their organizations, anticipating or responding as necessary.

Reason 6: Increasing the Pool of Promotable Employees

A planned MD program can help ensure an adequate supply of management talent to meet an organization's demands over time. In this sense it is particularly valuable since nearly three-fourths of all management talent in the United States is promoted from within.[6] That makes it essential to develop sufficient resources at lower levels in an organization to meet management requirements at higher levels over time.

Reason 7: Providing General Training

Management skills, once necessary only for a handpicked elite, are becoming more closely integrated with the daily work of nonmanagement employees. Over one-fourth of all organizations in North America are experimenting with self-directed work teams.[7] Increasingly, then, employees are expected to be self-managing. Employees need to master management principles if they are to do their jobs more effectively and with less intrusive overt or direct supervision. A planned MD program can be a means by which to build the management skills of everyone and thereby diffuse those skills throughout organizations.

Reason 8: Implementing Succession Plans

A planned MD program is a tool for implementing succession plans to ensure the orderly replacement of management talent. A succession plan addresses such questions as: (1) Who will replace a key executive in the event of sudden death, disability, or other loss? (2) How can successors be prepared to assume the responsibilities of key positions permanently or temporarily? A planned MD program helps answer these questions and address these issues.

Reason 9: Improving Management Morale

Individuals experience all kinds of feelings about their employment situations. They have feelings about their jobs, their immediate organizational superiors, the organization for which they work, their chances for advancement, and other issues. The term *morale* is used to describe a group's level of job satisfaction.

The relationship between work performance and individual job satisfaction or group morale has long been investigated, but so far, no strong correlation between them has been shown.[8] However, there is a correlation between voluntary staff turnover and individual job satisfaction and group morale. In other words, people do not have to be happy or pleased with their jobs to perform competently. But if they become dissatisfied and if alternative job opportunities become available, they will not long remain tied to a work environment where they feel dissatisfied.

Individual job satisfaction, group morale, and work performance are complex subjects. They are influenced by many factors. In recent years, evidence has surfaced to suggest that management employees—particularly those in middle management—are increasingly dissatisfied, experiencing lower morale than has been traditional at that level. Nor should that trend be too surprising. American corporations, weathering storms of mergers, acquisitions, takeovers, and buyouts in the 1980s, frequently experienced widespread white-collar layoffs and, on more than one occasion, cutbacks at the middle-management level. (And middle managers were not protected, as their top-management counterparts were, by golden parachutes to soften the blow of involuntary terminations.) In the 1990s, corporations are downsizing. Middle managers have been singled out as a particular target: "Middle managers make up 5–8 percent of the work force yet have accounted for 17 percent of all persons laid off in the past three years."[9] While management experts point to distinct advantages resulting from cutbacks in the middle-management ranks—such as improved communication between top managers and hourly workers—these gains have not been made without significant cost: Middle managers feel more insecure about their jobs and careers than ever before. Their insecurity is contagious, affecting the attitudes of others and sending the distressing message to supervisors that promotions for them may be unlikely.

Against this backdrop, a planned MD program can help management employees improve and update their knowledge, skills, and abilities. It also raises their self-esteem and promotes the view that top managers care about them. Even better, a planned MD program keeps management employees attractive in the labor market. It can furnish management employees at all levels with the knowledge and skills they need to advance *inside* their organizations—or survive *outside* them in the event of unexpected job loss. As a result, a planned MD program can boost management morale at a time when such a boost may be desperately needed.

Reason 10: Responding to Technological Change

Technology, meaning the application of know-how and machinery to work processes, affects the skills that workers need to perform. Its

influence on the knowledge and skills required of management employees is as great as its influence on other employees. Moreover, management employees are often expected to spearhead the introduction of
new technology to the workplace. A planned MD program is one way to
equip management employees with knowledge about technology and
its potential applications to work processes.

Reason 11: Increasing Opportunities for High-Potential Workers

Definitions of *high-potential workers* (HiPos) vary by management
philosophy and organizational culture, just as definitions of *poor-
potential workers* (PoPos) do. In one sense, a HiPo is anyone capable of
eventual promotion—a definition that can encompass many employees.
HiPos may also be defined as individuals who are:

  ‣ Capable of jumping two or more levels in a short time span
  ‣ Listed on replacement charts or succession planning forms as
    likely replacements for incumbents in key jobs or positions
  ‣ More highly educated or experienced than others in comparable
    positions in the organization
  ‣ Outstanding performers

There are other ways to define HiPos, and most organizations must
come to grips with establishing their own definitions.

A planned MD program can focus on developing HiPos so that their
exceptional abilities are cultivated and harvested in a way that would
not happen as quickly or as effectively with unstructured and unplanned methods. A planned MD program is a means by which to speed
up the development of the best and the brightest so that they are
capable of realizing their potential for their own benefit as well as for
that of their employer.

Reason 12: Realizing Career Plans

In most organizations there are two career ladders. First there is a
management career ladder, in which status and responsibility are tied
to position on a vertical chain of command. The higher the position, the
more people a job incumbent supervises and the more responsibility he
or she shoulders. "Supervisor" is the first rung on the management
career ladder in most organizations. Then there is a *technical career
ladder*, in which status and position are tied to position on a horizontal
continuum of knowledge, skill, and ability; that is, position level is tied
to level of expertise and experience. Although individuals remain at

the same desks and continue performing the same duties, they are promoted as they gain increasing organization-specific, job-specific, and occupation-specific knowledge and experience.

A planned MD program can be a tool to promote personal growth and career advancement for employees on both career ladders. For example, it can prepare *nonexempt employees*—those covered by the federal Fair Labor Standards Act (the FLSA)—to enter and advance vertically through the management ranks. Further, MD can prepare *exempt employees*—those not covered by the FLSA—to advance from supervisor to manager to executive. After all, individuals must acquire new knowledge and skills if they are to qualify for new responsibilities and positions. A planned MD program can be one means by which to provide them with new knowledge and skills through training, education, or development activities.

The same principle applies to a technical career ladder, typical in technical occupations such as data processing. Pay-for-knowledge compensation programs are based on assumptions about the workings of technical career ladders, in which individuals become more valuable to an organization as they increase their knowledge and experience in their functional specialties. Promotions recognize their achievements. A planned MD program, geared to individuals who supervise others in their functional specialties, can be a tool to help them acquire knowhow.

Reason 13: Increasing Opportunities for Women

If participation in planned MD programs is an avenue leading into or up the ranks of management, then it can provide passage into those ranks for women. At present, fewer than 5 percent of all senior management positions in Fortune 500 organizations are held by women, though women occupy approximately one-half of all positions in those organizations.[10] At this writing, the U.S. Department of Labor is studying the "glass ceiling" that prevents women from entering higher-level management ranks. As women continue to enter the work force in record numbers, socially responsible organizations are taking steps to open management opportunities to them. A planned MD program, while not a panacea, can nevertheless help achieve this socially desirable goal.

Reason 14: Increasing Opportunities for Minorities

With the passage of the Civil Rights Act of 1991, which restored many protections to minorities that had been eroded by U.S. Supreme Court decisions since 1980, organizations are under increasing pressure to open management ranks to protected labor groups. A planned MD program can help to serve that purpose, demonstrating an organization's genuine commitment to social justice by helping minorities advance and by providing an avenue to increase the speed by which that advancement can occur.

Scope of MD Programs

There are an estimated 12.5 million executives, managers, and supervisors in the United States.[11] Taken together, these job categories comprise approximately 10 percent of the U.S. work force, numbering about 120 million workers. Supervisors, managers, and executives oversee productive work activities and mobilize resources to achieve planned results.

Management Development needs, methods, and evaluation techniques differ by management job category. In the supervisory ranks, which have the highest concentration of management employees, the tendency is to focus on group-oriented training to meet organizational and individual needs. In the executive ranks, where the fewest people straddle the top of the organizational pyramid, the tendency is to focus on individually oriented developmental experiences.

Supervisors and MD

Supervisors occupy the first tier of management. Numbering about 5 million in the U.S. work force, they oversee the daily work activities of nonexempt employees. They have traditionally been responsible for the work of one unit, function, or assembly line. They devote their time to orienting and training workers, conducting employee performance appraisals, issuing orders, disciplining wayward employees, and dealing with union representatives about daily work in their units. They plan, organize, control, and schedule the work flow of their units. Central to their role is the ability to give direction to other people.[12]

In recent years the supervisor's role has been changing due to improved technology, greater emphasis on product and service quality, and increased expectations about employee participation in decision making. Supervisors are less often expected to tell others what to do and more often expected to coach, counsel, and advise others. Ordering people around, long the stereotypical activity associated with the traditional "straw boss" supervisor, is less common among today's supervisors than empowering individual workers and facilitating employee teams. In some organizations, the job title Supervisor has been replaced by Work Leader, Team Leader, or Work Coordinator. This changing role means that supervisors must become more skilled at handling individual counseling, group dynamics, and structured problem-solving methods. These skills are gradually supplanting the traditional management functions of planning, organizing, scheduling, and controlling.

The precise nature of supervisory duties vary, however, depending on the following:

- *Function.* Differences exist between supervision in marketing, manufacturing (operations), and administration.
- *Industry.* Differences sometimes exist between supervision in manufacturing companies and in service organizations.
- *Union status.* Differences exist between supervision in union and nonunion settings.
- *Organizational culture.* Differences exist between supervisory skills needed in authoritarian cultures and those needed in participative or empowering cultures.

Generally speaking, supervisors in different functions, such as manufacturing, marketing, and administration, devote different percentages of their time to instructing subordinates, managing individuals, representing their staff to higher-level management, planning and allocating resources, coordinating and managing groups, and monitoring the outside environment.[13] Supervisors in manufacturing companies deal with the organization's customers less often than do their counterparts in service organizations. Supervisors in unionized settings must often be prepared to defend their decisions against second-guessing by union representatives, an issue that does not confront supervisors in nonunionized settings. In authoritarian cultures supervisors shoulder total responsibility for decision making and receive credit or blame for the performance of their work units; in participative cultures supervisors delegate responsibility to those reporting to them, and employees receive credit or blame for their individual or team contributions.

Supervisors occupy a critical juncture between supervisory and nonsupervisory work. They are the organization's direct representative to their nonexempt employees; they are the nonexempt employees' direct representative to the employer. This dual responsibility can produce considerable stress, since supervisors often feel squeezed between employee and employer concerns. For instance, supervisors recognize keenly when their employees are not enthused about changes in organizational policies, procedures, technology, work methods, or working conditions. Likewise, supervisors are sensitive to employer concerns, appreciating the need for difficult business decisions on layoffs or cost cutting in ways that sometimes escape nonexempt employees who fear for their jobs or fear change itself.

Nearly 75 percent of all supervisors in the United States are promoted from inside their organizations.[14] Most supervisors begin their careers as nonexempt (hourly) employees and are eventually promoted. In the remaining 25 percent of cases, supervisors enter their positions after gaining experience in other organizations or transferring from other positions or locations.

Despite persisting interest in business and public management careers among college students, fewer than 20 percent of supervisors in U.S. organizations today prepare for their jobs through formal schooling.[15] More often, people enter these jobs from the nonsupervisory ranks. Employers devote less time and money to preparing individuals for supervision than they allocate for middle management, even though supervisors often have more direct contact with employees, customers, suppliers, and distributors.

Nonexempt employees prepare themselves to enter supervision in various ways. Apart from maintaining exemplary performance records in their jobs, they may:

- Enroll full-time or part-time in formal degree programs in management, business, or public administration at two-year community colleges or four-year colleges or universities.
- Attend nondegree-related seminars offered by colleges, professional associations (such as the American Management Association), private vendors, industry groups, or other sponsors.
- View public television programs about supervision.
- Listen to audiotape programs.
- Take correspondence courses.
- Attend conferences.
- Read about supervision on their own time.
- Talk to experienced supervisors about effective ways to prepare for entering supervision, asking such questions as "What do you know now that you wished you had known before entering supervision?" and "How would you suggest I prepare myself to enter supervision?"

Employers also sponsor training, education, and development to help promising individuals qualify for supervision. For example, employers may:

- Encourage experienced supervisors to identify and prepare promising individuals for promotion through planned or unplanned on-the-job coaching over extended time periods.

‣ Handpick promising individuals to attend carefully selected off-the-job college courses, public seminars, or industry-sponsored educational programs.

‣ Sponsor in-house training to meet the most common needs of people aspiring to enter supervision.

‣ Identify and encourage individuals to attend off-the-job college courses in supervision or management, perhaps using an organization's tuition reimbursement program as a funding source.

‣ Identify job assignments and other activities designed to expose individuals to experiences that will help them learn to deal with special assignments, handle difficult people, mobilize and deploy resources, and master other key skills deemed necessary to succeed in supervision.

Of course, these methods may be combined.

Large corporations devote substantial resources to supervisory training. Nearly 60 percent of all large U.S. corporations offer some form of in-house supervisory training, and the average supervisor in large corporations receives about thirty-three hours of training time each year on supervision.[16] But recent studies show that supervisors need more, rather than less, training, education, and development to meet daunting future challenges.[17] Unfortunately, expenditures on supervisory training were the second hardest hit by cutbacks—following middle-manager training—during the recession of 1990.[18]

Organizations need to do more than sponsor planned MD programs that are tightly focused on preparing people to enter supervision or to master new job duties immediately after promotion. Technology, social issues, laws, and other matters change so rapidly that supervisors—like all U.S. workers—need continual upgrading if their skills are to remain up-to-date. For this reason, some form of continuing education is necessary.

To help supervisors stay abreast of new developments, organizations should offer regular briefings, training sessions, and other information-sharing sessions to help supervisors learn about issues affecting their work and their employees' work. Among the issues in which supervisors should be regularly briefed are:

‣ Changes in the organization's plans, policies, or work procedures
‣ New laws, rules, or regulations
‣ New labor agreements
‣ Common problems
‣ New supervisory techniques that work especially well in other parts of the organization or in other organizations

Managers and MD

Middle managers occupy the second tier of management. They number about 5 million in the U.S. work force. They report to senior or top managers, directly oversee the work activities of exempt employees, and, through their role as the immediate organizational superiors of supervisors, indirectly oversee work activities of nonexempt employees. Central to their role is "linking groups."[19]

Managers are traditionally responsible for the work of several related work units or departments. While their specific duties may vary by *functional specialty* (manufacturing/operations, finance, marketing, or human resources), *geographic area* (regions within the United States or abroad), or *product/service line* (type of product or service), their general duties usually involve:

- Establishing intermediate-term goals and objectives to implement strategic plans
- Creating and monitoring budgets and other cost-control methods for their areas of responsibility
- Monitoring the industry and the organization's external environment to identify trends affecting their functions, geographic areas, or product/service lines
- Developing and overseeing annual and sometimes multiyear plans and strategies within their areas to achieve desired results and improved profitability, customer service, and product or service quality
- Staffing key positions within their areas
- Developing people for supervisory and managerial positions
- Structuring their areas of responsibility in ways designed to improve productivity, individual job satisfaction, and group morale
- Establishing policies, procedures, and standards for the work performed in their areas
- Rewarding individuals and groups, within established guidelines of their organizations, for achieving desired results

Job descriptions for managers usually underscore their responsibilities rather than define the specific tasks they perform.[20]

While organizations occasionally hire managers from competitors or from other companies within the same industry in order to gain fresh perspectives and to avoid "inbreeding," many managers in the United States are promoted from the supervisory ranks. By working in supervision first, managers increase their understanding of:

‣ *The organization's purpose.* What is the organization's reason for existence?
‣ *Structure.* How is the organization's work divided up, and who does what?
‣ *Rewards.* What are the organization's rewards, and how are they gained?
‣ *Technology.* How is the organization's work performed?
‣ *Leadership.* Who are the organization's formal and informal leaders, and what do they value?
‣ *Culture.* How are decisions made, and what does the organization really value?

As managers plan to implement organizational strategy, their familiarity with these and other issues serves them in good stead.

Most managers possess a college degree, which usually provides an important educational foundation on which to build industry- and organization-specific knowledge and skills. While the relationship between a college degree in business and subsequent success in management is difficult to prove, the credential provides the holder with awareness of basic business terminology, credibility with others, a social network of acquaintances who graduated from the same school, and awareness of proven methods for approaching problem finding and problem solving.

Individuals prepare themselves to enter managerial positions by demonstrating exemplary performance at lower levels of the organizational hierarchy, advertising their interest in advancement to others, building a network of supporters, and acquiring the skills they need to qualify for advancement.

Research consistently shows that managers rank at or near the top of all occupational groups in the amount of training they receive.[21] Most of that training is intended to help managers qualify for promotion or to succeed immediately after promotion. As in the case of supervisors, managers who have just been promoted are usually highly motivated to learn about their new roles, and they view MD efforts as a means to help them master their new responsibilities.

Large corporations devote substantial resources to the training of managers. Indeed, nearly 75 percent of all large U.S. corporations offer some form of in-house management training. The average manager in a large corporation receives about thirty-seven hours of training in management annually.[22] The budget for manager training exceeds that for any other occupational group,[23] although 32 percent of organizations in *Training Magazine*'s 1991 survey reduced expenditures on middle-manager training during the 1990 recession.[24]

Executives and MD

Executives occupy the highest tier of management in most organizations. They number about 2.5 million in the U.S. work force. They report to, and include, the highest level in the organization, such as the senior managers responsible for functions such as finance and human resources. The executive level also includes the chief operating officer (COO), the chief executive officer (CEO), and the board of directors. Executives directly oversee the work activities of middle managers and indirectly oversee the work of supervisors and hourly employees.

Executives are traditionally responsible for the work of several related departments. They chart the course for their organizations, and an organization's survival and success may depend on the course they chart. Like managers, their specific duties may vary by *functional specialty* (manufacturing/operations, finance, marketing, or human resources), *geographic area* (regions within the United States or abroad), or *product/service line* (type of product or service). Their general duties usually involve:

- Formulating the strategic plan of the organization
- Creating incentives and allocating resources to help realize strategic objectives
- Using their knowledge of the industry to identify and to anticipate trends affecting the organization
- Identifying organizational strengths and weaknesses relative to competitors and working to build on strengths or to overcome weaknesses
- Staffing key managerial positions within their areas
- Developing managers
- Structuring the organization and their own areas of responsibility to conform to the organization's strategic direction

Increasingly, executives find it necessary to think strategically in a world in which global competition is the norm rather than the exception.[25] In the United States, unlike Japan, executives are also expected to produce quarterly profits that spiral constantly upward. Some executives are viewed as villains as they downsize their organizations to hold down direct labor and employee benefit costs, a process that can adversely influence the economies of entire communities, regions of the United States, or third-world nations. Socially insulated from the pressures of daily operations, problems with nonexempt employees, and routine customer concerns, executives must find ways to gather accurate information about what is happening inside and outside their organizations so they can make informed decisions. That challenge is all the more difficult because, as chief controllers of organizational reward and incentive systems, executives are positioned in such a way that managers, supervisors, and nonexempt employees have a vested interest in attaching a positive spin to events that are not always positive.

Individuals prepare themselves to enter executive positions in the same ways they prepare themselves to enter middle management. Apart from maintaining exemplary performance records, they advertise their interest in advancement and build a coalition of supporters among their peers (other managers), their subordinates (supervisors), and their desired peers (executives). For managers to enter the executive ranks, they need luck (available positions), support (people who want them to become executives), and requisite knowledge and skills (knowledge of the industry, function, organization, people, and culture).

Preparing people for executive positions is often a matter of great concern to CEOs, COOs, and boards of directors. Methods of preparation are usually highly individualized, tailored to unique strengths and weaknesses of each person. An Individual Development Plan (IDP) may be prepared to plan for the individual's growth. IDPs may call for international assignments, short courses at Ivy League schools, executive MBA programs, domestic and international job rotations, vendor-sponsored education, and other learning activities targeted to meet specific individual needs. Though reviewed annually, an IDP may have a duration exceeding one year, especially if tied to a succession plan and designed to groom replacements for key positions.

Prospective executives are rarely prepared for advancement through classroom training offered by in-house training departments. There are several reasons for this:

  ‣ Their numbers are small, making it difficult to justify devoting substantial in-house training resources to meet their needs.

  ‣ Their needs vary widely and are often best met through individualized, rather than group, learning methods.

  ‣ Their high-level positions may pose a problem for in-house MD specialists, who (in some organizations) are not positioned to command respect or authority in their dealings with executives.

Large corporations spend substantial sums of money and devote much time to executive training. About 70 percent of all large U.S. corporations make planned efforts to train executives, who receive an average of 36.3 hours of training per year.[26] Manufacturers tend to be the most organized in their executive development efforts; financial institutions tend to be the least organized.[27]

Like supervisors and managers, executives must be kept abreast of changes in the external environment if they are to make informed decisions and plan strategically. Organizations are making various attempts to do that, though many efforts to deliver *continuing education* to executives are not labeled by that term. More often than not, executives are kept updated by serving on committees, task forces, or project groups assigned to scan the organization's environment and to recommend changes designed to keep the organization competitive. They may also be developed, in part, by employer-sponsored service in community, charitable, or industry-related organizations.

Planned and Unplanned MD

Planned MD is a deliberate, conscious effort to identify how many people with what skills will be needed by an organization to carry out supervisory, management, and executive duties and to meet those human resources needs through carefully crafted training, education, and development activities. In organizations that have adopted a philosophy of planned MD, a continuous effort is made to identify and to meet future organizational and individual learning needs.

On the other hand, *unplanned MD* is a form of crisis management in which no effort is made to identify future management needs, and vacancies in the supervisory, management, and executive ranks prompt hectic scrambling to find qualified replacements. Sometimes the best applicants are selected, promoted, or transferred; sometimes expediency governs. No preparation is made for filling predictable vacancies stemming from such organizational factors as growth, diversification, or other charges wrought by external conditions and strategic plans. Nor is there preparation for filling vacancies caused by death, disability, retirement, transfer, or termination.

Unplanned MD is often the first position on a six-step continuum of MD:[28]

1. *Unplanned MD.*
2. *Isolated tactical MD.* Ad hoc efforts are made to address special problems and to meet pressing immediate needs (such as unanticipated vacancies).
3. *Integrated and coordinated structural and development tactics.* Steps are taken to anticipate MD needs.
4. *A Management Development strategy to implement corporate policy.* MD strategy plays a part in implementing corporate strategy.

5. *MD strategy input to corporate policy formation.* Information about the organization's MD needs influences the formulation of an organization's strategic plans.
6. *Strategic development of the management of corporate policy.* MD "processes enhance the nature and quality of corporate policy-forming processes, which they also inform and help implement."[29]

Few organizations fit neatly into one position along this continuum. Indeed, some organizations are positioned at a different place along the continuum for different groups, perhaps planning MD for supervisors but not for managers or executives. Some sponsor planned MD for managers or executives but not for supervisors. Even within a particular organization, some management employees do a better job than others of preparing their subordinates for entry into management ranks and helping them to master work responsibilities upon promotion, to update skills in light of changing conditions, and to prepare for subsequent advancement to higher levels.

Few academic research studies have been conducted to compare the value of planned and unplanned MD for:

- Improving organizational profitability
- Increasing the chances of competitive success
- Ensuring that the right people are at the right places at the right times to meet the organization's needs for management talent
- Holding down turnover in the management ranks
- Encouraging people to enter management
- Reducing the personal anxiety experienced by individuals who move into supervisory, managerial, or executive positions
- Improving an organization's track record to promote women, minorities, and members of other protected labor groups

However, it just seems to make sense that *planned* MD efforts will be more effective than *unplanned* efforts in meeting these goals. As the old saying goes, "If you don't know where you're going, you'll have a tough time getting there." The same principle applies to MD. If nobody plans to achieve results, then results will be difficult to achieve.

Barriers to MD

What barriers stand in the way of successful implementation of a planned MD program? Three seem to loom over all others: (1) lack of management support; (2) lack of expertise to design or implement MD; and (3) lack of resources, such as staff or funds.

1. *Lack of management support.* The organization's management sees no good reason to approach MD in a planned, systematic way. Citing other important priorities or their own preferences, executives do not believe that MD should be planned. Some believe a "sink-or-swim" approach works best to prepare people to enter management ranks, meet job challenges upon promotion, keep skills current, or prepare people for subsequent advancement. Others are uncomfortable with planned MD programs because they worry that such programs may build unrealistic expectations, creating a "crown prince" syndrome.

2. *Lack of expertise.* The organization does not possess the capability to start and operate a planned MD program successfully. Nor, perhaps, do executives know whom to approach to find and tap such expertise. Obviously, lack of expertise can be a real problem in smaller organizations in which nobody is given full-time responsibility to coordinate MD efforts.

3. *Lack of resources.* The organization does not possess the wherewithal to carry out a planned MD program, even if support exists and expertise can be found. The willingness of an organization's management to find the resources for a planned MD program indicates support; on the other hand, the inability to find the resources suggests that executives do not attach much significance to planned MD efforts. Only organizations in bankruptcy truly lack the resources for a planned MD program, because much can be done at low cost.

Overcoming Barriers to MD

How do organizations surmount the barriers to MD? The answer depends on how many barriers must be overcome.

To overcome lack of support, key members of the organization's management must become aware of how planned and unplanned MD efforts differ and must be convinced that planned MD is worth undertaking. Moreover, they must consider the following questions:

- What's in it for them if planned MD is undertaken? What will they gain from it?
- How will planned MD contribute to achieving strategic plans, meet needs identified in succession or replacement plans, and help the organization achieve greater competitive success?
- What problems, if any, result from the organization's unplanned approach to MD? What is happening now?

‣ What solutions will planned MD offer for those problems, and how will the benefits of planned MD match up to its costs?

To convince an organization's leaders to sponsor planned MD, some individual or some group must assume a leadership role and become an idea champion or a cheering section favoring it. That person or group must build management awareness of planned MD by circulating articles and books (like this one) favoring planned MD, researching what other organizations are doing through *benchmarking*, gathering complaints about unplanned MD practices from the organization's current job incumbents, and identifying possible benefits of a planned MD program.

To overcome lack of expertise, someone—or some group—must be given responsibility for coordinating a planned MD program. It is important to understand, however, that this individual or committee cannot be given sole authority or delegated the responsibility to "do" MD, since many people rightfully have a role to play in "growing" talent. Rather, the individual who is designated MD leader, or the committee assigned the role of overseeing MD functions, is a focal point for planning activities, carrying them out, and following up to see what works and what does not. Without someone spearheading these efforts, they will usually lack focus. They may not even be launched.

Few academic programs exist to train people to enter and to carry out the role of director or coordinator of a planned MD program. Organizations lacking the expertise internally usually need to find qualified individuals externally. Sources of talent include leaders of MD programs for other organizations in the same or another industry, leaders of MD programs serving industry or professional associations, faculty or continuing education directors in universities or community colleges, and consultants who have worked on MD programs in other organizations.

To overcome lack of resources, the organization's top managers must set the tone by committing their support to a planned MD program. Paying lip service to it or playing wait-and-see will not work. What is needed is a leap of faith at the outset, deciding that such an effort is worth vesting with adequate resources to start up and function.

Summary

We introduced this chapter with a case study to dramatize one problem that can lead to the introduction of a planned MD program. We then defined a planned MD program as a systematic effort to train, educate, and develop individuals who aspire to—or are already functioning in— the management ranks. It is conducted on the job or off the job to meet individual, group, and organizational learning needs and to improve individual, group, and organizational performance. We pointed out that learning needs may be met through training, education, or development. Training is job-oriented; education is individual-oriented; development is organization-oriented.

A planned MD program is undertaken for many reasons. When the introduction of such a program is contemplated, the benefits should be weighed against the costs. Generally, however, we believe that it is important to plan MD rather than to leave it unplanned. After all, if you don't know where you are going, you'll have a tough time getting there!

Introducing a planned MD program is no quick, simple, or easy matter. Proponents face many barriers. Three barriers generally emerge as most significant: (1) lack of management support; (2) lack of expertise to design or implement MD; and (3) lack of resources. Each must be overcome before the organization can proceed to the next steps.

Part II

Planning and Designing the Management Development Program

INTRODUCTION TO PART II

In Part II, we introduce key issues to consider when setting up and operating a planned MD program.

In most organizations, introducing a planned MD program requires a change of culture. Leaders must come to grips with what they want from the program, realizing that having a planned MD program means that they will have to minimize favoritism and begin to think about the knowledge and the experience necessary for individuals to perform effectively as supervisors, managers, and executives. This process can be more difficult than it sounds but is absolutely essential if a planned MD program is to meet the needs of the organization and the learners it serves.

The four key issues covered in this part are

1. Establishing program purpose
2. Identifying MD needs
3. Establishing an MD curriculum
4. Administering the planned MD program

Chapter 2 describes how to establish the program's purpose, goals, and objectives and how to identify the program's targeted market. Chapter 3 describes how to assess MD needs for individuals and groups. Chapter 4 explains how to establish a curriculum (long-term instructional plan) to guide the planned MD program. Chapter 5 describes how to set up the administrative support system for a planned MD program.

Chapter 2

Focusing a Management Development Program

The impetus for a planned MD program, like other organizational changes, frequently begins when people:

> • *Complain about the way things are being done.* "Here we just turn desks around and call people supervisors. That's no way to run a company! We should issue each of them a costume consisting of a red cape, red boots, and a blue suit with a big yellow *S* emblazoned on the chest. They will need it!"

> • *Are hurting due to crisis.* "Now that Mary is quitting for another job, we have nobody ready to take over for her. Finding and training a replacement is going to be a real mess! Why didn't we plan for a backup and prepare someone? Let's do something to avoid a similar problem in the future!"

> • *Experience pain in making a transition.* "When I took over this job, nobody trained me. I didn't even know where the restroom was located, and nobody was willing to take time to show me. I don't want anybody to go through that kind of anguish again. I have a stomach full of ulcers from that wrenching experience. Surely that's not how we want to do business!"

> • *Discover that major barriers discourage entry to the management ranks.* "Nobody here wants to be a supervisor, manager, or executive. People can simply earn more as hourly employees eligible for overtime. They end up taking a pay cut just to get a fancy title. That's nonsense! Do we really want to create a disincentive for working in management?"

Events of these kinds create windows of opportunity: that is, times when the organization may well be open to the idea of a planned MD program.

Changing the Corporate Culture

To introduce a planned MD program, you must start out with the support of the organization's leaders. You need their mandate to explore what purpose(s) MD should serve, what goals it should seek to accomplish, how it should be initially operated, and whose needs it should meet. Introducing a planned MD program requires a culture change.

Culture change has figured prominently in books and articles on management in recent years. If published accounts have anything in common, it is the idea that making a culture change is a difficult, gut-wrenching, and time-consuming experience. Managers frequently underestimate what it involves. In reality, introducing and consolidating change is like riding a bucking bronco at a rodeo: It is exceedingly difficult at first. However, if people stand to gain personally from a change and are involved in the change process, they will leap on the bronco, and their added weight will make taming the beast all the easier.

This chapter is about leaping on the bucking bronco. More specifically, consider this question: What do you have to do to lay the foundation for a planned MD program in your organization? Assuming leaders of the organization agree that it is worth exploring or undertaking—and, if they do not, then their initial support must be secured before leaping on the bronco!—the first step is to conceptualize the MD program, clarifying why it should exist, what results it should initially achieve, and whose needs it should try to meet.

We suggest you begin your planned MD program by taking the following steps:

1. Form a group or committee.
2. Determine the program's purpose.
3. Establish program goals and objectives.
4. Target groups to be served.
5. Prepare a program policy and philosophy.
6. Prepare a flexible action plan to guide program start-up.
7. Establish a regular schedule to review program results.

While we plan to address these steps in this chapter, let's add a caveat at the outset: *There is nothing sacred about these steps.* They are suggestions only. What works in one organizational setting may not work in others. Therefore, consider these steps in light of previous successful changes introduced in your organization. Modify the steps for introducing a planned MD program on the basis of what has worked before in your organization. Examples of previous successful change efforts might include the introduction of new technology, work methods, self-directed work teams, employee benefits programs, or new products or services. Ponder these questions:

- What steps were taken to introduce those changes successfully?
- Who was involved in making those changes?
- What were the most important steps and milestones in that change effort?
- What made the change effort successful?

Armed with the answers to these questions, you should be able to modify your steps in introducing a planned MD program so they follow proven approaches to introducing change and innovation in your organization's unique culture.

Forming a Group

Once top managers agree to explore a planned MD program, they will want solid information about problems to be solved, action plans, and estimates of costs. To get that information, an administrative structure of some kind is usually required. Such structures include steering committees, task forces, and project teams. The results of our 1992 survey of MD professionals reveal that committees are relatively common (see Exhibit 2-1).

A group can take initial steps, formulating guidelines for a planned MD program and presenting them to top executives and other stakeholders. The group members also form a nucleus of supporters for introducing and consolidating the change, building a core of support for it in the organization. If the group members include at least one powerful individual, such as the owner of the business or the chief executive officer, the group's existence also creates a political impetus for change, demonstrating that it enjoys top-level sponsorship.

An additional payoff from using a group structure is that the group activity itself provides an opportunity for management development. Those participating in the group are directly exposed to setting up a new program, managing significant change, leading a group of people, and other activities that transfer directly to their management jobs. It offers a chance to "learn by doing"—or even "do by learning"[1]—and also builds the participants' stake in the success of the program.

Exhibit 2-1. Use of MD committees.

Question: Does your organization use any special methods to encourage participation/management ownership in Management Development programs? For each method listed in the left column below, check yes or no in the right column.

	Yes		No	
	Frequency	**Percentage**	**Frequency**	**Percentage**
Rely on one or more MD committees composed of representatives from various groups inside your organization?	24	38.71%	38	61.29%
Rely on one or more MD committees composed of representatives from various groups outside your organization?	3	4.84%	59	95.16

Source: William J. Rothwell and H. C. Kazanas, "Results of 1992 Survey on Management Development Practices in the U. S." (Urbana, Ill.: Department of Vocational and Technical Education, 1992, unpublished).

Types of Groups

Different types of groups can be formed to support a planned MD program in the early stages.

‣ A *steering committee*, as its name implies, is formed to guide and navigate. Such a committee usually includes higher-level managers, such as top executives. In small organizations, one committee of four to nine people should be sufficient, and the leader should be chosen—or at least appointed—by the business owner. In large corporations with many work sites, one committee should be formed at the corporate level, another at the division or strategic business unit (SBU) level, and still others at each work site and/or for each level or function of management to be served. Leaders at each level should be appointed by the top manager in charge of the facility or plant.

‣ An *advisory committee* or *coordinating committee* is formed to offer advice or coordinate the MD program. It has no power or formal authority to direct others. It exists to make useful recommendations to the chief executive, board of directors, management employees, or director of MD. It should be formed only with the blessing of the chief executive. (The CEO need not be a member, although his or her membership is desirable.) It establishes initial guidelines for the organization's planned MD program, approving the selection (as necessary) of external consultants to provide assistance and/or appointing a full-time MD director to administer the MD program. The leader of the committee is usually appointed by the owner in a small business or by the CEO or the board of directors in a corporate setting. Members are handpicked for their knowledge of management in the organization, their interest in a planned MD program, and their credibility with others in management.

▸ A *task force* is temporary, unlike steering or advisory committees that endure even as individual members rotate on or off them. Once an initial plan for an MD program has been developed and implemented, the task force is disbanded. A task force is usually composed of a representative cross section of employees, including, for example, an executive, a manager, a supervisor, and several nonexempt employees. The leader is appointed by a top manager or is elected by task force members.

▸ An *annual task force* is a variation of the task force. It is formed at the beginning of the year, completes an annual cycle of assigned tasks, and then disbands. Annual task forces are sometimes used to review MD needs in light of strategic plans, succession plans, or other plans. (Some top managers favor annual task forces for MD since they exist only long enough to complete a specific assignment. They do not contribute to the phenomenon of proliferating committees, a common problem in some corporations.)

▸ A *project team* is temporary. Composed of four to six individuals and headed by a leader elected by the members, its focus is narrower than that of a committee or task force. Indeed, project team members may be asked to direct their attention to a handful of issues only. To cite some examples:

- ▸ Articulating the purpose of a planned MD program for an organization or work site
- ▸ Determining the annual goals or objectives of the program
- ▸ Expressing a policy or philosophy to guide the program
- ▸ Identifying and interpreting MD needs for an organization, work site, or targeted market
- ▸ Planning and scheduling specific MD practices, such as an internal group training program, an external group training program, or a management job rotation program

When the task is completed, the project team disbands. Project teams are frequently used to design and deliver internal group training on such subjects as production scheduling, statistical process control, or budgeting.

  ‣ A *focus group* is a special, temporary group. Originally used by marketing managers to determine how well a proposed product or service would be received by randomly selected potential customers, they are still widely used in marketing, public relations, and other fields in which public reaction is important. They may also be formed to assess the value of proposed MD activities. Participants are chosen to represent different groups, such as executives, managers, supervisors, and aspiring supervisors. They are called together for a short time, such as from one to four hours, and are asked to make recommendations about the need for training, education, or development on specific issues. Alternatively, members may be asked to attend a preview of a training course and to offer their reactions. If members of the focus group give an effort their stamp of approval, then it proceeds as planned; if they express reservations, their suggestions for change are used to improve the effort.

Selecting the Group Members

The qualities to look for in the people chosen to serve on a steering committee, advisory or coordinating committee, task force, project team, or focus group vary, depending on the purpose of the group.

  The choice of committee or task force members should be based on the following:

  ‣ *Their interest.* Does each member favor planned MD? If so, he or she will probably be motivated to help make it work.
  ‣ *Their knowledge of MD practices.* Is each member familiar with MD practices in the corporation and the industry or in businesses generally? The greater the group's knowledge of benchmarks, the faster it can progress by relating practices in other settings to its own situation.
  ‣ *Their own successful track records in management.* How successful has each member been in entering and progressing through the management ranks? What is each member's potential for future advancement?
  ‣ *Their own breadth and depth of management experience.* How broad and deep is each member's management experience as practiced in this, or other, organizations? Broad experience is

gained by many moves; deep experience is gained by long-term exposure to one function or specialty.

- *Their credibility.* How well respected is each group member by the organization's other management employees? Well-respected members usually give a committee or task force significant influence in the organization.
- *Their willingness to make recommendations and follow through with action.* How willing is each group member to explore new ideas and, more important, to follow through to see them put into practice?

In contrast, members of project teams should be chosen for their knowledge and skills concerning the task at hand, whatever that may be. Each member should be thoroughly familiar with the subject matter and should possess the skills to follow through on whatever tasks the project requires. Members of focus groups should represent a target market or audience. Their collective reactions should provide reliable clues about how a Management Development method, such as an internal group training program or a management job rotation program, will be received.

Determining Program Purpose

A *purpose* is essentially a *mission*, a reason for being. In recent years, the concept of purpose has received much attention. It is, after all, a starting point for formulating—or changing—strategic plans.

An MD program should also have a purpose. It can perhaps be best understood as the answer to this question: *Why is the organization undertaking a planned MD program?* The answer to the question will provide clarity of direction and suggest goals to be achieved by the program.

Components of Purpose

The purpose of an MD program should be stated in writing.[2] Like an organization's written purpose statement prepared during strategic planning, a written purpose statement for an MD program should provide answers to the following questions:[3]

- What needs should be met by the program?
- What should be the program's major areas of service?

‣ Whose needs should the program be designed to meet?
‣ Whose needs should be given priority?
‣ What should be the responsibilities of participants, sponsors, the organization, and other stakeholders in ensuring program success?

Methods for Determining Purpose

An MD program should serve the purposes of the organization and its target market. There are at least three key sources of information about the program's purpose: (1) the organization's leaders; (2) members of management; and (3) employees. Information should be gathered from each source. Appropriate methods for gathering information about program purpose vary according to the source.

The organization's leaders are the first key source of information about program purpose. A planned MD program has the potential to change the culture of an organization by changing the knowledge, skills, and attitudes of its leadership. Consequently, MD is frequently linked to *Organization Development* (OD),[4] otherwise known as a long-term, top-down approach to introducing and consolidating organizational change by energizing and empowering employees.[5]

OD is a process of effecting change that is supported by the organization's top managers. With this view in mind, top managers should be polled about their opinions on the desirable purpose(s) of a planned MD program. Indeed, starting with these managers is wise, for it can build top-level interest, awareness, and support. Better yet, if top managers can help kick off efforts to collect information about the desirable purpose(s) of the program, their participation will send a strong signal of support. That is one reason many organizations form a steering committee composed of top executives to begin the MD effort by clarifying its initial purpose, goals, and objectives. Steering committee meetings are ideal settings for gathering information about the desirable purpose(s) of a planned MD program (see Exhibit 2-2).

Members of management are the second key source of information about program purpose. Few experienced managers in the United States today would dispute that *participation* is a key to building *ownership* and *support*.[6] That principle is no less true for the success of a planned MD program than for improving product quality or customer service. Consequently, it is important to build support for MD by enlisting participation in the process, particularly when formulating the program's purpose.

But how is that done?

Exhibit 2-2. Questions about the purpose of a planned MD program.

---

1. In your opinion, what should be the single most important reason for this organization to begin a planned MD program? What needs should be met by the program?
2. Why did you provide the answer you did to question 1? Explain your reason(s).
3. What problems has the organization been experiencing by *not* planning its MD efforts?
4. What should be the MD program's major areas of service?
5. Whose needs should the program be designed to meet?
6. Whose needs should be given priority? (Are some groups or individuals more important than others, at least at the outset?)
7. In your opinion, what should be the responsibilities of participants, their immediate organizational superiors, the organization, and other stakeholders in ensuring program success? (List responsibilities for each group you list.)

One way is to release information on program purpose gathered from the organization's leaders and to request comments from other members of management. Such information can be presented in "white papers," during informal briefings, or through short electronic mail messages. Experienced managers or supervisors may then be asked for additions, deletions, or modifications.

Another way is to survey or interview experienced executives, managers, or supervisors individually about the desirable purposes to be served by a planned MD program. (The questions posed in Exhibit 2-2 can become the starting point for writing a survey or preparing a list of questions for individual interviews.) The results can then be compiled and fed back to the respondents until the responses begin to converge around common issues. This approach, essentially a Delphi procedure, is advantageous because it:

- Uses a process in which almost everyone affected by a planned MD program is given a chance to participate in developing its purpose.
- Keeps everyone informed as information is gathered and decisions are made.
- Builds consensus around a few simple issues, thereby galvanizing support and interest.

Employees are a third key source of information about program purpose. They are, after all, affected by a planned MD program because their immediate organizational superiors are prospective participants. Moreover, employees have a unique perspective, too seldom valued, from which to identify the unique strengths and weaknesses of their own immediate organizational superiors.

Personal interviewing is probably the best method for gathering information from employees about the desirable purpose(s) of a planned MD program. Few employees want to write down their thoughts, even in organizations where jobs are secure and morale is high. They may fear reprisal from their immediate organizational superiors, so their anonymity should be ensured and protected. The interviewer must be perceived as a trustworthy individual, perhaps someone from outside the organization who is viewed as unbiased. Faculty from local colleges can be employed at reasonable cost to conduct such studies.

First, ask the CEO to notify exempt and nonexempt employees about the study in order to give it legitimacy, emphasize its importance, and allay whatever fears may exist about it. Second, select employees randomly from an employee roster or a payroll record. Third, contact employees for individual meetings before, during, or after work—or even during lunch hours. Fourth, pose questions similar to those in Exhibit 2-2. Fifth, feed back the results to managers and employees, starting from the CEO and progressing downward. In light of the results, pose the questions in Exhibit 2-3 to each layer of management, recording reactions and feeding them downward to the next layer each time. Sixth and finally, close the feedback loop by conveying the reactions of each layer back to top management. Ask top managers to synthesize the results and to finalize the purpose of the MD program. Through this approach, all employees participate in establishing the purpose of the planned MD program, increasing its visibility and building commitment at all levels.

Exhibit 2-3. Questions for employees about the purpose(s) of a planned MD program.

---

1. In your opinion, what is the best thing about the way supervisors, managers, or executives perform in this organization? (Cite an example and explain your reasoning, if possible.)

2. What is your biggest single complaint about the way supervisors, managers, or executives perform in this organization? (Cite an example and explain your reasoning, if possible.)

3. Assume for a moment that you were the "boss" of your boss for one day. What orders would you issue to him or her? What training would you see that he or she attends? Why?

Establishing Goals and Objectives

A *goal* is a result to be achieved. Goals are seldom specific. They grow out of purpose, indicating generally what should be achieved. In some instances, goals may actually be stated as part of a written purpose statement for an organization, division, department, or program.

Examples of goals for a planned MD program might include:

- Improving the preparation of individuals for supervisory, management, or executive positions
- Establishing and carrying out programs to ease the transition of individuals hired into, promoted into, or transferred into the jobs of supervisor, manager, or executive
- Helping supervisors, managers, and executives keep their skills current
- Planning and carrying out programs intended to give individuals the skills they need to advance in their management careers

Goals may also be linked directly to the various purposes of planned MD programs. For instance, a planned MD program may be intended to:

- Contribute to implementing the organization's succession plans.
- Contribute to implementing the organization's strategic plans.
- Develop individuals for increased responsibility.
- Help individuals realize their career plans within an organization.
- Improve the morale of management employees.
- Improve the organization's ability to respond to environmental change.
- Improve the organization's ability to respond to technological change.
- Increase the pool of promotable management employees.
- Increase the productivity of management employees.
- Provide general training to individuals inside the organization.
- Build skills in managing people for individuals who have never received formal instruction on supervision or management.
- Increase opportunities for women.
- Increase opportunities for minorities.
- Increase opportunities for "high-potential" workers.[7]

It is rarely possible for a planned MD program to meet *all* these goals. For this reason, you should limit the goals to the most important ones only. These goals should then be presented for review and approval by higher-level managers and targeted groups.

Objectives are directly related to, but more specific than, goals. Objectives add elements of time and measurement to goals. Answering the questions in Exhibit 2-4 will help you to convert the general goals of a planned MD program to specific objectives.

Targeting Groups to Serve

A planned MD program can serve the needs of any or all management groups. However, during the start-up of a program, you will usually find it necessary to establish priorities and to target specific groups for immediate attention. Later, as the program proves its success and is accepted, additional target groups may be added. The effect is the same as that attained by a juggler who starts out with a few items but, as a rhythm is achieved, adds more and more items to be juggled.

But how can you conceptualize the various groups to which a planned MD program can be targeted? Generally, there are four ways: (1) by job category; (2) by special group; (3) by special needs; and (4) by a combination of criteria. Each of these groupings can be used to establish initial program priorities.

Job Category

Job category is one way to organize a planned MD program in an organization. After all, jobs are the nexus, or connecting point, between individual abilities and organizational responsibilities. By definition, a job is composed of various *duties* or *tasks* (activities with discernible starting and ending points), *desired results* (outcomes to be achieved), or *responsibilities* (continuing results to be achieved). *Job titles* or *job categories* are identifiers for groups of related tasks, desired results, or responsibilities across an organization.

Generally speaking, management jobs are commonly distinguished by level of responsibility or by proximity to nonexempt workers or the CEO. As we pointed out in Chapter 1, supervisors are frontline management employees whose work typically involves overseeing the daily activities of nonexempt workers. They must usually have a detailed grasp of how the work is performed. Managers are the next line of management employees; their work involves overseeing the activities of both supervisors and nonexempt workers. They require less detailed technical knowledge of how the work is performed but do need more

text continues on page 47

Exhibit 2-4. Worksheet for converting MD goals to objectives.

Directions: Use this worksheet to help you structure your thinking about the goals and objectives of a planned MD program for your organization. For each goal listed, rank its importance on the line next to it. Then convert the goal to an objective by answering the questions appearing below it. Add paper as necessary. There are no right or wrong answers for this worksheet. However, some answers may be more or less useful, depending on the needs of your organization and its management employees. When you finish, present your results for discussion to members of a steering committee, advisory/coordinating committee, task force, project team, or other group assigned to help establish and operate the planned MD program in your organization. Repeat this activity on a regular and periodic basis, such as once a year.

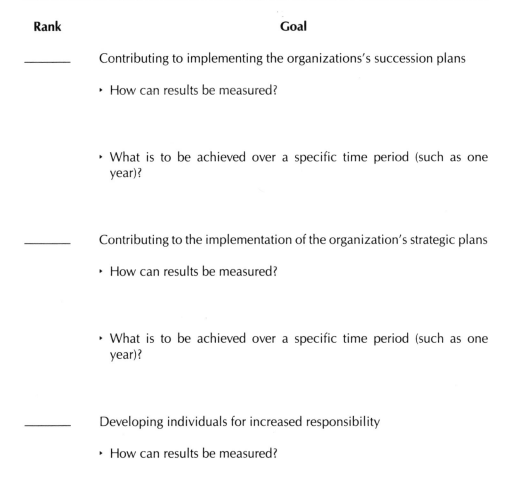

Rank	Goal
_____	Contributing to implementing the organizations's succession plans

‣ How can results be measured?

‣ What is to be achieved over a specific time period (such as one year)?

| _____ | Contributing to the implementation of the organization's strategic plans |

‣ How can results be measured?

‣ What is to be achieved over a specific time period (such as one year)?

| _____ | Developing individuals for increased responsibility |

‣ How can results be measured?

(continues)

Exhibit 2-4 (*continued*).

Rank	Goal
	‣ What is to be achieved over a specific time period (such as one year)?
_____	Helping individuals realize their career plans within an organization
	‣ How can results be measured?
	‣ What is to be achieved over a specific time period (such as one year)?
_____	Improving morale of management employees
	‣ How can results be measured?
	‣ What is to be achieved over a specific time period (such as one year)?
_____	Improving the organization's ability to respond to environmental change
	‣ How can results be measured?
	‣ What is to be achieved over a specific time period (such as one year)?

Rank	Goal

Rank   **Goal**

_____ Improving the organization's ability to respond to technological change

‣ How can results be measured?

‣ What is to be achieved over a specific time period (such as one year)?

_____ Increasing the pool of promotable management employees

‣ How can results be measured?

‣ What is to be achieved over a specific time period (such as one year)?

_____ Increasing the productivity of management employees

‣ How can results be measured?

‣ What is to be achieved over a specific time period (such as one year)?

_____ Providing general training to individuals inside the organization

‣ How can results be measured?

(continues)

Exhibit 2-4 *(continued)*.

Rank	Goal
	‣ What is to be achieved over a specific time period (such as one year)?
_____	Building skills in "people management" for individuals who have never received formal instruction on supervision or management
	‣ How can results be measured?
	‣ What is to be achieved over a specific time period (such as one year)?
_____	Providing increased opportunities for women
	‣ How can results be measured?
	‣ What is to be achieved over a specific time period (such as one year)?
_____	Providing increased opportunities for "high-potential" workers
	‣ How can results be measured?
	‣ What is to be achieved over a specific time period (such as one year)?

analytical and conceptual skills. Executives are the highest-level management employees. Their work is heavily focused on conceptualizing and planning.

When a planned MD program is targeted by job category, MD efforts are designed to help individuals:

- Prepare to enter management jobs.
- Orient themselves to the management level to which they have recently been promoted or transferred.
- Remain current in knowledge, skills, or attitudes appropriate to their job category.
- Advance to a new, higher-level job.

When targeted by job category, a planned MD program must be based on the present and/or future tasks, duties, or desired results of such job categories as supervisor, manager, or executive.

There are several good reasons to focus a planned MD program on meeting the needs of learners on the basis of their job categories:

- It is relatively easy to distinguish between job categories and to explain those distinctions to others.

- Many other organizations base their MD programs on job category, making it easier to benchmark program initiatives across an industry or a geographical area.

- Few skeptics can seriously question the relevance of basing MD activities on job-related tasks, duties, and responsibilities.

- Various government regulatory agencies—such as the Equal Employment Opportunity Commission—rely on job categories as a basis for comparing the advancement and training opportunities offered to protected and nonprotected labor groups. Consequently, if you base your planned MD program on job categories, you should find it relatively easy to report on—and, if necessary, legally defend—affirmative action and equal employment opportunity efforts in your organization.

Of course, there are several drawbacks to using job categories to target groups for planned MD. One is that management job categories are changing in the United States. It is therefore very important to avoid basing MD programs solely on *past* (historical) rather than on *current* or *future* responsibilities by job category.[8] At one time a sharp dividing line separated the tasks and duties of different management levels. That line is blurring as a result of corporate downsizing and advances in information technology. These trends are likely to continue.

A second drawback is that many organizations have more than just three levels of management. For this reason, you must exercise care to classify management job categories in ways that reflect reality in your organizational culture. Indeed, you must start out by identifying the significant management job categories in your organization. One way to do that is to examine an organization chart, identifying how many and what kinds of management positions exist in the organization. Very real differences in duties may also be apparent between *line* (production-oriented) and *staff* (professional, technical, and advisory) supervisory, management, and executive positions. These differences should be taken into account when you decide what job category or categories are to become the target for an initial planned MD program.

Special Groups

Another way to target your market is by special group membership. For example, in an effort to address the so-called glass ceiling that limits advancement opportunities for women and other protected labor groups, some corporations have directed their MD program to improving the opportunities available to these groups. Many large corporations have begun special MD programs to increase advancement opportunities for women, minorities, the aged, and the disabled.

To plan a Management Development program geared to meeting the needs of special groups, you should consider several questions:

- *Why is such a program needed for the special group?* What is the special purpose of the program? Why is it needed?
- *Who is included in the group?* Can you identify members of the special group to be served by a planned MD program?
- *Where are they?* Identify their locations.
- *What do they need?* Identify their special needs, particularly those arising from their protected labor status.
- *Who should plan and operate the program?* Special programs gain credibility if they have significant involvement from members of the special groups to which they are targeted.

However, some evidence suggests that these targeted programs in corporations have been turning into *diversity programs* open to all. One reason for this trend is the desire to avoid excluding people from the programs. People who are deliberately excluded may begin to harbor suspicion about members of protected labor groups and the "special treatment" accorded to them, a reaction just the reverse of the intended goal. By including nonprotected groups, organizations build their sensitivity to the special needs of protected groups and thereby promote increased understanding and harmonious relations.

Special Needs

Companies may design special programs to meet the unique needs of different classes of performers in the management ranks. The underlying assumption is that a corporation may gain special payoffs by concentrating efforts on different groups of performers. For instance, high-potential (HiPo) employees participate in programs designed to help them build on their strengths and realize their potential more quickly; poor-potential (PoPo) employees participate in programs designed to help them overcome their deficiencies. Many corporations operate special high-potential Management Development programs designed to place selected individuals on the fast track to advancement.[9]

If you choose to target your planned MD program by special program, consider these questions:

> • *What desired payoffs are to be achieved by a special program?* Why do you want to direct your initial efforts to performance levels?
> • *How may employees be classified by their performance?* How do you define *high-potential performer, high performer, poor-potential performer,* or *low performer?*
> • *What MD needs exist for each group of performers?* What should be done for each group?
> • *Which special group or groups should receive primary attention?* How are priorities decided? By whom are they authorized?

Like targeting special groups, however, special programs can also produce significant resentment if not properly handled. If, for example, participants in HiPo programs are viewed as "crown princes" or "water walkers"—and receive much special attention, high visibility, and choice job assignments—then they may well be disliked intensely by others. Worse yet, some people may deliberately sabotage their work. Great care must be taken to avoid favoritism and bias in advancement opportunities and job assignments. There is a special challenge in establishing and operating HiPo programs successfully.

Combination of Criteria

Of course, it is possible to use a combination of methods to select initial target groups for MD programs. Indeed, it is possible to target efforts by job category, special group, *and* special need. One example: a minority-oriented management trainee program for HiPos. The questions in Exhibit 2-5 give you the opportunity to structure your thinking about which—or how many—groups you wish to target for your initial efforts.

Preparing a Policy and Philosophy

In the context of MD, a *policy* is a written description intended to coordinate action and fix responsibility, and a *philosophy* is an expression of values. The available research suggests that few organizations have prepared a written *policy and philosophy statement* to govern

Exhibit 2-5. Worksheet for targeting groups for a planned MD program.

Directions: Use this worksheet to structure your thinking about whose needs to serve at the outset of a planned MD program. Answer the questions, and then compare your responses to the responses provided by other members of management in your organization.

---

1. It is not possible to meet the MD needs of all members of management at the same time. What group or groups do you feel should receive initial emphasis for an MD program? (By *groups* we mean job categories such as individuals aspiring to become supervisors, newly promoted supervisors, experienced supervisors, individuals aspiring to become managers, newly promoted managers, experienced managers, individuals aspiring to executive positions, newly promoted executives, or experienced executives. We may also mean special groups, such as women or minorities, or special classes of performers, such as exceptionally high or low performers.)

2. Why do you feel the way you do? In other words, how do you justify your answer to question 1?

training, education, or development efforts.[10] For example, one research study revealed that only "22 percent of the companies reported having a written policy requiring managers to attend formal training and education programs. In 93 percent of these companies, this policy requires first-level supervisors to participate in formal training/education programs, and in 48 percent of these companies, this policy also applies to top-level managers. This policy is new within the past five years for 60 percent of these respondents."[11]

Although few organizations have a written policy and philosophy statement to guide MD, having one offers distinct advantages.

Advantages of a Written Policy and Philosophy Statement

A written MD policy and philosophy statement is worth having for several reasons. First, it puts the organization on the record about what the program is intended to achieve. Second, it clarifies the responsibilities of supervisors, managers, and executives in such efforts. Third, it is a starting point for building interest, attention, and ownership in the program. Fourth and finally, it is a tool for communicating about the program to participants, their immediate organizational superiors, and others who are interested.

Without a policy and philosophy statement, an organization may well flounder in its efforts to establish a planned MD program. Powerful executives may bend the program to suit their whims. MD directors, once hired to lead such programs, will have no clear mandate and may find themselves buffeted by differing and possibly conflicting expectations. The result: The MD program will not be as effective as it could have been.

Components of a Policy and Philosophy Statement

What should be included in a written policy and philosophy statement for a planned MD program? There is no simple answer to that question, because the desirable issues to be addressed may vary across organizations. However, it is possible to list nine questions that should be answered in a policy and philosophy statement:[12]

1. What basic philosophic principles should guide a planned MD program?
2. What should be the program's purpose?
3. What should be the program's goals?
4. What should be the relationship between the program and the organization's other human resources practices for management employees?

5. Whose needs should the program be designed to serve?
6. What should be the program's components?
7. How should planned MD activities be delivered?
8. How should the program be supported by the organization?
9. What should be the responsibilities of program participants, their immediate organizational superiors, and others?

The first question will prompt decision makers and program architects to articulate a credo, a statement of the values that the MD program is designed to support. The second and third questions will help clarify the program's purpose and goals, showing how the program is designed to support the philosophy. The fourth question will clear up the relationship between a planned MD program and other human resources policies such as those on management performance appraisal, compensation, benefits, and selection. The answer to the fifth question will identify the program's targeted groups; the answer to the sixth question will identify program activities; and the answer to the seventh will clarify how MD activities will be delivered. Questions eight and nine will clarify how much support the program will enjoy and the roles of people who affect program success.

Preparing a Policy and Philosophy Statement

It's a good idea to begin drafting a policy and philosophy statement as soon as top managers signal support for establishing the MD program. Drafting such a statement should become a central focus of a steering committee or other group early on. The reasons: The writing process brings key issues to the surface and crystallizes committee thinking.

Committee members can use the worksheet in Exhibit 2-6 to structure their thinking on key program issues. The worksheet should be distributed before the initial group meeting, and members should be asked to jot down ideas to be shared in that meeting. This should start the group off with a problem-solving focus.

Preparing a Flexible Action Plan

A written policy and philosophy statement is only an early step in establishing a planned MD program. Another is the development of a flexible *action plan,* a description of steps that must be taken to achieve desired results. You might liken it to a business plan for a small enterprise. An action plan is the product of a focused *vision* about

text continues on page 55

Exhibit 2-6. Worksheet for preparing a policy and philosophy statement for a planned MD program.

Directions: Use this worksheet to structure your thinking about key issues to be considered when introducing a planned MD program. Jot down your answers for each question posed. Be prepared to share your thoughts with others. The results of this worksheet should become the basis for a written policy and philosophy statement to guide the planned MD program. Attach more paper if necessary.

---

1. What basic philosophical principles should guide the planned MD program?

   ‣ What do we believe about the nature of management in this organization?

   ‣ What do we believe about the value of preparing management employees to do their jobs?

2. What should be the program's purpose?

   ‣ What is the *chief* reason for sponsoring this program?

3. What should be the program's goals?

   ‣ What do we hope to achieve from this program?

4. What should be the relationship between the program and the organization's human resources practices for management employees?

   ‣ What should be the relationship between planned MD and:

   —Management job descriptions?

   —Management performance appraisals?

(continues)

Exhibit 2-6 (*continued*).

———————————————————————————————

—Management compensation practices?

—Management recruitment?

—Equal employment opportunity and affirmative action?

5. Whose needs should the program be designed to serve?

  ‣ Should the program be designed primarily to meet the needs of:

    ☐ Job categories?
    ☐ Special, protected labor groups?
    ☐ High, low, or intermediate-range performers in the management ranks?
    ☐ A combination?

6. What should be the program's components?

  ‣ Should the program rely on such methods as:

    ☐ Internal group training?
    ☐ External group training?
    ☐ External education?
    ☐ Job rotation?
    ☐ On-the-job training?
    ☐ Coaching?
    ☐ Mentoring?
    ☐ Other methods?

7. How should planned MD activities be delivered?

  ‣ Is there a preference for MD:

    ☐ On the job?
    ☐ Off the job?
    ☐ Some combination?

‣ What is the reason for this preference?

8. How should the program be supported by the organization?

‣ How will it be funded and budgeted for?

9. What should be the general responsibilities of participants in the program, their immediate organizational superiors, and others?

‣ What are the responsibilities of those who participate in the MD program?

‣ What are the responsibilities of the bosses of those participating in the MD program?

‣ What should be the top managers' responsibilities in the MD program?

‣ How will people be informed of their responsibilities?

‣ How will people be held accountable for their MD program responsibilities?

---

desired results to be achieved, a picture of what a planned MD program should eventually look like.

An action plan answers this question: *How will goals, objectives, or desired results be achieved?* It usually specifies what goals or objectives will be achieved, specific steps to take, and the time required. It may also identify who is responsible for doing what.

Why Is an Action Plan Important?

An action plan reduces the likelihood that a desired goal or objective will not be achieved because of uncertainty about who should do what. It also economizes on steps, making sure that each step directly contributes to achieving a desired goal or objective. Further, it becomes a basis for judging group and individual performance. On a philosophical level, an action plan is important because it makes an otherwise vague vision of the future concrete and attainable.

When introducing any change in organizations, it's wise to try to engineer one or more quick successes to build enthusiasm and support. This principle applies when introducing a planned MD program. One or more action plans should be prepared right away. These plans should be geared to achieving quick, highly visible results. Preferably, the plan should be designed to satisfy a long-standing but relatively simple MD problem that has given rise to complaints among supervisors, managers, or executives. While such problems may vary across organizations, one example might be a training course on budgeting for those who are expected to budget but who have never received training on budgeting. Another example is a training course on employee discipline for those who are responsible for administering progressive discipline but are unsure how to apply it.

Why Is Flexibility Important?

Don't expect the action plan to cover every problem that will be encountered in starting the MD program. Be flexible. Be willing to modify the action plan as events unfold.

On the other hand, try to anticipate problems. The introduction of any change produces side effects. Some side effects can be predicted; some cannot. Some are positive; others are not.

The same principles apply to introducing a planned MD program in an organization that has always promoted from within or relied heavily on unplanned on-the-job training or informal coaching to prepare individuals for management. Some problems can be anticipated, and strategies for dealing with them should be thought out ahead of time. For instance, upon the introduction of a planned MD program, it is common for experienced employees at all levels to worry about how the change will affect them personally. Those most worried are likely to be people who would have otherwise expected advancement based on their seniority, popularity, or performance. It is important to allay their fears as much as possible. Do that by communicating about program initiatives and involving as many people as possible.

Exhibit 2-7. Worksheet for establishing a vision for a planned MD program.

Directions: Use this activity to help you establish a vision and a flexible action plan to introduce a planned MD program in your organization. Starting from the left side of the line appearing below, identify different time periods (for example, 5 months, 7 months, 9 months, 12 months, and 5 years). Then, below each vertical line, describe what should be happening in the MD program and what results should be achieved. Finally, under the last line on the right, describe the ultimate results to be achieved—what should be happening, how the program should be functioning, and what results should have been achieved. (Add paper as necessary.)

_____ Months   _____ Months   _____ Months   _____ Months   _____ Years

---

You can use the activity in Exhibit 2-7 to build flexibility into program planning. Then plan one quick success for the planned MD program.

Establishing a Regular Review Schedule

As a final step in introducing a planned MD program, you should establish a schedule for evaluating program success and achievement periodically. The idea is to build in a means to track, and communicate, program successes and achievements. Without such a schedule, it will be easy to forget to review the program's impact amid daily work pressures. But if this step is forgotten, MD program activities may be scaled back during periods of retrenchment. Unfortunately, this has happened in many businesses in the past.

We have more to say about evaluation in Chapter 10. For now, however, it is sufficient to note that the foundation for program evaluation should be planned from the outset in order to protect the program from budget slashing. A demonstrated track record, widely communicated, goes a long way toward building and maintaining program support. Evaluation is one way to demonstrate that track record.

Summary

In this chapter, we emphasized the importance of establishing a core group of committed people to work on launching a planned MD program. We also explained how to clarify program purpose, goals, and objectives and how to select a target group to be served by the program. Finally, we described the value of preparing a program policy and philosophy, a flexible action plan for program start-up, and a schedule to review program results.

Chapter 3

Identifying Management Development Needs

Once you have clarified the purpose of a planned MD program, you should begin identifying management learning needs. This step has no definite beginning or end, since we assume that your aim is to improve management performance continuously. To emphasize the importance of this step, which is the focus of this chapter, we start out with a brief but realistic case study.

INTRODUCTORY CASE STUDY

George Smithers was hired to establish a planned MD program for a conservative service organization employing 1,500 people. George was hired from outside the company and the industry, but he started with significant experience in MD and in college teaching. The company had never planned MD before, having relied on promotion from within and on-the-job coaching to help employees advance.

On his first day George was introduced to members of the company's MD steering committee, which had been authorized by the company's board of directors and CEO to oversee the start-up of a planned MD program. The committee members consisted of the company's executive in charge of management information systems, the second-in-command of company finance, two key middle managers from operations, and the top human resources executive (George's immediate organizational superior).

George was pleasantly surprised to learn that committee members had already clarified the purpose of the MD program, established program goals and objectives, and identified prospective and experienced supervisors as initial target groups. Managers and executives were to be served by the program later, after initial success had been achieved with supervisors.

George felt that his next steps were clear. He would coordinate the preparation of a program policy and philosophy statement, establish a flexible action plan for program start-up, and prepare a schedule of learning experiences. These steps would not only give direction to the fledgling MD program but provide George with a means to orient himself to the company and build support for the program.

George also felt that he should conduct a management needs assessment to uncover gaps between what the targeted learners already knew or did and what they needed to know or do. George was aware, after all, that the term "supervisor" does not have a universal meaning. Supervisory duties, tasks, and responsibilities vary dramatically across industries and organizations and are different for people working for different managers in the same organization.

As a first step in needs assessment, George planned to review supervisory job descriptions and recent supervisory performance appraisals. He knew that the information they contained would shed light on what supervisors were expected to do in the organization and how well they had been doing it. He would then be able to assess individual and group needs in view of organizational requirements.

Unfortunately, George soon learned that the organization had no written supervisory job descriptions. Nor, it seemed, did the organization make it a regular practice to require supervisory performance appraisals. Although dismayed by the lack of information, George was undaunted: He decided to conduct a supervisory needs assessment in several steps. First, he would interview a small, randomly selected group of supervisors and their immediate organizational superiors regarding supervisory responsibilities. From the interview results he would draft a supervisory job description and use it as a basis for a written needs assessment survey questionnaire. After having both reviewed by a small group of experienced supervisors and their immediate organizational superiors, he would finalize the questionnaire and send it out to all supervisors and their immediate organizational superiors in the organization. He would use the survey results to identify supervisory learning needs and to establish initial priorities for the planned MD program. Finally, he decided to feed back the results of his efforts to members of the steering committee and survey respondents. Doing so would communicate the necessity of the MD program and validate a direction for it.

In time, George also wanted to establish a management curriculum in the organization to meet predictable learning needs resulting from promotions to supervisory positions. Comprising planned learning experiences, it would be flexible, lending itself to individualized planned learning experiences as necessary.

Defining Needs

As the introductory case study implies, a *need* is traditionally viewed as a performance gap separating *what is* from *what should be*. In this context, *performance* means *the desired results of job activities*. Performance should not be confused with the observable or unobservable behavior or activities of job incumbents.

Learning vs. Nonlearning Needs

There are three categories of needs:

1. *Learning needs.* A performance gap is caused by lack of necessary knowledge or skill.

2. *Nonlearning needs.* A performance gap is caused by an obstacle in the work environment.
3. *Learning and nonlearning needs.* A performance gap is caused in part by lack of necessary knowledge or skill and in part by an obstacle in the work environment.[1]

A simple example should help clarify these differences. Newly promoted supervisors experience learning needs when they *do not know how* to fill out reports, conduct employee performance appraisals, or prepare work schedules. But they experience nonlearning needs when they already know how to perform these supervisory tasks but fail to do so for other reasons—such as lack of proper tools (e.g., because they aren't given necessary equipment to write out reports), insufficient time (e.g., because of conflicting work assignments), or improper attitude and motivation (e.g., they don't consider these tasks important enough to warrant attention).

More often than not, MD focuses on meeting individual or group learning needs. Its typical purpose is to equip people with the knowledge and skills they need to perform their management jobs competently. However, those concerned about MD should also pay close attention to nonlearning needs stemming from problematic recruitment, selection, and reward practices. Questions that can help distinguish learning from nonlearning needs appear in Exhibit 3-1.

Sources of Learning Needs

Where do learning needs come from? Most authorities agree with the view, first proposed in 1961,[2] that needs stem from at least three primary sources:

1. *The organization.* What performance is required of an individual or group by the organization's strategic plan, culture, and activities?
2. *The job.* What do people have to know or do to be able to perform their jobs competently?
3. *The individual.* What does the individual or group already know or do? How does that compare to what the individual must know or do to perform competently?

Since 1961, authorities have added a fourth source of learning needs: *the external environment,* or the world outside the organization. The external environment affects learning needs through requirements posed by customers, stockholders, competitors, regulators, and other

text continues on page 64

Exhibit 3-1. Distinguishing learning from nonlearning needs.

When confronted with a problem performance or a problem situation, pose the following questions to find out more about the problem and its causes:

What is happening?	‣ What is happening now? (Describe the situation) ‣ Who first reported the problem? ‣ When was the problem first noticed? ‣ How was the problem first noticed?
What should be happening?	‣ What is the desirable or ideal state? ‣ What performance or behavior is expected? ‣ What performance standards or objectives provide benchmarks against which to measure what should be happening? ‣ What organizational policies, common business practices, or governmental laws, rules, or regulations apply to this situation or problem?
How wide is the performance gap between what is happening and what should be happening?	‣ What is the difference between *what is happening* and *what should be happening*? ‣ What are the consequences of this performance gap?
How important is the performance gap between what is happening and what should be happening?	‣ How important is the performance gap to — Customers, suppliers, or other external stakeholders? — The organization? — Divisions, departments, work groups, or work teams? — Individual management employees? — Other individuals or groups? (If the problem is not important, ignore it. Otherwise, continue to the next step.)
What is the cause of the performance gap?	‣ Is the problem caused *chiefly* by — Lack of knowledge or skill? (Do people know what to do in situations like this one?) — An obstacle to performance? (Do people have the resources they

need to perform? Do they want to perform? Are they capable of performing?)
— A combination of a lack of knowledge or skill and an obstacle to performance?

<table>
<tr><td>What solutions will address the cause(s) of the performance gap most effectively?</td></tr>
</table>

‣ If the performance problem is caused chiefly by lack of knowledge or skill, can it be addressed most cost-effectively by
— Designing and delivering training?
— Designing and offering job aids to help people comply with a policy or to follow procedure at the time they need to perform?
— Giving people an opportunity to practice a skill or to master knowledge on their own, either on the job or off the job?
— Modifying selection practices to choose people who have more knowledge or skills at the time of a job change, such as at time of hire, promotion, or transfer?
— Modifying job duties so that only those already possessing appropriate knowledge or skills handle problems?
— Establishing expert systems to minimize the need for human decisions and/or actions?
— Choosing another strategy to address the deficiency of knowledge or skill?

‣ If the performance problem is caused chiefly by an obstacle to performance, can it be cost-effectively addressed by
— Clarifying work standards?
— Improving feedback about individual or group performance?
— Providing more appropriate tools, materials, procedures, policies, or other resources to support the work?
— Holding individuals or groups more accountable for their performance by

(continues)

Exhibit 3-1 (*continued*).

---

applying disciplinary methods when appropriate?
— Changing/improving the match between performance and rewards or incentives?
— Choosing another strategy designed to overcome obstacles to performance that are outside the immediate control of individuals?

‣ If the performance problem is caused by a combination of lack of knowledge or skill and a barrier to performance, can the problem be broken down into components based on their causes and can appropriate, cost-effective solutions be selected for each component?
— If yes, continue to the next step.
— If no, devote time to analyzing the problem so it can be broken down into components suitable for corrective action.

‣ What problems are likely to result from the corrective action that is planned?

What negative or unintended side effects may result from the solution(s) selected, how can they be anticipated, and how can their effects be minimized?

‣ What can be done before or during corrective action to minimize problems or negative or unintended side effects?

---

stakeholder groups. Identifying stakeholders' expectations for an organization and/or its products or services can be a vital first step in formulating organizational strategic plans, establishing a total quality management (TQM) effort, re-engineering work processes, and identifying the learning needs of exempt and nonexempt employees.

Organizational, job, individual, and external environmental requirements should be clarified and then compared to existing conditions to determine the gap between what is and what should be.

Defining Learning Needs Assessment

In the most general sense, *learning needs assessment* is the process of identifying performance gaps, caused by lack of either knowledge or skill, that separate *what is* and *what should be*. It answers such questions as:

- How large is the performance gap?
- How important is the performance gap at present and in the future?

Management Development learning needs assessment (MDNA) is the process of identifying the learning needs of management employees. It is a crucial starting point for planning learning experiences.[3] Without MDNA, it is not possible to determine what learning needs exist—or which needs deserve priority attention.

Unfortunately, relatively few organizations make it policy to conduct systematic MDNA routinely. A 1987 survey study revealed that only 27 percent of the survey respondents' organizations conduct needs assessment for management employees.[4] Needs assessment is most often conducted for supervisors and least often conducted for top managers. Large organizations are more likely than small ones to use needs assessment to identify the learning needs of management employees.

Determining Whose Needs to Assess

Begin MDNA by identifying the learning needs of the first group targeted for attention in your planned MD program. For instance, you may choose to start with MDNA for aspiring supervisors, high-potential employees (HiPos), or protected labor classes. Start with the group whose needs are perceived to be greatest.

In addition—or, as an alternative—conduct a *benchmarking* study.[5] Identify well-known competitors or organizations renowned for their MD programs. Prepare questions to determine (among other issues) which management groups in those organizations are receiving priority attention. Contact representatives of those organizations. Visit them, if at all possible, to see firsthand what they are doing. Take along representatives of key stakeholder groups in your organization—such as members of the MD steering committee, top managers, and targeted learners—to build an impetus for change and for program success. Presently, a small but growing number of organizations are benchmarking their MD programs. The organizations most frequently benchmarked, as identified in a 1992 survey sponsored by the American

Society for Training and Development, are Motorola, General Electric, and Xerox.[6]

Macro and Micro Learning Needs

MDNA may be conducted for long-term or short-term learning needs. Long-term needs are relatively enduring or may affect many people. They are called *macro needs*.[7] On the other hand, short-term needs may change rapidly. They are created by topical problems facing an organization, individual, or job category. They may also result from individual deficiencies. These needs are called *micro needs*.[8]

Examples of macro and micro needs are easy to point out. Suppose supervisors, the initial targets of a planned MD program, interview job applicants. When supervisors are hired, promoted, or transferred into their positions, few know how to conduct legally defensible employment interviews. Hence, employment interviewing presents a *macro learning need* because it affects all supervisors in the organization; that is, it will endure as long as supervisors are expected to conduct employment interviews.

Suppose that new laws are enacted, court rulings are handed down, or company policies are instituted that affect employment interviewing practices—as has recently occurred with the enactment of the Americans with Disabilities Act.[9] Such a change affects everyone, including those experienced in employment interviewing. Changes of this kind also create macro learning needs affecting many people.

On the other hand, individuals vary in the knowledge and skills they bring to their jobs. Some newly promoted supervisors may know already how to conduct employment interviews in conformance with company policy and legal requirements. Forcing them into learning the basics is a waste of time. Others may not be conducting interviews properly, even though they have been doing them for some time without receiving training first. They experience *micro needs*, unique needs stemming from their individual strengths and weaknesses.

Three Approaches to MDNA

There are three general ways to conduct MDNA: the *top-down approach*, the *bottom-up approach*, and the *combination approach*.

1. The *top-down approach* focuses primarily on macro needs. A plan is prepared to guide the preparation, orientation, and training of all members of an identified group. All group members participate in the learning experiences identified as appropriate for them. In short, it

is a one-size-fits-all approach. Recent critics of MD complain that this approach is used far too often and is usually ineffective.[10]

2. The *bottom-up approach* focuses on micro needs. Individual needs are assessed, and the information gained is fed upward to higher-level management levels and/or to a centralized MD function. When aggregated, individual needs become the basis for a collective learning plan. This is a way of identifying common needs shared by individuals so that appropriate action can be taken to address them. Individual needs falling outside the envelope of common needs for the group can be met by sending individuals outside the organization to attend public seminars sponsored by local colleges, universities, or training vendors.

3. The *combination approach* strikes a balance between the top-down and the bottom-up approaches. First a plan is prepared to guide the preparation and orientation of a group. Then individual needs are compared to group needs. Individuals participate only in learning experiences appropriate to *their* needs. Planned learning experiences are selected from a smorgasbord of available options.

Conducting MDNA

MDNA is conducted by systematically collecting, analyzing, and using information about learning needs. Various techniques may be used to compare what management employees already know or do and what they should know or do to perform efficiently and effectively. The most common approaches to collecting information about management learning needs are listed and summarized in Exhibit 3-2. Each has distinct advantages and disadvantages, as the exhibit shows. Some are used more often than others, as we found in our 1992 survey of MD specialists. (A summary of our survey results appears in Exhibit 3-3.)

How Often Should MDNA Be Conducted?

Ideally, MDNA should be conducted at least annually. Both macro and micro needs should be examined at that time. It is also important to integrate the planned MD program with the organization's needs as expressed in strategic plans and succession plans. Consequently, MDNA should be conducted on a schedule linked to those other organizational activities.

Individual (micro) needs should be assessed at least once each year, at the end of projects, or upon the discovery of individual deficiencies. Some organizations tie individual needs assessment to management

text continues on page 80

Exhibit 3-2. Techniques for conducting MD needs assessment.

ASSESSMENT CENTER

A process rather than a place, an assessment center usually consists of a series of activities based on the requirements of a job in an organizational setting. Assessment centers are often associated with the process of selecting those deemed suitable for promotion into the management ranks, but they can also be used to identify individual learning needs.

<table>
<tr><th>Steps in Conducting
MDNA Using the Technique</th><th>Advantages and Disadvantages</th></tr>
<tr><td>

1. Conduct a detailed job analysis for the job category (such as supervisor, manager, or executive).
2. Design management activities—such as in-basket exercises, simulations, or role plays—to assess an individual's abilities to meet the requirements of each job.
3. Train assessors, who are usually experienced job incumbents from the client organization.
4. Test out the activities.
5. Implement the assessment center.
6. Evaluate results of the assessment center over time.
7. Use the assessment center to:
   - Select individuals for management positions.
   - Identify individual training needs.

</td><td>

Advantages:
- The results are usually easily accepted by management.
- The approach is based on job requirements, and assessment centers can be more effective than selection interviews and other methods for selecting management employees and/or identifying their training needs.

Disadvantages:
- Expensive to design and to set up.
- Tend to perpetuate existing management methods and organizational culture.

</td></tr>
</table>

COMPETENCY MODEL

A description of desirable knowledge, skills, and abilities of job incumbents in an entire job category—such as supervisor, manager, or executive. A competency model, once agreed upon, can be immensely useful in selecting management employees, training them, and preparing them for advancement from one management level to another.

<table>
<tr><th>Steps in Conducting
MDNA Using the Technique</th><th>Advantages and Disadvantages</th></tr>
<tr><td>

1. Review literature on previous competency models of management.

</td><td>

Advantages:
- Results have high face validity and are accepted by management easily.

</td></tr>
</table>

Steps in Conducting MDNA Using the Technique	**Advantages and Disadvantages**

2. Identify exemplary performers in the organization to participate in the study.
3. Draft a survey for use with exemplary performers to capture their views about essential roles, competencies, work outputs, and quality requirements for each management job category.
4. Test the survey for clarity.
5. Conduct the survey.
6. Compile the results.
7. Compare individual profiles to the ideal profiles in the competency model.
8. Use the competency model to:
   ‣ Select individuals for management positions
   ‣ Identify individual training needs
	‣ The approach lends itself to meeting future requirements (implied by strategic plans) as well as past requirements.
	
	Disadvantages:
	‣ A vendor or other outside assistance may be required to establish a valid competency model.
	‣ The results of the competency model may be too general to be helpful.

DACUM METHOD

An acronym formed from letters in the phrase *Developing A CurriculUM*, DACUM has been widely used in establishing vocational and paraprofessional curricula in community colleges. This approach can also be used to help a group of experienced job incumbents focus on changes they need to make in preparation for adopting a new role for management—such as the new role for management implicit in a team environment.

Steps in Conducting MDNA Using the Technique	**Advantages and Disadvantages**
1. Assemble a panel of experienced job incumbents, preferably the best performers. 2. Set up an agenda for a 1- or 2-day meeting for each job category to be analyzed. 3. Begin the meeting by explaining that its purpose is to focus on what incumbents *do* on their jobs. 4. Go around the panel of partici-	*Advantages:* ‣ The results are usually easily accepted by management. ‣ The approach is fast and relatively inexpensive. ‣ A body of knowledge exists about using the approach. *Disadvantages:* ‣ The approach is limited to the

(continues)

Exhibit 3-2 (*continued*).

Steps in Conducting MDNA Using the Technique	Advantages and Disadvantages
pants, and ask for activities or tasks performed (one from each participant initially).	experience and knowledge of the participants.
5. Record tasks on large index cards or on sheets of paper, and affix them to a wall.	‣ The approach tends to be based on present or past duties, rather than future ones (although DACUM can be modified to focus on future work requirements).
6. Adjourn the group briefly and establish several general descriptive categories in which to classify two or more activities/tasks each.	
7. Change the wall chart to reflect the categories established.	
8. Convene the group and ask group members to verify that the descriptive categories are appropriate to use, making changes as needed.	
9. Go through each activity or task again, asking panel members to verify, revise, or delete them.	
10. Adjourn the meeting and reduce the wall chart to a 1-page handout (called a DACUM chart).	
11. Create a written questionnaire based on the DACUM chart for use in assessing individual knowledge, skills, and abilities.	
12. Ask each job incumbent and each organizational superior of a job incumbent to use the questionnaire for assessing skill levels.	
13. Use the survey results to: ‣ Identify selection criteria. ‣ Identify individual training needs. ‣ Establish an internal group training curriculum.	

FOCUS GROUPS

A focus group is a small group formed to "focus" on an issue of concern to group members. This approach has proved its value in marketing research. A focus group typically consists of a randomly selected group of customers called together to assess reactions to a new product or service. A focus group may also be established to examine management learning needs. Such a group may consist of external stakeholders (customers, suppliers, or distributors) or internal stakeholders (exempt or nonexempt employees).

Steps in Conducting MDNA Using the Technique

1. Select a small group of people at random from:
   - External stakeholders (customers, suppliers, distributors), and/or
   - Internal stakeholders (nonexempt *or* exempt employees).
2. Call the group together in a central location.
3. Ask group members to list:
   - Problems they have encountered in doing business with the organization and/or in performing in the organization.
   - Management learning needs they can infer from those problems (this assumes management is responsible for all such problems).
4. Compile results from the focus group, using them as a basis for:
   - Establishing learning plans for management.
   - Feeding back results to management employees as they plan their own learning activities.

Advantages and Disadvantages

Advantages:
- Fast.
- Relatively inexpensive.
- Offers a unique perspective that is difficult to obtain from other methods.

Disadvantages:
- It can be difficult for members of a focus group to separate management learning needs/performance from organizational needs/performance.
- Employees in a focus group may not "open up" to identify problems/concerns.

INDIVIDUAL DEVELOPMENT PLANS (IDP)

An IDP, synonymous with an *individualized learning plan*, is designed to orient one person to a new job, upgrade skills in preparation for a new job, or rectify a deficiency of knowledge and skill for an experienced performer. Learning needs are individually assessed on some periodic basis, such as once a year.

(continues)

Exhibit 3-2 *(continued)*.

Steps in Conducting MDNA Using the Technique	**Advantages and Disadvantages**
1. Prepare a form and procedures to encourage periodic discussions between management employees and their immediate organizational superiors, focusing on: • Individual needs (stemming from job requirements, personal strengths and weaknesses, and organizational requirements/ issues). • Learning objectives to meet the needs. • Learning methods (how to meet the needs). • Evaluation methods. 2. Encourage management employees and their immediate organizational superiors to meet to discuss learning needs on some regular basis. 3. Offer advice and support in meeting the learning needs, ensuring some kind of follow-up.	*Advantages:* • Highly individualized. • Easily administered. • Easily focused on needs stemming from the job, the individual, and/or the organization. • Capable of aggregation so that macro needs, shared by more than one person, can be identified and met. *Disadvantages:* • Requires time commitment by each management employee and his/her immediate organizational superior. • Depends heavily on the interaction of superior/subordinate and their ability to identify learning needs.

INTERVIEWS

An interview is a planned or unplanned conversation. When used in needs assessment, an interview may be conducted with randomly selected members of a targeted learner group—such as supervisors or managers—and/or with their immediate organizational superiors for the purpose of identifying the common learning needs of that group.

Steps in Conducting MDNA Using the Technique	**Advantages and Disadvantages**
1. Randomly select for interviews group members from any/all of these groups: • Targeted learners (such as supervisors, managers, or executives).	*Advantages:* • Easy. • Simple. • Fast. • Dialogue with others serves to build interest and expectations for change.

Steps in Conducting MDNA Using the Technique	**Advantages and Disadvantages**
‣ Immediate organizational superiors of the targeted learners. ‣ Peers of the targeted learners. ‣ Subordinates of the targeted learners. 2. Meet with them, asking what they perceive to be the greatest learning needs/performance deficiencies/improvement possibilities of the targeted learners. 3. Identify common themes identified across interviews, considering them to be learning needs typical of the job category in the organization.	*Disadvantages:* ‣ Tends to be heavily influenced by past or present problems rather than future organizational requirements. ‣ May build unrealistic expectations for improvement/change.

MANAGEMENT DIAGNOSTIC QUESTIONNAIRES

In recent years much interest has been expressed in numerous management diagnostic questionnaires that purport to identify individual styles of interacting with others. The best known is the Myers-Briggs Type Indicator, though others are also frequently used.

Steps in Conducting MDNA Using the Technique	**Advantages and Disadvantages**

1. Purchase questionnaires from an external vendor.
2. Target individuals to take the questionnaires, explaining beforehand:
  ‣ What the results do and do not mean.
  ‣ How the results will be used—and by whom.
3. Administer the questionnaires.
4. Score results and/or allow individuals to self-score.
5. Facilitate discussion about:
  ‣ What the results mean.
  ‣ How the results may be used appropriately.
	Advantages:
	‣ May increase individual motivation to learn.
	‣ May heighten individual appreciation of learning styles.
	‣ May lead to experimentation in interpersonal interaction.
	
	Disadvantages:
	‣ Unethical or unschooled users may misuse the results.

(continues)

Exhibit 3-2 (*continued*).

Steps in Conducting MDNA Using the Technique	Advantages and Disadvantages
‣ Issues of ethics and confidentiality.	
6. Plan learning activities, if learners desire, to meet identified group/individual learning needs.	

MANAGEMENT TESTS

Written—or performance—tests of:
‣ Management theories

and/or

‣ Individual approaches to common (or unusual) problems encountered in the practice of management.

Individual learning needs are identified by comparing an individual's test score to some absolute score (national benchmark), the average score of other management employees in the organization, or the score of the "best" management employees in the organization.

Steps in Conducting MDNA Using the Technique	Advantages and Disadvantages
1. Purchase examinations from an external vendor or prepare examinations in-house.	*Advantages:* ‣ May heighten individual motivation to learn. ‣ Job-related testing is more "objective" than relying on the perceptions of others.
2. Target individuals to take the tests, explaining beforehand: ‣ What the results do and do not mean. ‣ How the results will be used—and by whom.	
3. Administer the test.	*Disadvantages:*
4. Score results and/or allow individuals to self-score.	‣ Test scores may be misused by unschooled or unethical people.
5. Facilitate discussion about: ‣ What the results mean. ‣ How the results may be used appropriately. ‣ Issues of ethics and confidentiality.	‣ May create disparate impact (that is, produce discriminatory results).
6. Plan learning activities, if desired,	

Steps in Conducting MDNA Using the Technique	Advantages and Disadvantages
to meet identified group/individual learning needs.	

WRITTEN NEEDS ASSESSMENT SURVEYS

A very popular method of collecting information about learning needs for MD, as well as for employee training generally, a written needs assessment survey typically consists of a series of questions about the need for different training courses (or other planned learning experiences). Such a survey is usually sent to targeted learners, their immediate organizational superiors, and/or other stakeholders in MD. Written surveys may be regarded as "interviews reduced to written form."

Steps in Conducting MDNA Using the Technique	Advantages and Disadvantages

Steps in Conducting MDNA Using the Technique

1. Draft a written survey to assess management learning needs in one or more management job categories in an organization by:
   - Purchasing (or locating) a survey questionnaire from a publisher or other source and modifying it in a way that is in compliance with copyright restrictions, or
   - Using results of interview questions to draft a tailor-made survey.
2. Pretest the survey by calling together a group of stakeholders (prospective learners, their immediate organizational superiors, or their immediate subordinates) and, going through the survey item by item, working to improve the clarity of the questions posed before the survey is sent out.
3. Select a sample to receive the survey.
4. Select analytical methods for processing results.
5. Test the survey, if appropriate, by selecting a small group of stakeholders at random and sending

Advantages and Disadvantages

Advantages:
- Allows much information to be collected and analyzed quickly.
- Heightens expectations for change by involving many people in the needs assessment process.
- Relatively inexpensive (compared to cost of conducting on-site interviews).

Disadvantages:
- May build unrealistic expectations for change.
- Not everyone sends in a completed survey, leading to incomplete results.

(continues)

Exhibit 3-2 (*continued*).

Steps in Conducting MDNA Using the Technique	Advantages and Disadvantages
the survey to them. Use the test results to assess response rates and to identify questions needing possible revision. 6. Revise the survey, as appropriate. 7. Administer the survey. 8. Analyze the survey results. 9. Feed back the survey results to stakeholders. 10. Plan learning activities based on identified learning needs.	

CRITICAL INCIDENT TECHNIQUE

A very effective approach to collecting information about MD needs, the critical incident technique was first used to train military pilots and spies. The aim of this method is to collect information about needs that are of life-and-death importance (hence the use of the term *critical*) on the basis of specific and relatively common situations encountered in the past (hence the term *incident*). In its purest form the method is quite simple: Ask experienced management employees about the worst situations they have encountered in the past, and use their answers to ensure that the newly hired, newly promoted, or newly transferred are trained how to handle those situations.

Steps in Conducting MDNA Using the Technique	Advantages and Disadvantages

1. Select a group or panel (6–15 people) of experienced job incumbents, such as supervisors, managers, or executives.
2. Call a meeting of the panel.
3. Answer these questions:
  ‣ What is the critical incident technique?
  ‣ How can the results be used?
  ‣ What will be done in the meeting?
4. Ask panel members to write down:
  ‣ A description of the most difficult situations each of them has
	Advantages:
	‣ Fast.
	‣ Very appealing to no-nonsense/skeptical management employees.
	‣ Focused on the most difficult, hard-to-handle issues/situations.
	
	Disadvantages:
	‣ Tends to be oriented to past or current problems rather than those that may arise in the uncertain future.
	‣ Lacks a logical flow from one incident to others (that flow must be imposed).

Steps in Conducting MDNA Using the Technique	**Advantages and Disadvantages**

   encountered in his or her management career.
   ‣ A description of how the situa-
      tions were handled.
   ‣ A description of how the situa-
      tions should be handled if they
      should happen in the future.
5. Share the situations with the
   group.
6. Prioritize the training on the situations (on the basis of group members' input).
7. Include coverage of critical incidents in:
   ‣ Classroom training.
   ‣ On-the-job training.
   ‣ Other methods.

THE DELPHI PROCEDURE

This method of collecting information about learning needs takes its name from the ancient Greek oracle of Delphi. The method is not solely associated with MD; rather, it has been widely applied to futures research. When using the Delphi procedure, choose a panel of experts in the job category and conduct numerous rounds of surveys until results converge around common themes.

Steps in Conducting MDNA Using the Technuque	**Advantages and Disadvantages**

1. Select a group or panel (6–15
   people) of stakeholders in MD—
   such as experienced job incumbents, their organizational superiors, their organizational subordinates, customers, and/or others.
2. Ask the group members to participate in a Delphi study of management learning needs by job category—that is, for such groups as
   supervisors, managers, or executives.
3. Draft a written survey about issues
   of importance to the organization,

Advantages:
‣ Has a long and venerable history.
‣ Lends itself to examinations of the
   future as well as of the past or
   present.
‣ Requires minimal time commitment
   from busy management employees.

Disadvantages:
‣ Takes some time to reach a
   conclusion.
‣ May require several rounds of
   surveys to obtain good results for all
   management job categories.

(continues)

Exhibit 3-2 (*continued*).

Steps in Conducting MDNA Using the Technique	**Advantages and Disadvantages**
individuals, and job categories and/or about perceived MD needs for each job category.	‣ Results may become outdated quickly as new challenges face the organization.

4. Ask a small group (2–3 people) to review the survey's clarity and contents before it is shared with the Delphi panel.
5. Revise the survey.
6. Send out the survey to the Delphi panel.
7. Compile results and develop a second survey based on key issues and/or needs identified in the first survey.
8. Ask a small group (2–3 people) to review the clarity and contents of the second survey before it is shared with the full Delphi panel.
9. Revise the second survey.
10. Send out the results of the first survey and the second survey to the Delphi panel.
11. Repeat steps 7 through 10 until the responses of the Delphi panel converge around common issues of importance and/or learning needs by job category.
12. Use results of the Delphi panel to identify issues/needs affecting each job category and to assess individuals' learning needs against those results.

NOMINAL GROUP TECHNIQUE (NGT)

NGT, like the Delphi procedure, has been widely used in assessing the learning needs of employee groups other than management. The basic idea is to call together a group of experienced employees and/or their immediate organizational superiors and to give them a series of questions to which they respond in writing. Then the responses are shared.

Steps in Conducting MDNA Using the Technique

1. Select a group or panel of (6–15) people who are knowledgeable about a management job category in the organization.
2. Ask the group members to participate in a Nominal Group to identify:
   - Key issues affecting management employees.
   - Learning needs for each job category of management employees in an organization.
3. Call a meeting of the group or panel.
4. Hand each panel member a 3" × 5" index card and ask him or her to identify key issues affecting a management job category in the organization.
5. Ask panel members to:
   - Place one issue on each card.
   - Work in silence.
   - Hand in their cards as they finish them.
6. Place the ideas on a flipchart, blackboard, or overhead transparency.
7. Ask group members to vote on the relative importance of each issue (the highest vote "wins" top priority).
8. Ask group members to vote on issues they believe should be the focus of planned learning experiences (MD activities) for one job category—such as supervisor, manager, or executive (the highest vote "wins" top priority).
9. Compile the results after the meeting, and distribute them to participants and other stakeholders.
10. Use the results as a starting point for setting MD priorities and for

Advantages and Disadvantages

Advantages:
- Same as for the Delphi procedure.

Disadvantages:
- Same as for the Delphi procedure.

(continues)

Exhibit 3-2 *(continued)*.

Steps in Conducting MDNA Using the Technique	**Advantages and Disadvantages**
assessing individual, group, and organizational learning needs by job category.	
11. Repeat the approach for other job categories.	

---

performance appraisals; others keep them separate, preferring instead to tie individual needs assessment to management career planning or succession planning activities. Individual Development Plans (IDPs), prepared annually, are often a guiding force for MDNA.

Who Should Participate in MDNA?

Participants in MDNA, like those in assessing learning needs for other occupational groups in organizations,[11] may include:

- Targeted participants
- Immediate organizational superiors of targeted participants
- Peers
- Organizational subordinates
- Professional or industry associates
- Customers, suppliers, or other stakeholders
- Spouses or family members of targeted participants
- Predecessors
- Mentors or sponsors of targeted participants

When all these groups participate in MDNA, it is called *360-degree needs assessment* because the providers form a circle of acquaintances around the targeted learners.[12]

Targeted participants are an important source of information about their needs. Their perceptions should not be minimized, and their participation and involvement in MDNA can build their ownership and support. Immediate organizational superiors are uniquely positioned to detect individual needs, provide coaching, and identify individual strengths and weaknesses. They can also assess the individual's potential for advancement. Peers, organizational subordinates, professional associates, industry associates, customers, spouses, family members,

Exhibit 3-3. Frequency of use for different techniques of MD needs assessment.

Question: There are various ways by which to assess training and development needs for management employees of an organization. For each method listed in the left column, circle an appropriate response in the right column. Use these codes for your responses:

1 = Not at all
2 = Seldom
3 = Sometimes
4 = Frequently
5 = With all management employees

Needs Assessment Method	Number of Occurrences	Mean Frequency of Use
1. Individual development plans	62	3.58
2. Interviews	63	3.38
3. Written/phone needs assessment surveys	63	2.78
4. Focus groups	60	2.67
5. Management diagnostic questionnaires	63	2.51
6. Succession plans	63	2.46
7. Competence model for management positions	63	2.24
8. Management tests	61	1.62
9. Assessment center(s)	63	1.56
10. DACUM method	53	1.21

Source: William J. Rothwell and H. C. Kazanas, "Results of a 1992 Survey on Management Development Practices in the U.S." (Urbana, Ill.: Department of Vocational and Technical Education, 1992, unpublished).

predecessors, and mentors or sponsors are uniquely positioned to observe management employees in other ways. Generally, the more opinions collected and the more perspectives taken into account, the more powerful and rounded the needs assessment of individuals—or groups.

Summary

In this chapter we defined needs as performance gaps separating what management employees already know or do and what they should know or do. Needs are identified through an assessment process designed to uncover and prioritize those performance gaps. Many different methods may be used to collect and analyze information about learning needs.

Chapter 4

Establishing a Management Development Curriculum

As we explained in Chapter 3, MD learning needs are performance gaps indicating differences between what management employees already know or do and what they should know or do to perform competently. Nonlearning needs should be met by removing obstacles to individual or group performance; learning needs should be met through planned learning experiences such as training, education, or development. This chapter focuses on establishing a long-term learning or instructional plan, otherwise known as a *curriculum*, to guide a planned MD program and to meet predictable learning needs.

Identifying and Meeting Learning Needs

When you set out to meet learning needs, you will soon discover that it makes sense to approach the task in an organized way. By structuring and planning what you do, you will make the process of meeting learning needs more efficient for you and more understandable to learners. In contrast, a disorganized approach leaves you unsure about what needs to meet or how to know precisely when you have met them. Worse, it subjects learners to anxiety about when they know enough to perform competently on their own.

Perhaps a simple example will dramatize the importance of identifying and meeting learning needs in an organized way.

EXAMPLE

You are a manager setting out to train two recently promoted supervisors. One way you can approach their training is to cover problems as they come up. You simply tell them what to do and how to do it as the need arises. If you use this approach, you do not have to invest any time planning their training. But you will have to keep your fingers crossed and hope that they eventually learn their jobs well enough to function on their own through gradual and unstructured exposure to everyday work experience. Only after an extended time will the learners develop to the point that you will trust them to handle typical daily problems on their own. In the meantime, they will be tortured by self-doubts and may grow dissatisfied. You may have trouble remembering what training they have received, and that will complicate your ability to hold them accountable for what they have learned. After all, you will be unsure just what problems they have experienced through exposure to daily crises. Too much—or too little—of your valuable time will be devoted to their individualized coaching. On occasion you may not be available when they need help, and they will be forced to muddle through emergencies they have not been trained to deal with or mentally prepared to handle.

Another way to approach their training is to cover work duties and responsibilities logically, scheduling activities so that individual progress will be clear. You begin by preparing a detailed job description and deciding how you will judge supervisory performance on each responsibility or desired result. Through this process you clarify your own expectations. By examining the job description carefully, you see that some supervisory responsibilities are shared by all supervisors in the organization; some are shared only by supervisors in one division or department; and, some are unique to one work unit or function. You also see that it will be relatively easy to train newcomers on some issues but not so easy to train them on others. Some responsibilities listed on the job description are logically related and can be effectively treated at the same time. Others are not logically related, and training will require special instructions and more time.

From this information you can begin to prepare an individualized training plan to guide the orientation of each new supervisor. That plan should sequence learning activities logically and should be based on a detailed job description, individual strengths and weaknesses, organizational needs or plans, and external environmental trends or demands. It should clearly establish a basis for accountability by listing what training your new supervisors will receive, when the training will be offered, how it will be handled, and how results will be evaluated. You should share the entire learning plan with each new supervisor at the outset of training, thereby reinforcing the plan's importance and establishing learner accountability. Armed with this plan, you should be able to proceed through new supervisory training in an organized fashion. Even better, you can sidestep the necessity of wasting time on spoon-feeding or hand-holding.

If you follow the approach just outlined, you will have taken the first steps toward devising a *management training curriculum*. The same approach can be usefully applied to the training of newly hired, newly transferred, or newly promoted managers and executives. Alternatively, it can be designed to meet the learning needs of a special group or contribute to the implementation of a special program. On a broad conceptual level, then, a *management development curriculum* goes beyond a training curriculum to integrate management training, education, and development.

The Role of a Centralized MD Function in Meeting Learning Needs

Macro learning needs can be more economically, efficiently, and consistently met by a centralized MD function or department than by numerous managers who separately sponsor their own learning experiences for their employees. A centralized MD function usually focuses on meeting shared learning needs across a job category, special group, or special program. That frees individual managers to devote more attention to meeting learning needs unique to their work functions and to the individuals reporting to them.

Defining Curriculum

Curriculum is derived from the Latin word for *foot race*.[1] The term eventually became associated with a course of study rather than with the course of a foot race. Today it is widely applied to educational course requirements that students must meet before they are eligible to graduate from elementary school, secondary school, trade school, or college.

Taken more generally, a curriculum simply means a *learning* or an *instructional plan*. It need not refer solely to programs sponsored by degree-granting educational institutions. A curriculum may refer to *any* planned learning—whether delivered to learners on the job, off the job, or in some combination of on-the-job and off-the-job learning experiences. These learning experiences may range in length from one minute to many years.

Curriculum development implies an evolutionary process of discovering appropriate learning experiences; *curriculum design* implies a systematic approach to the planning of learning experiences.

Training, Educational, and Developmental Curricula

In Chapter 1 we said that training is job-oriented, education is individual-oriented, and development is organization-oriented. In practice, that means training focuses on helping people meet their job responsibilities, education focuses on preparing individuals for advancement, and development focuses on evoking new insights about the organization, industry, community, society, or culture of which the learners are members.

A curriculum can be designed to meet any or all these needs. It is thus a broad plan for orienting people to new jobs, correcting problems with present performance, upgrading skills, preparing people for advancement, and evoking new ideas.

Reasons for Establishing a Management Development Curriculum

As individuals enter—or prepare to enter—new positions, they must change and adapt to meet new job and organizational requirements. Most people adapt to change best when they are gradually prepared to assume new responsibilities and challenges. Few are capable of making a quantum leap from performing one job to performing a very different job without any help.

The same principles apply to MD. By using an MD curriculum to prepare, orient, and upgrade the skills of management employees, organizations ensure that key people are properly equipped to meet new responsibilities. As Julia Galosy observed, "Curriculum design requires that we view the whole fabric of management learning in its totality; learning experiences are created from this holistic perspective. The challenge of curriculum design is to build a coherent, sequential plan which will provide structure and unity to the full gamut of planned learning experiences."[2] The idea is thus to create a unified view of learning experiences that can help exempt employees meet their learning needs.

Approaches to Curriculum Design for MD

There is no one best way to design an MD curriculum. In fact, there are four basic approaches to developing a curriculum:

1. The subject-centered approach
2. The objectives-centered approach
3. The experience-centered approach
4. The opportunity-centered approach[3]

Their labels suggest the chief distinctions among the approaches. A subject-centered approach bases learning plans on topics or subjects; an objectives-centered approach bases activities on the knowledge or skills the learners are expected to possess after participating in planned learning experiences; the experience-centered approach makes the planning of learning an experience of its own; and the opportunity-centered approach provides individuals with choices about what they learn, leaving it up to them and their immediate organizational superiors to discover opportunities.

The Subject-Centered Approach

The subject-centered approach to curriculum design is perhaps best known, even among people who know little about how to plan learning experiences. It is widely used in American education. Consequently, most people have at least a rudimentary grasp of how it works.

Put simply, the subject-centered approach bases instruction on subjects or course titles. Students in educational institutions take courses geared to grade level. Needs assessment is carried out centrally, the province of state boards of education (at the elementary or secondary level) and accrediting bodies (at the college level). Planning course details within a curriculum is left to teachers, and instructional delivery methods rarely vary. Despite advancing technology, educators still rely heavily on classroom delivery rather than video-based, audio-based, or computer-based alternatives. Nor is hands-on field experience common. Instructional evaluation is often minimal and indirect; students take tests and receive individual grades. Little is done to evaluate the daily performance of individual students or teachers to provide prompt, specific feedback that might be of use in improving their performance.

As a simple example of a subject-centered curriculum, consider the courses required to earn a master of business administration degree. Many public and private schools allow entry into M.B.A. programs through two routes: one for those who completed an undergraduate major in business administration, the other for those who completed an undergraduate major in another discipline. The core subjects in a typical M.B.A. curriculum include production/operations management, marketing, finance, organizational behavior, and business policy/strategic planning. Students with undergraduate business majors take these courses and electives; students without undergraduate business majors also complete prerequisite courses in economics, statistics, accounting, and other business-related subjects.

The subject-centered approach to curriculum design can also be applied to developing curricula for people in designated job categories, special groups, or special programs in a planned MD program. Needs assessment is carried out centrally—and sometimes informally—by an MD director, an MD coordinator, a steering committee, a coordinating committee, or a project team. Planned learning experiences are identified to correspond to the major job responsibilities of the targeted learners. Methods of planning each learning experience are left up to trainers or vendors. Instructional delivery methods may vary. Evaluation is carried out chiefly by participants.

To design a subject-centered MD curriculum, take the following steps:

1. Update job descriptions for the targeted job category, making sure to obtain a list of key responsibilities.
2. Formulate a course title to correspond to the knowledge or skills needed to meet each key responsibility identified on the job description.
3. Group, as appropriate, related knowledge or skills to reduce the course titles to a manageable number.
4. Sequence the course titles in the order of their importance to meet the needs of individuals who are:
   a. Preparing to enter the job category. (What "subjects" should the participants learn about first, second, and so on?)
   b. Orienting themselves to the job category.
   c. Upgrading their skills, having already gained experience.
   d. Preparing for movement to other job categories or making other life changes.
5. Design each planned learning experience in the subject-centered curriculum in greater detail, focusing on the individual or collective group needs of the participants.[4]

See Exhibit 4-1 for a worksheet to use in devising a subject-centered management curriculum for supervisors. The same approach can be used to design a management curriculum for managers or executives.

The subject-centered approach has unique advantages and disadvantages. The chief advantages are that it is quick, dirty, and cheap. You can prepare a curriculum in short order for aspiring supervisors, experienced supervisors, aspiring managers, experienced managers, aspiring executives, and experienced executives. People who want to see quick results are generally happy with how quickly a subject-centered approach can produce a unified MD curriculum.

There are disadvantages, however. Because the curriculum design process is handled quickly and rarely permits much participation, only a few people feel any ownership in the results. Others may complain that the subjects have little or nothing to do with daily work activities— and that is a significant problem. The subjects identified may not be treated consistently, varying across instructors or vendors, leading to inconsistencies in preparation and subsequent work performance of program participants. If internal group training is the primary vehicle for delivering the instruction, then scheduling can become problematic in today's lean organizations, in which the management ranks have

text continues on page 90

Exhibit 4-1. Worksheet for creating a subject-centered MD curriculum.

Directions: Use this worksheet to practice creating a subject-centered MD curriculum on the basis of the supervisory job description. For each responsibility listed in the left column of Part I, write a course title in the right column. Then, in Part II, group all related or similar responsibilities under a reduced number of course titles. Finally, in Part III, establish a tentative supervisory training curriculum by sequencing the course titles as you feel they should be delivered to aspiring, to newly promoted, and to experienced supervisors.

Part I

Supervisory Responsibility Listed on Job Description	Course Title
1. Take daily attendance of employees.	
2. Schedule work flow, exceptions to normal work flow, and work on backlogs.	
3. Manage time of self and workers.	
4. Monitor productivity of workers assigned.	
5. Train employees on procedures and products.	
6. Coordinate unit activities with other units and departments.	
7. Document changes in work procedures.	
8. Perform cost/benefit analysis of projects.	
9. Conduct employee performance appraisals.	
10. Coach and positively reinforce employees.	
11. Correspond with suppliers, wholesalers, retailers, and customers.	
12. Set goals and objectives with employees.	
13. Interview prospective employees.	
14. Discipline and, on occasion, terminate employees in compliance with organizational policy and applicable laws, rules, and regulations.	
15. Prepare budget for the work unit in consultation with manager.	

Supervisory Responsibility Listed on Job Description	Course Title
16. Identify need for backup workers and oversee worker cross-training.	
17. Order supplies and raw materials.	
18. Conduct staff meetings with employees.	
19. Prepare payroll for the work unit.	
20. Schedule vacations.	
21. Authorize overtime.	
22. Perform overtime calculations for employees.	
23. Ensure employee compliance with general safety and accident procedures for assigned employees.	

Part II

Group all related or similar responsibilities under a reduced number of course titles, based on your response to Part I.

Related Responsibilities	Course Title

Part III

Basing your work on the results of Part II, sequence the course titles as you feel they should be delivered.

Job Categories/Targeted Groups	Course Titles in the Appropriate Sequence
‣ Aspiring supervisors preparing for promotion	1. _____
	2. _____

(continues)

Exhibit 4-1 (*continued*).

Job Categories/Targeted Groups	Course Titles in the Appropriate Sequence
	3. _____
	4. _____
	5. _____
‣ Newly hired, promoted, or transferred supervisors	1. _____
	2. _____
	3. _____
	4. _____
	5. _____
‣ Experienced supervisors who require updating, retraining, or preparation for advancement	1. _____
	2. _____
	3. _____
	4. _____
	5. _____

been cut so dramatically that it becomes difficult for people to steal time from daily work pressures to attend planned learning experiences away from their work sites. Every hour spent in the classroom is an hour away from the job. If training is offered on nonworking time, some people will not show up—and it will be difficult to force them to do so. Course evaluations based on participant reactions will carry little weight with results-oriented managers who want to know how much money was saved or what performance problems were solved as a result of investments in planned learning experiences.

The Objectives-Centered Approach

The objectives-centered approach to curriculum design is widely associated with technical training. However, it can also be applied to planned MD. It takes its name from its emphasis on *performance objectives*. Objectives are the explicit results to be achieved from planned learning activities. They are articulated in writing. Performance objectives are matched directly to meeting learning needs; each objective presents a desired *solution* to an identified need, problem, or deficiency of individual knowledge, skill, or attitude.

The objectives-centered approach is usually based on existing work requirements, although it is possible to identify possible *future* work requirements and to base the curriculum on those. Needs assessment focuses on identifying performance gaps between actual and desired work performance and organizational requirements. As needs are identified, they become the basis for performance objectives; objectives are grouped and logically sequenced to form courses and other planned learning experiences. Learning experiences are based on the objectives and leave little room for the subjective opinions of MD specialists, participants, or top managers.

To design an objectives-centered MD curriculum, take the following steps:

1. Assess:
   a. Management work requirements.
   b. Organizational requirements.
   c. Individual strengths and weaknesses.
2. Analyze:
   a. The group targeted for participation.
   b. The work environment.
3. Conduct MD needs assessment.
4. Develop performance objectives on the basis of needs.
5. Prepare written or performance-based tests to assess learner achievement on the basis of performance objectives.
6. Identify strategies to meet the performance objectives.
7. Prepare, locate, and, if necessary, modify materials to meet the objectives and thereby help participants to meet the learning needs.
8. Deliver or facilitate planned learning experiences.
9. Evaluate MD methods and/or the MD program.[5]

These steps are systematic because the results (*outputs*) of each step become the starting points (*inputs*) for subsequent steps.

The objectives-centered approach has its own advantages and disadvantages. A chief advantage is its focus on job-related performance and learner accountability. After all, performance objectives signify the results to be achieved from planned learning, and they are directly linked to needs, instructional content, and tests. This approach is very detailed, and skeptical managers who want to see effective results are generally pleased with it. That is a major selling point.

However, there is one big disadvantage to the objectives-centered approach: The process of designing planned learning experiences can be very time-consuming and costly. Effectiveness is achieved at the cost of speed. Targeted participants and their immediate organizational superiors may complain that it takes too long to prepare and to deliver planned learning experiences designed in this way, though few question their value once they have been designed.

The Experience-Centered Approach

The experience-centered approach is often linked to Organization Development (OD), a long-term approach to planned organizational change that relies heavily on behavioral science techniques. Like OD, the experience-centered approach:

‣ Bases planned MD experiences on the highly participative *action research model* that consists of such phases as data collection, feedback, problem solving, implementation, and evaluation. Needs are identified by learners and other stakeholders; strategies for meeting needs are identified by the same group. The steps of this process are continuous, making them ideal to integrate with increasingly popular total quality management (TQM) efforts, employee involvement (EI) programs, and work-team directed efforts.

‣ Is geared to achieving long-term cultural and organizational change. MD becomes a tool for changing organizations by involving the leadership in a highly participative and long-term planned learning experience.

To design an experience-centered MD curriculum, take the following steps:

1. Identify performance problems in management, separating what management employees should know and do from what they already know or can do.
2. Feed the results of step 1 back to each level of management.
3. Facilitate efforts by each level of management to:
   a. Diagnose the cause(s) of these gaps.
   b. Plan MD experiences designed to solve the problems and thereby meet needs.
4. Involve members of management in each step of implementing planned MD experiences. These steps include:
   a. Assessing learning needs.

    b. Selecting methods to meet the needs.

    c. Delivering planned learning experiences.

    d. Evaluating results.

5. Feed the results of steps 1 through 4 back to all members of management to ensure that the process is highly participative and oriented toward continuous improvement.[6]

The experience-centered approach is advantageous for one major reason. Since developing an experience-centered curriculum is highly participative, the process builds strong ownership among those it serves. In time, aspiring and experienced supervisors, managers, and executives will come to accept an MD curriculum that they and their predecessors have established and have continued to refine.

But there are two major disadvantages to using this approach: It tends to be very time-consuming, and it focuses on solving *past* performance problems. A participative approach simply takes more time than other approaches to design and deliver. And, because a participative approach involves management employees in identifying needs, there is a tendency to base learning experiences on performance problems experienced in the past, particularly worst-case situations that are more easily remembered than routine ones.

The Opportunity-Centered Approach

Identifying and meeting *individual* MD needs is the chief focus of the opportunity-centered approach, which is customarily designed from the bottom up. The centerpiece of the opportunity-centered approach is an *individualized learning plan* (IDP) or *learning contract* prepared for each management employee each year. (The terms *individualized learning plan* and *learning contract* are synonymous.)

To design an opportunity-centered MD curriculum, take the following steps:

1. Establish a program in which management employees meet with their immediate organizational superiors at some regular interval, usually once each year, in order to discuss:

    a. Individual performance gaps (needs stemming from past and current performance).

    b. Individual career goals (needs stemming from future aspirations).

    c. The organization's future goals (needs stemming from plans).

2. Establish an individualized plan to meet the needs through planned MD experiences. This plan should be reached by mu-

tual agreement between individuals and their immediate organizational superiors.

3. Establish a means by which to hold both individuals and their
    immediate organizational superiors accountable for achieving
    results.
4. Feed the results of IDPs at all levels to:
    a. Top managers.
    b. The MD director, MD coordinator, or MD committee.
5. Aggregate the IDPs to identify common needs shared by many
    people.
6. Prepare an instructional plan to meet common needs through
    internal group training, external group training, or other MD
    methods.
7. Establish a means by which to offer consulting advice to meet
    uniquely individual needs, as needed.
8. Track and monitor activities and results against IDPs to provide
    information for future planning.[7]

One big advantage of the opportunity-centered approach is that it
is directed toward *individualizing* learning plans. Supervisors, managers, and executives—as leaders in each of their functions—often face
unique challenges. As leaders, their influence over others makes their
individual strengths and weaknesses critical to organizational success.
Indeed, as people advance to higher-level responsibilities, how they
personalize their jobs becomes more important. One value of the opportunity-centered approach is that it is tailor-made to deal with uniquely
individual needs, dovetailing nicely with strategic and succession
plans.

Another big advantage of the opportunity-centered approach is
that it is highly participative, giving management employees a chance
to meet with their immediate organizational superiors to identify needs
and to plan for short- and long-term training, education, and development to meet those needs. The results of IDPs are, in turn, fed back to:

- Higher-level managers, so they are familiar with individual and
  group MD needs and issues
- A centralized MD function that can track individual and group
  needs, monitor achievement, and provide support and technical
  assistance to meet the needs

Finally, an opportunity-centered approach does not preclude the
use of other approaches. For instance, the organization can establish a
subject-centered MD curriculum for training courses. When an IDP

Exhibit 4-2. Prevalence of MD curricula at different levels.

Question: A *curriculum* is a long-term, standing series of planned learning experiences—such as training courses—for individuals, work units, or job categories. Indicate groups for which your organization has a curriculum.

	Yes		No	
	Frequency	**Percentages**	**Frequency**	**Percentages**
Individuals just promoted to supervision?	54	87.10%	8	12.90%
Experienced supervisors?	48	77.42	14	22.58
Individuals just promoted to middle management?	45	71.43	18	28.57
Experienced middle managers?	39	62.90	23	37.10
Individuals aspiring to become supervisors?	32	50.79	31	49.21
Individuals aspiring to become middle managers?	28	46.67	32	53.33
Individuals just promoted to top management?	20	32.79	41	67.21
Experienced top managers?	18	29.03	44	70.97
Individuals aspiring to become top managers?	13	21.67	47	78.33

Source: William J. Rothwell and H. C. Kazanas, "Results of a 1992 Survey on Management Development Practices in the U.S." (Urbana, Ill.: Department of Vocational and Technical Education, 1992, unpublished).

indicates that an individual experiences a learning need that can be met by a regularly scheduled internal group training session, the individual merely signs up to participate.

There is one major disadvantage to the opportunity-centered approach: It places heavy emphasis on the relationship between individuals and their immediate organizational superiors. While few can dispute that the employee-boss relationship exerts profound influence over individual development, not all organizational superiors are equally adept at or motivated to develop those reporting to them. In addition, management employees—like all employees—are subject to a pigeon holing or stereotyping effect in which their immediate organizational superiors' impressions of their current performance and future potential can be difficult to change. If those impressions are unfair or inaccurate, they pose a very real stumbling block to individual development.

The MD Curriculum: What Are Other Organizations Doing?

Research reveals that organizations are not adequately planning their MD efforts,[8] even though more money per employee is spent on developing supervisors, managers, and executives than is spent on developing individuals in other occupational groups.

In our 1992 survey (described in Chapter 1), we learned that recently promoted and experienced supervisors are the two groups for which most organizations have established a curriculum (see Exhibit 4-2). Thus, MD curricula exist more often at lower than at higher management levels. This fact supports the conclusion that higher-level management employees tend to receive more individualized attention and to participate in more individualized planned learning experiences than do lower-level management employees.

Summary

In this chapter we explained that curriculum design means planning learning experiences, a process intended to satisfy needs. There are four basic approaches to curriculum design for MD. Each approach implies different steps. They are not mutually exclusive and may be used in combination. A curriculum is implemented through specific MD activities, including on-the-job or off-the-job training, education, and developmental experiences.

Chapter 5

Administering a Management Development Program

This chapter describes how to set up an *administrative support system* consisting of the policies, procedures, and activities necessary to ensure that a planned MD program is carried out. With an administrative support system, an organization's action on MD will be an outgrowth of coordinated, consistent, and effective action.

What to Consider

As you establish a planned MD program, consider the following questions:

1. Where should the MD function be positioned in the organization's reporting structure?
2. What rewards or incentives should be offered to management to encourage members to accept responsibility for developing their own skills and knowledge and those of the employees who report to them?
3. What kind of leader should direct the planned MD program?
4. How should the program leader be recruited, selected, and oriented?
5. How should internal staff members and external vendors be selected, oriented, and trained?
6. How should planned MD activities be scheduled?
7. How should budgeting be handled?
8. What records of MD activities should be kept?
9. How should MD program activities be publicized?

In this chapter we address these questions. Before reading the chapter, however, pause a moment to formulate your own answers by completing

Exhibit 5-1. Worksheet for listing administrative issues regarding a planned MD program.

Directions: Use this worksheet to structure your thinking about important administrative issues to consider when establishing and operating a planned MD program. For each question, jot down your answer(s) in the space below. Add paper as necessary. There are no "right" or "wrong" answers in any absolute sense, although some questions may be more or less appropriate, depending on the organization's culture, top managers' attitudes about MD, and the organization's expressed policy and philosophy for MD.

---

1. Where should the MD function be positioned in the organization's reporting structure?

2. What rewards or incentives should be offered to members of management to encourage them to accept responsibility for their development and that of their management subordinates?

3. What kind of leader should direct the planned MD program?

4. How should the program leader be recruited, selected, and oriented?

5. How should internal staff members and external vendors be selected, oriented, and trained?

6. How should planned MD activities be scheduled?

7. How should budgeting be handled?

8. What records of MD activities should be kept?

9. How should MD program activities be publicized?

---

the worksheet in Exhibit 5-1. As you complete the worksheet, think about the written program policy and philosophy governing your planned MD program. Does it provide clues to answer the questions? If not, you may wish to modify it so that it does. Pose the questions on the worksheet to members of a committee, task force, or project group involved in the MD program.

Positioning MD

Where should the MD function be positioned in the organization's reporting structure? That is an important first question to answer about the administrative support structure. The best answer may depend on the size of the organization, the issue of responsibility, and the options available.

Differences by Organizational Size

Large organizations of 1,000 or more employees often have a unit or a department charged with responsibility for coordinating MD; smaller organizations, which rarely have an MD unit or department, are more likely to make operations a committee or task force responsibility. In both cases, however, somebody *must* be charged with program responsibility. Otherwise grand ideas will founder on crude procedures. Indeed, MD will soon be forgotten amid the daily pressures to get the work out. One result of such neglect is that, in smaller organizations, no successors will be prepared to carry on after the company founder's death, retirement, or disability. In larger organizations, the inability to place the right leaders in the right places at the right times will sound the death knell for strategic plans. In addition, because managers tend to hire and promote individuals like themselves and because the management ranks of most organizations are dominated by white males, the lack of planned MD may limit advancement opportunities for women, minorities, the disabled, and people over age 40.

Who Bears Responsibility?

It seems logical to position MD where greatest responsibility for it rests. However, in an important sense, MD is pervasive: All supervisors, managers, and executives bear an important responsibility to develop their own skills and those of the people reporting to them. An organization's ultimate responsibility for MD, like that for strategic planning, rests with the highest official. In large organizations that is usually the CEO; in small organizations it is the owner, founder, or proprietor.

Options for Positioning

Even though MD is a pervasive responsibility, someone must be charged with the responsibility for coordinating and carrying out MD activities, ensuring they are scheduled and managed. Most often, MD can be positioned within the following departments or units:

1. Training and development
2. Human resource management
3. Planning or development
4. The office of the chief executive
5. A line department
6. A department reporting to the CEO
7. The corporate board of directors

Each placement has advantages and disadvantages.

When placed in the training and development (T&D) or the human resources development (HRD) department, MD is linked to the key function with which it is commonly associated—planned learning activities carried out for performance improvement. That is a major advantage. It can lead to a desirable cross-fertilization of ideas about an organization's employee training, education, and development activities. Moreover, it can produce a powerful integration of all HRD efforts, including technical development, sales development, management development, and professional development.

But this placement can be disadvantageous if T&D or HRD is placed two or more levels below the CEO in the organization's chain of command. That placement complicates access to top managers. One result: a predictable focus on the needs of target groups at or below the placement of the person carrying out MD-related activities.

A second disadvantage can arise if MD is placed with T&D or HRD. Some T&D or HRD specialists view their function *solely* as providing a "corporate schoolhouse" offering classroom courses.[1] Off-the-job, rather than on-the-job, learning experiences are emphasized. When linked to a department holding to that philosophy, the MD function may emphasize management *training* at the expense of management *education* or management *development*. Yet most Management Development, like most employee learning generally, occurs outside classrooms and on the job.

Placing MD in the human resources management (HRM) or personnel department links it to an important function that contributes to planning and meeting the organization's leadership needs. That placement can produce a results-focused orientation in which the planned MD program is linked directly to HR plans. Moreover, placement in HRM connects MD with other important activities that influence it, among them job/work analysis, performance appraisal, compensation, benefits, recruitment, selection, and Organization Development.

There are two primary disadvantages to this placement, however. First, MD is removed from the CEO by at least one level, as is also true when MD is placed with T&D. Making matters worse, some HR managers are hesitant to allow the director of MD to work directly with other managers in the organization, serving as a resource person and an internal consultant. They prefer that communication be handled formally through the chain of command so that all messages from higher-level managers pass through the HR manager first. That practice can compromise the value of MD as a means to offer consulting services and advice to others. Second, placing MD with HRM encourages managers to view MD as a staff or advisory function. That turns out to be a spot with low credibility in many organizations. Conflict between "line" and "staff" managerial officers has been the subject of problems—and discussions[2]—for many years.

At first glance it would seem natural to place MD with an organization's planning or development function. MD should be viewed from a long-term perspective, a view that should be common among planners and developers. When the organization's planning or development function coordinates strategic planning and MD efforts are linked to it, important long-term benefits can be realized.

Unfortunately, planners and developers often focus their attention on financial forecasting or budgeting issues and exclude or downplay HR issues. Some do not know *how* to plan for HR. (Indeed, one chief of planning in a very large corporation once told us that "we tried HR planning and systematic MD activities, and we couldn't make them work.") If there is no willingness to attempt MD in a systematic way tied to the organization's needs and strategies, then placing MD with corporate planning or development will not usually work out.

Placing MD in the office of the CEO can achieve goodness of fit only when the CEO is a champion and supporter of planned MD. Such a placement gives the director of MD access to the individual who, by virtue of position, should be most interested in MD and also enables the director of MD to work comfortably with top- and middle-level managers.

But this placement also has its drawbacks. Chief among them is that, if the CEO is not a supporter of MD, the director of MD will not feel secure in the position—and probably will not last long. Another drawback is that the closeness to the CEO may create reluctance among managers to discuss their subordinates and themselves realistically. They will hesitate to be frank. Some will be tempted to paint an overly optimistic picture for the CEO's benefit, thereby creating a positive impression about MD in various divisions in which conditions are not positive.

Placing MD directly in a line management department, such as marketing, finance, operations, or production, puts it near the largest group of potential customers. After all, line management departments traditionally have more supervisors, managers, and executives than staff departments do.

But this placement is not ideal. Whatever line department MD is placed in will tend to become the prime—and sometimes the only—"customer." Managers in other departments will be reluctant to ask for help from an MD director whom they may view as tied to one organizational function, since they may reason that he or she is involved with that function exclusively. Even when that is not true, this kind of placement can lead to an unfortunate reluctance among others to ask for support.

MD can be a department in its own right but yet not be part of the CEO's office. In this case, the director of MD reports directly to the CEO and appears on the organization chart as a peer of other first-tier managers.

There can be real benefits to this placement. The director of MD has access to the CEO and to other first-tier managers but is not viewed as a member of the CEO's staff. Managers in other parts of the organization are likely to view MD as a source of help, and assurances of confidentiality are easier for them to believe.

Finally, the MD function can be placed directly under the board of directors, perhaps as a board-authorized committee. This placement gives the function the aura of the board's power and gives MD an independence from other activities that is hard to find anywhere else. Unfortunately, too few boards of directors take a firsthand interest in MD, as they do in financial matters. As a result, this placement is most unusual. Nevertheless, it is worthy of exploration.

Encouraging MD Through Rewards and Incentives

While theories of motivation differ dramatically, two conclusions about motivation seem inescapable: People will do what they are rewarded for doing and will not do what they are punished for doing. These principles apply to MD: Executives, managers, and supervisors will take a dedicated interest in the training, education, and development of themselves and of the employees reporting to them only when they are rewarded for doing so. If they are overtly or inadvertently punished for such action, they will avoid it. It is important to understand that the success or failure of any planned MD program rests heavily in the hands of the participants and their immediate organizational superiors. Moreover, it should *not* be viewed as the sole responsibility of an MD director or MD coordinator. The responsibility for MD cannot and should not be delegated down an organization's chain of command or shoved onto a staff administrator; rather, that responsibility must be shouldered by *every* executive, manager, and supervisor.

But how does an organization encourage management employees to take an interest in self-development and in the development of those reporting to them? There are at least four basic approaches:

1. Responsibility for MD can be made explicit, and management employees at all levels can be routinely held accountable for it.
2. The organization can offer incentive bonuses for MD.
3. The organization can offer nonpecuniary rewards for MD results.
4. The three approaches can be combined.

One way to encourage management employees to take a personal interest in self-development and in the development of management employees reporting to them is to make that responsibility explicit and subject to periodic review.

For instance, the responsibility for MD can be listed on management job descriptions. That makes it clear that the responsibility is an important one. If this approach is chosen, it is important to make clear that management employees are responsible for their own development as well as sharing responsibility for employees reporting to them.

You can also determine how well the responsibility is being carried out by making MD an item for discussion during performance appraisals, salary reviews, and career counseling sessions. Management employees, like most employees, will be influenced by whatever they believe affects their salary raises and their chances for advancement.

By listing MD as an issue for consideration in employment decisions, the organization demonstrates powerful support for it.

Another approach: Put in place an organizational policy that management employees can be promoted or transferred only when they have groomed their own replacements. While extremely powerful, this policy must be monitored carefully. It may not produce dependable or consistently reliable results because some management employees will not be sure how to interpret its requirements. Specific directions must be given about how to groom a replacement and how satisfactory results will be measured.

One alternative to imposing explicit requirements for MD is to create incentives for it. An incentive is perhaps best understood as an inducement or a means of encouragement. An incentive system, as the term is commonly used in compensation practice, is based on the assumptions that people:

- Are able to perform what is desired
- Believe they can perform what is desired
- Believe that what they do will result in more money—or other rewards—for them
- Value the rewards they will receive
- Will not be forced into pursuing conflicting priorities by the incentives

Finally, incentives must be based on measurable results that vary across people.

At least two kinds of incentive programs, both using managerial bonuses, can be established to encourage MD:

1. A program geared to the immediate organizational superiors of one or more targeted management individuals, groups, or job categories
2. A program directly geared to the targeted individuals, groups, or job categories

In both cases, funds are allocated from the organization's profits—or, in the case of government agencies or not-for-profit enterprises, from appropriations or revenues—to pay for the bonuses, which usually range from 20 percent to 80 percent of base pay, depending on the job category of the person receiving them.[3]

In both cases, objectives for MD are established at the beginning of a year. They should be based on measurable criteria, including:

• *Number of hours.* How much time is spent by each management employee each year participating in internal group training, external group training, external education, or other learning experiences?

• *Planned objectives vs. achieved results.* What planned learning objectives were negotiated between management employees and their immediate organizational superiors? What results were achieved? How well do results match objectives?

• *Fulfillment of management certification requirements.* A certification program is a curriculum of planned learning experiences, with certification meaning that the individual has completed a program related to individual, job, or organizational requirements or plans. Management employees should be allowed to progress at their own speeds but minimal progress should be a requirement for a pay raise. If they progress faster than expected and their job performance is at least satisfactory, then they become eligible for higher-than-average pay raises. This approach is comparable to a pay-for-knowledge program.[4]

• *Number of management employees promoted to other responsible positions in the organization.* Some organizations recognize, and encourage, management employees who prepare their people for advancement to other positions in the organization. Such managers acquire a reputation as "people developers," and those who work for them are sometimes sought out by others in the organization.

There are good reasons to establish incentive programs both for employees and for their immediate organizational superiors. Such programs encourage employees to develop their skills, and their immediate organizational superiors are also encouraged to support that development.

When most people think of rewards, money is usually the first thought that crosses their minds. But money has long been viewed as a questionable motivator. Its effects are short-lived. Once people receive raises, they want others almost immediately. Using money as a reward is also difficult in today's cost-conscious organizational environments, where it is becoming increasingly difficult to fund the swelling expenses of employee health-care benefits and still offer salary increases sufficiently over the annual inflation rate that they are viewed by employees as real rewards for exemplary performance. In many organizations, pay raises for exemplary performers seldom exceed 5 percent at a time when annual inflation averages between 3 and 5 percent in the United States. It is small wonder that many employees confuse merit raises with cost-of-living adjustments.

For this reason and others, some organizations adopt *nonpecuniary rewards* as a means of recognizing and encouraging those who develop themselves or their employees. There are two types: *intrinsic* (those stemming from the work itself) and *extrinsic* (those stemming from the job environment).[5] Intrinsic rewards include increased job autonomy, task control, power, influence, visibility, or achievement. Extrinsic rewards include organizational or supervisory recognition and social interaction.

Exhibit 5-2 lists various rewards that may be offered to management employees who develop their skills or who encourage the development of those reporting to them. Note that while some rewards are inexpensive, they do acknowledge that participation in MD is important and worthwhile.

Exhibit 5-2. Examples of nonpecuniary rewards to encourage MD.

Activities That May Be Rewarded	Nonpecuniary Rewards
‣ Encouraging employees to plan their careers ‣ Providing management employees with job-related and career-related coaching ‣ Serving as mentor or sponsor for management employees who are or are not reporting directly to a supervisor, manager, or officer ‣ Attending or delivering training in organizationally sponsored training courses ‣ Serving on steering committees, advisory committees, project teams, or other MD groups in —organizational settings —community colleges or university settings ‣ Participating in, or providing support for, planned job rotation programs ‣ Participating in, or delivering presentations at, management conferences ‣ Serving on industry-related education committees ‣ Publishing books or articles	‣ Seeing that memos/letters are sent from the CEO or others ‣ Awarding desired job assignments ‣ Awarding high-visibility assignments ‣ Allowing desired geographical transfers ‣ Setting up executive mentoring for the employee ‣ Providing the opportunity to serve in loaned executive programs ‣ Awarding certificates ‣ Reporting about the person in the organization's in-house publications ‣ Honoring people at banquets or giving other special recognition

Finally, if sufficient support exists to offer encouragement for MD, the approaches may be combined. While that can be an expense strategy, it can pay off by creating conditions in which management employees really *want* to develop their skills and to help others develop.

Identifying the Right Kind of Leader

CEOs often say that finding the right leader at the right time is crucial to the strategic success of new ventures, start-ups, or turn-arounds. This principle applies as much to the leadership of a planned MD program as to other ventures. If a program lacks the right leader— someone possessing the right mix of skills and positive attitudes—then it is doomed to failure from the outset. In fact, if you wish to destroy a program, a fast way to do it is to place someone in charge of it who lacks the right skills, lacks a positive attitude, or lacks credibility.

MD Director or Coordinator?

Many large organizations employ at least one person to oversee and coordinate MD efforts. In the largest corporations, there may even be separate full-time positions devoted to supervisory development, manager development, and executive development. However, for the sake of simplicity, we use the term *MD director* to refer to a full-time professional assigned to MD. Of course, other job titles are also possible: director of executive education and development, assistant vice-president of management development, vice-president of executive development, or senior vice-president of corporate executive development.

MD directors are full-time professionals assigned to spearhead planned MD programs. They work directly with executives, managers, and supervisors, and they have usually received previous education or training in MD. They conduct management development needs assessment, design and/or deliver training geared to the management ranks, and locate sources to meet identified MD needs.

On the other hand, small organizations rarely employ enough management employees to justify full-time positions to oversee and coordinate their planned MD programs. In those cases, a committee oversees MD activities. For want of a better term, we use the title *MD coordinator* to refer to the elected or appointed chairperson of such a committee. The coordinator carries out committee recommendations, ensuring they are implemented, and communicates about committee initiatives with other management employees.

MD coordinators devote only part of their time to the planned MD program. They work full-time in other capacities. They have rarely participated in previous education, training, or work experience focused on administering a planned MD program, although they are usually enthusiastic advocates of MD.

What to Look For

Before selecting an MD director or appointing an MD coordinator, key decision makers in the organization and/or members of an in-house MD committee should first decide what they want from the planned MD program. It is at this point that a written program policy and philosophy statement and a tentative first-year action plan become invaluable. Armed with this information, committee members can draft a *job description* for an MD director or a *role description* for an MD coordinator and then circulate it among decision makers for additions or other modifications.

A *job description* is a list of responsibilities. Since an MD director is a management employee, his or her responsibilities should be summarized in such a description. But MD coordinators work only part-time at that position. Coordinators already have job descriptions for their full-time jobs in the organization, but they do need guidelines for enacting their roles as MD committee leaders. These are called *role descriptions*.

The purpose and philosophy driving the planned MD program greatly affects the appropriate knowledge, skills, and attitudes of the ideal candidate chosen to spearhead the program. For instance, if the program's purpose is to offer internal group training, it makes sense to recruit someone as MD director who has previously designed and delivered training of that kind. If the program's purpose centers around executive development, someone should be chosen for the job who feels comfortable working with executives. If the program's purpose centers around starting and operating a management job rotation program or a high-potential program, then the best candidate will be someone who has already done that. If the MD program is to be *comprehensive*—meaning that it is intended to meet the needs of many targeted learners through a combination of training, education, and development methods—then the ideal candidate should possess education and experience commensurate with such a challenging undertaking.

As a starting point, review the sample job description in Exhibit 5-3. Modify it as necessary to meet the demands of the planned MD program in your organization. You may also narrow it to create a role description for an MD Coordinator.

text continues on page 111

Exhibit 5-3. Job description of an MD director.

Summary

Administers MD activities for the organization; oversees internal training and external education for all management levels; coordinates participation in industry-related, association-related, and university-related management programs.

Responsibilities

1. Analyzes management performance problems, distinguishing learning from nonlearning needs.
2. Assesses job-specific learning needs for supervisors, managers, and executives, using needs assessment results to establish and maintain a planned MD program.
3. Establishes performance objectives for training programs.
4. Offers consulting assistance to determine whether the learning needs of supervisors, managers, or executives will be met best through internal or external group training or through other methods.
5. Designs and delivers internal supervisory, management, and executive training programs to meet identified needs.
6. Sources external training, education, or development programs as necessary to meet individual needs.
7. Prepares and negotiates contracts with external vendors or consultants, as appropriate, to meet supervisory, management, and executive learning needs.
8. Manages and oversees assigned external vendors and consultants, ensuring they meet contractual requirements.
9. Selects media for planned learning activities, choosing classroom-based, video-based, audio-based, or computer-based individualized instruction or other delivery methods when appropriate.
10. Selects and purchases audiovisual equipment, as necessary, to support internal training for supervisors, managers, and executives.
11. Establishes and maintains close working relationships with key executives, managers, and supervisors as appropriate to build ownership in—and support for—the planned MD program.
12. Sets up and coordinates various management and project committees to support the MD program.
13. Prepares instructional materials for internal training, including trainer guides, participant workbooks, checklists, videotape scripts, audiotape scripts, participant activities, and on-the-job checklists.
14. Prepares training schedules.
15. Provides individualized assistance to line managers to address the specialized MD needs of their management employees.
16. Prepares and distributes invitations to internal group training and briefing sessions for executives, managers, supervisors, and aspiring supervisors.

(continues)

Exhibit 5-3 (*continued*).

17. Oversees a specialized management trainee program for high-potential talent, recruiting and overseeing selection of such employees.
18. Oversees internship and summer programs for individuals with management potential.
19. Provides special advice and assistance on recruiting, selecting, and orienting management talent for the organization.
20. Arranges meeting facilities, as appropriate, to support classroom sessions, self-study, management briefings, and other activities.
21. Budgets for the MD program.
22. Delivers training programs and briefings to aspiring supervisors, experienced supervisors, managers, and executives—including (but not limited to) such topics as orientation to supervision, conducting performance appraisals, communicating effectively, motivating employees, on-the-job training and coaching, career planning, selection and interviewing methods, and discipline methods.
23. Conducts rehearsals of training programs to elicit reviews and suggestions for improvement by supervisors, managers, and executives.
24. Evaluates training, education, and development programs.
25. Ensures transfer of learning from training, education, or developmental settings to on-the-job work settings.
26. Establishes and maintains a management skill inventory for use in succession planning and HR planning and in the organization's strategic planning.
27. Offers career counseling to aspiring and experienced supervisors, managers, and executives.
28. Provides outplacement and decruitment services, when necessary, for management employees.
29. Promotes and coordinates external educational activities linked to such efforts as executive MBA programs, night-school MBA programs, and other educational activities linked to MD.
30. Identifies and coordinates policy for external management seminars and conferences.
31. Coordinates efforts to develop company management talent via work experience through planned job rotations and other methods.
32. Educates management employees about their responsibility to train, educate, and develop their subordinates.
33. Provides advice and suggestions about management job descriptions, management performance appraisals, and management compensation.

Qualifications

1. Requires the knowledge, skill, and mental development equivalent to the completion of a master's degree with specialized courses in employee training, human resources management, adult learning, and instructional design.

2. Requires general knowledge of the history, structure, and operations of the organization and the industry of which it is part.
3. Requires experience in leading training, education, and/or development activities.
4. Requires ability to establish and maintain effective interpersonal relations with employees at all levels of the organization, with external vendors, with college faculty, and with other groups.
5. Requires strong writing and oral communication skills.
6. Requires familiarity with such instructional media as video-based, computer-based, and self-study instruction.

Date Prepared: _____ , 19____

Recruiting, Selecting, and Orienting a Program Leader

There are several steps to take when recruiting, selecting, and orienting a program leader:

1. Decide first whether to recruit a full-time MD director or a part-time MD coordinator.
2. On the basis of the MD program's purpose, goals, policy, philosophy, and first-year tentative action plan, prepare a job or role description for the MD director or MD coordinator.
3. Ask others in the organization to review and finalize the job or role description to build ownership in the selection process.
4. Receive approval to fund the job, setting the salary at a competitive level (for salary information about MD specialists, consult the annual survey results in any November issue of *Training Magazine*).
5. Position the job within the organization's chain of command, involving the immediate organizational superior of the MD director.

After taking these actions, prepare to recruit, select, and orient the MD director or MD coordinator.

Recruitment Strategy

There are two primary sources for recruiting an MD director or MD coordinator—outside and inside the organization. Decide at the outset where to look for the best applicant. Typically, a full-time MD director is hired from *outside*, assuming the organization employs no one with the requisite expertise to meet the program's unique requirements. On the other hand, a part-time MD coordinator is usually selected from *inside*, often by appointment by the CEO or by election by the members of an MD steering or advisory committee.

If the decision is made to undertake an outside search for an MD director, start by looking at recent employment applications already on file. List the position with the local job service; advertise in local newspapers and in newsletters of local chapters of the American Society for Training and Development (1640 King Street, Box 1443, Alexandria, Va. 22313-2043; telephone, 703-683-8100). If necessary, extend the search nationally through search firms specializing in training and development that advertise regularly in *Training and Development*, *Training*, *Personnel Journal*, *HRMagazine*, and *HR Executive*. List the position with the referral service of the National Society for Performance and Instruction (1126 Sixteenth Street NW, Suite 102, Washington, D.C. 20036; telephone, 202-861-0777).

On the other hand, if the decision is made to restrict the search to *inside* the organization only, begin by posting a job description on bulletin boards or listing it in the organization's internal publications. Do not be shy about using other sources, such as word-of-mouth recruitment. It is also advisable to list the opening with the organization's equal employment opportunity or affirmative action office.

No matter where the advertisements are placed, they should indicate *minimum* job qualifications. If special restrictions apply, those should be listed; so, too, should *essential job functions* as defined in the Americans with Disabilities Act. The salary range should also be listed to prompt inquiries and applications from serious candidates only.

Selection Strategy

Clarify selection strategy and criteria before applications or résumés are received. Decide how to weight applicant education and experience, screen résumés or applications, conduct job interviews with applicants, and make the hiring decision. If more than one person will participate in making the selection decision—an advisable move—be sure it is clear who is to do what in the selection process.

Start developing selection strategy with the job or role description. Involve members of the MD steering or advisory committee in the screening, interviewing, and hiring process. Formulate interview questions on the basis of the responsibilities listed in the job description, adding questions about each applicant's background to a core of questions that will be posed to all applicants. If possible, ask applicants to provide relevant work samples, such as management courses they have designed and delivered. You may even wish to request videotapes of group presentations from applicants, assuming the job requires platform skill. Have several people interview each applicant and write down their observations immediately and independently after each interview. Then compare the observations later. Make an offer only to the one applicant who is most positively received.

Orientation Strategy

Orientation is designed to increase the speed of the socialization process, reducing the unproductive breaking-in period during which a newcomer learns about the job, role, department, and organization. A well-planned orientation can also reduce the chance of avoidable turnover. Of all training and development activities, orientation is the one activity that is the most commonly sponsored by organizations.[6] Several practical guides to employee orientation have been published and are readily available.

The most important question to ask before formulating orientation strategy is: *Was the leader for the MD program hired from inside or outside the organization?* Generally, someone hired from outside requires a more thorough orientation than someone transferred or promoted from inside. Plan the orientation to ensure success. Never assume success will happen on its own.

To orient an MD director hired from outside the organization, begin by sending him or her to the organization's in-house orientation. (Many organizations offer such in-house programs, sponsored by the human resources department, to summarize key employee benefits and to outline the organization's work rules.) The newcomer should also receive the following:

- The organization's human resources manual
- Recent annual reports
- The organization's written MD policy and philosophy
- Tentative action plans for MD
- Minutes of an in-house MD committee

Then give the newcomer an orientation to the area of the organization in which the job is positioned. If possible, convene a special meeting of the MD steering or advisory committee to offer initial suggestions about the newcomer's orientation.

It can also be very helpful to arrange one-on-one informational interviews between the newcomer and key people. Such interviews serve several purposes. First, they help socialize the newcomer quickly so he or she knows—and is known to—key people. Second, they provide an opportunity for the newcomer to hear many views about MD in a short time. Third, they can help the newcomer learn about the organization's culture, history, structure, and strategic plan.

Orienting an MD director or an MD coordinator hired from inside the organization should be easier. He or she should already be familiar with the organization's rules, benefits, culture, history, structure, and strategic plan. But it will still be necessary to provide detailed background information about the MD program. (This step may not be necessary if the person has been serving as a member of an MD steering or advisory committee.)

Selecting, Orienting, and Training Staff and Vendors

Internal staff members consist of full-time or part-time people hired to support the planned MD program; *external vendors* are consultants or other service suppliers whose special skills are needed for the MD program. Both internal staff members and external vendors support the program and report to the MD director or coordinator. They carry out varied activities, such as conducting needs assessment, writing performance objectives, preparing performance tests or written tests based on objectives, locating or writing instructional materials for on- or off-the-job use, identifying sources of planned learning experiences to meet macro or micro needs, delivering instruction, and evaluating instruction.

When Are They Needed?

Full-time internal staff members should be hired for MD only when the number of targeted learners is sufficiently large to warrant it. Otherwise, external vendors or part-time staff members can be used to meet short-term, one-time, or specialized needs. Use the guidelines in Exhibit 5-4 to help decide whether to hire internal staff members, rely on external vendors, or use a combination of internal staff and external vendors.

Recruiting and Preparing Staff or Vendors

The process of selecting, orienting, and training internal staff members and external vendors does not differ markedly from the process of

Exhibit 5-4. Flowchart used to decide whether to hire internal staff or find external vendors.

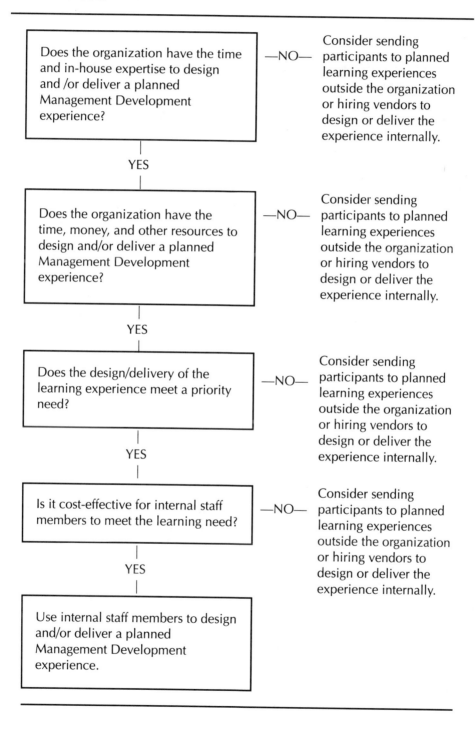

selecting and orienting an MD director or coordinator. Typically, staff and vendors are recruited and selected by the MD director or coordinator, often after consultation with other people who have a stake in these decisions.

1. The MD director or coordinator should decide just what the staff members or vendors will be expected to do. Many MD staff members and vendors assist in developing instructional materials or delivering classroom presentations. The demand for MD specialists is expected to increase through the year 2000.[7]

2. The MD director or coordinator should draft a job description (for staff members) or a work plan (for external vendors). Circulate the plan to interested people for their suggestions and modifications before finalizing it. This process builds ownership through participation. A job description or work plan should list the primary responsibilities to be shouldered by the prospective staff member or vendor.

3. The MD director or coordinator should obtain approval to hire the staff member or to contract with the vendor. Approval to hire usually requires completion and approval of a job requisition. Approval to contract usually begins with a "Request for a Proposal" that lays out project requirements for a vendor.

4. The MD director or coordinator should plot out and implement recruitment strategy. As in recruiting an MD director or MD coordinator, talent may be found inside or outside the organization. Internal recruitment may be carried out through job posting, word-of-mouth recruiting, and searches of skill inventories. External recruitment may be carried out through newspaper advertising, newsletter announcements, personal contacts, or specialized search firms. Vendors may be identified through published sources, professional contacts of the MD director/coordinator, or professional advertising.

5. The MD director or coordinator should use a job description or a work plan as the basis for preparing selection criteria and interview questions. Applicants for internal staff positions should be screened and interviewed; prospective vendors should be screened on the basis of their proposals and then interviewed.

6. The MD director or coordinator should select the staff member or vendor. The choice should be made as objectively as possible, preferably after interviews with several people. Once vendors are chosen, they should be required to sign a contract that clearly indicates project expectations, objectives, and time frames and the maximum amount to be spent on each activity.

7. The MD director or coordinator should orient the staff members

or vendors. If staff members are chosen from within, or if vendors have previously worked with the organization, then a lengthy orientation should not be necessary. Otherwise, a thorough orientation should be planned.

Scheduling

The scheduling of planned MD activities is more important than it may seem at first glance. Four issues are particularly important when scheduling:

1. Organizational needs
2. Work cycles
3. Individual needs
4. MD activities

Organizational Needs

When a planned MD activity is specifically designed to support an organizational need, then scheduling becomes critically important. Indeed, the organization's chances of meeting its needs may depend on MD activities. When that is true, then scheduling MD assumes a commanding position.

Consider driving issues identified in strategic plans, because they make organizational needs explicit. For instance, assume an organization's leaders have decided to make customer service training a high priority. It makes sense, then, to identify what managers and employees need to know or do to meet that goal. MD activities may be required, and they must be scheduled to help meet the need.

Work Cycles

Organizational work cycles vary, depending on the business. For instance, retailers are particularly busy during the holiday season. Manufacturers are busy when they receive larger-than-normal orders. Some financial service firms are busiest at year end—from October through December.

When possible, MD activities should not be scheduled during peak work cycles. If they are, targeted participants may face scheduling conflicts with their work and may not be able to participate in off-the-job learning experiences or to devote time to on-the-job experiences.

The point to bear in mind is that MD activities should be scheduled at times when they do not conflict with peak work cycles. If you are unsure when the peaks of the work cycle occur, ask others these questions:

- When is the organization's work cycle at its peak?
- When does the organization's work activity drop off?
- What is the best time of year for people to participate in planned MD activities?

Individual Needs

Individuals are eager to participate in MD activities when they feel the need to learn. This feeling, what adult educators call a *teachable moment*, is most intense just before and immediately after a change affects an individual. To ensure that the timing of MD activities matches predictable needs, scan the organization to determine if there will be any special time in the future when a larger-than-normal group is to be promoted or transferred. (Such changes can occur immediately after a large group leaves an organization due to an early retirement offer or a layoff.) Do this scanning at the beginning of each year, or immediately after announcements are made that have sweeping implications for the organization. Adjust planned MD activities accordingly.

The same principle applies when individuals are promoted, demoted, transferred, hired, or outplaced. Any change prompts individuals to learn more because learning is a mechanism for coping with change. Because people are often highly motivated to learn at such times, they may be particularly receptive to the idea of developing learning plans.

MD Activities

Not all MD methods require the same amount of time, and these different requirements affect scheduling. For instance, internal group training is finite: Each experience has a definite beginning and ending for participants. Job rotation programs often last longer than internal group training efforts and require advance timing and scheduling commitments. External group training may require on-the-job time commitments for study or learner follow-up. On the other hand, self-study efforts, on-the-job coaching, and other individualized learning activities are quite flexible, allowing participation as time permits.

When scheduling MD activities, avoid periods when group activities demand the most time from the largest groups. Schedule them so that they do not interfere with the organization's peak work cycles, and avoid periods of upheaval in the *immediate* aftermath of buyouts, mergers, acquisitions, or layoffs.

Program Budgeting

The budget for a planned MD program should grow out of an action plan, usually established on an annual basis. However, few organizations budget separately for MD, choosing instead to fund MD by "dividing costs among several participating departments so that digging the pertinent figures out of individual budgets can be a difficult task."[8] When MD programs are budgeted on a corporate or strategic business unit (SBU) level, they are often developed from a zero-based perspective because MD activities are not necessarily the same from year to year; rather, MD programs are driven by organizational, individual, and job needs that may vary somewhat over time.

Start the budgeting process by tentatively planning each project in each program area. In organizations that target MD participants by job categories, program areas mean *annual learning plans for each job category*, and projects are *specific planned learning experiences*. In organizations that target participants by special group or program, the group or the program becomes the basis for budgeting, and projects are specific activities for each group or program.

List the projects planned for each program area during the future year. If possible, develop a simple list of activities for each project. Then prepare a simple *project budget* based on the staff, equipment, and other necessary resources. Base estimates on information supplied by vendors or on historical experience. When you finish, tally the resources that will be required in each project in each program area and then budget for equipment, instructors' salaries, instructors' benefits, facilities, and travel. Be sure to follow organizational policies, practices, and accounting methods when preparing the final budget.

Keeping Records

Record keeping is essential to meet management and legal obligations.

Records are useful from a management perspective because they indicate *who* participated in *what* MD activities. Without records, management will not be able to access information about individual participation in MD activities to aid decision making about who should:

- Qualify for a promotion.
- Receive a higher-than-average pay raise.

- Receive a desirable transfer to another part of the organization to cultivate needed skills.
- Be assigned to particular jobs or short-term assignments.

Without records, MD specialists will also lose an important source of information about MD needs.

From a legal perspective, organizations are required to avoid discrimination in all employment matters. Under equal employment opportunity and affirmative action policies, people must be given equal access to hiring, promotion, and training. Without records of who participated in planned MD, your organization may not be able to defend itself against a charge of unfair employment discrimination if one is ever filed.

Some state governments require professionals to complete a specific number of continuing-education hours each year as a condition for maintaining their state licenses. If your organization functions in an industry in which continuing education is important, record keeping for MD can be critical.

Two sets of records should be kept: one about participants and one about programs.

Participant records may be linked to an organization's Human Resources Information System (HRIS), containing employment, payroll, and benefits information, or to confidential record keeping for succession plans. It is desirable to link the records if possible, although MD records may become so detailed that they become unwieldy. For each individual participating in a planned MD program, you may want to keep at least the following information:

- Complete name (and any changes resulting from marriage or divorce)
- Names and locations of schools attended
- College majors
- Degrees earned
- Degrees in progress
- Dates of graduation
- Fluency in foreign language(s)
- Professional designations earned or licenses held
- Professional designations in progress
- Training programs attended, including sponsor's name, dates of attendance, and location
- College courses attended (or in progress)
- Published articles and books

‣ Major presentations made to professional, industry, or organizational groups
‣ Jobs held in previous organizations, including job titles and dates of employment
‣ Jobs held in the current organization, including titles, dates of movement in and out of them, and location
‣ Other issues of particular interest and value for MD purposes, including performance appraisal results and identified individual learning needs

Program records should contain information about each MD program, organized according to participant group—job category, special group, or special program. At a minimum, each project record should contain information about:

‣ What it was (descriptive title)
‣ Who participated (list of participants)
‣ When it was held (dates)
‣ Where it was held (location)
‣ How it was held (delivery method)
‣ Why it was held (how did it satisfy a business or individual need?)
‣ What happened (what evaluation results are available? how were they gathered?)

Information about internal group training is easiest to record, while information about on-the-job training may be the most difficult. Additional information may have to be added to program records in order to satisfy continuing education requirements. For instance, management employees who are also accountants may need special information about each planned learning activity in which they participated in order to comply with statutory licensing requirements.

In small organizations with fewer than 100 management employees, paper records about individuals and MD programs will probably satisfy most requirements. But in large organizations employing more than 100 management employees, automated record keeping is essential. Numerous vendors sell computerized record keeping software, typically designed for use on a personal computer. You can locate vendors by consulting such publications as *The ASTD Buyer's Guide and Consultant Directory* (Alexandria, Va.: American Society for Training and Development, 1991) or *Training: Marketplace Directory* (Minneapolis: Lakewood Publications, 1991).

A software package can be purchased and installed quickly. How-

ever, not every software package for record keeping permits easy
modification to meet specific organizational needs, so be sure to check
out software carefully before making a purchase. (Most vendors will be
willing to supply you with a *demo disk*.) Review several software
packages before choosing one.

Publicizing MD Activities

It is not enough for an organization merely to sponsor a planned MD
program. Information about program activities and results should also
be publicized so targeted learners and their immediate organizational
superiors will be inclined to participate in it and to support it. Publicity
is thus a vital tool to build program support and visibility by trumpet-
ing successes.

Publicity and MD Philosophy

Not all organizations have cultures that are equally open; not all
organizations have top managers or middle managers who are equally
supportive of a planned MD program. Top managers or middle managers in some organizations may be unwilling to publicize information
about planned MD programs for fear they will be swamped by promo-
tion-seekers, only some of whom are worthy of promotion. In such
organizations, managers may prefer to make information about MD
activities available only to those they are willing to nominate and
sponsor for participation. For this reason, be sure to clarify the organization's philosophy about publicizing the MD program before doing so
through in-house periodicals or community newspapers.

Some managers may also consider MD activities proprietary and
may prefer to keep information about them confidential. Since the MD
program should be closely linked to corporate strategy and succession
plans, information about it may be treated as top secret. Prospective
participants and their immediate organizational superiors are clued
into program activities on a need-to-know basis.

The attitude toward publicizing an MD program can be a reflection
of an organization's general employment philosophy. Organizations
that take a secretive stance about MD usually shroud other employment matters in secrecy as well. For instance, they may be unwilling to
share information about pay ranges, job classifications, or job descriptions. They may also be unwilling to clarify the criteria used in making
promotion or pay decisions.

However, recent workplace trends favoring participative management generally discourage secretive approaches to MD. Managers are learning that employees want to know the reasons underlying employment decisions. When left in the dark, cynical and skeptical employees often assume that employment decisions are not being made fairly or legally. That perception can lead to costly litigation. For this reason, then, it is advisable for most organizations to be open about MD activities so long as proprietary organizational rights and individual rights to privacy are not violated.

How Should a Planned MD Program Be Publicized?

There are three methods by which to publicize a planned MD program:

1. Mass media
2. Group approaches
3. Personal selling

It is usually not a matter of choosing one method in preference to others; rather, most organizations seek an effective combination of methods.

Mass media are geared to reaching many people, usually with a simple message. The aim is to build awareness. In organizational settings, you can use the following mass media approaches to publicize MD efforts:

- Place articles in community newspapers or in-house publications.
- Place announcements on bulletin boards.
- Provide information about MD efforts by electronic mail bulletin boards.
- Sponsor career/education "fairs" in the organization.
- Provide large-group presentations to 100 or more employees.
- Send direct mail brochures and memos to everyone qualified to participate in MD experiences.

Direct mail methods are often most effective, although there is admittedly no assurance that people will read what is mailed to them.

Group approaches are focused on building awareness and interest for MD in a specific niche market. In organizational settings, group approaches might include presentations to all management employees working in the same function or department or reporting to the same person. These presentations may be made before, during, or after succession planning or individual career planning activities to reinforce the value of MD as a tool for realizing organizational and individual goals.

But our favorite approach is personal selling, though it is by far the most time-consuming. It involves one-on-one contact with prospective participants and/or their immediate organizational superiors. The aim is to target the message to the specific needs of a handful of individuals.

To do personal selling, arrange a meeting with managers in charge of various departments or work units. Then explain what the planned MD program can do for them and their management employees. Finally, ask for their support, cooperation, and participation. End the meeting, as any good salesperson would, by asking for enrollments, participation, or other evidence of a "sale."

Summary

In this chapter we described the administrative support system necessary to operate a planned MD program. As we explained, early issues to consider when starting up a planned MD program include any or all of the following:

1. Where should the MD function be positioned in the organization's reporting structure?
2. What rewards or incentives should be offered to induce people to accept responsibility for developing their skills and those of their management subordinates?
3. What kind of leader should direct the planned MD program?
4. How should the program leader be recruited, selected, and oriented?
5. How should internal staff members and external vendors be selected, oriented, and trained?
6. How should planned MD activities be scheduled?
7. How should budgeting be handled?
8. What records of MD activities should be kept?
9. How should MD program activities be publicized?

Part III

Selecting, Planning, and Using Formal, Informal, and Special Methods

INTRODUCTION TO PART III

In Part III we focus on methods for changing individuals or groups, providing them with the knowledge, skills, or attitudes they need to perform competently, prepare themselves for advancement, or gain new insights about the problems they face on their jobs.

Change rarely comes about on its own, in MD or in any other organizational change effort of which MD may be part. For this reason, many organizations use a combination of three methods to bring about change: formal methods, which occur off the job and lend themselves to group planning; informal methods, which occur on the job and require planning between one management employee and his or her immediate organizational superior; and special methods, which are often unique, cutting-edge, or controversial.

This part of the book, then, focuses on these methods. Chapter 6 provides two models for selecting appropriate MD methods. Chapter 7 describes how to select, plan, and use formal MD methods; Chapter 8 describes how to select, plan, and use informal MD methods; and Chapter 9 describes how to select, plan, and use special MD methods.

Chapter 6

Selecting MD Methods

In earlier chapters in this book, we indicated that the start-up of a planned MD program requires that many issues be addressed:

- What is the purpose of the planned MD program?
- What goals and objectives should the MD program strive to realize initially? eventually?
- What policy and philosophy should guide the MD program?
- What targeted job category, special group, or special program should be served by the MD program initially?
- What action plan should guide program start-up?
- What needs are evident for the targeted groups?
- What instructional plan (curriculum) should guide the organization's planned MD program?
- What administrative support will be necessary for the program?

Once these questions are answered, you are ready to pose these additional questions:

- By what methods should learning needs be met? (By *methods* we mean *modes of delivering planned MD activities.*)
- How should the MD curriculum be implemented?

When working in MD, you may be tempted to skip the preliminary questions and jump immediately to the questions about methods. By doing so, you will endear yourself to zealots who want to take immediate action. Unfortunately, the action taken may be ill-conceived because hastily contrived. It may fail to meet the MD needs of targeted management groups in the organization. Hasty action will only frustrate those you serve and damage the long-term credibility of the MD program in a way that will not be easy to repair.

We suggest you take a more deliberate course of action. Resist impatient zealots. Be thoughtful about what you do. While not falling into the paralysis of analysis, avoid the temptation to follow those who cry, "Fire, aim, ready." Instead, pick one important issue early on—and address it so extraordinarily well that you establish a reputation for quality.

With that thought in mind, we turn our attention in this chapter to the process of choosing methods designed to meet the learning needs of targeted groups. At this point our aim is simply to explain when to use methods common to MD. In the three chapters that follow, we describe these methods in detail.

Methods Used in MD Programs

According to a 1989 survey by the American Society for Training and Development (ASTD) that questioned 100 training executives employed by *Fortune* 500 companies, the most commonly used methods in MD for senior and upper-level executives are these:[1]

Method	Percentage of Organizations Using the Method
1. University-sponsored executive and MD programs	59%
2. Vendor-sponsored external programs	47
3. Classroom training	36
4. Succession planning	35
5. Cross-functional job rotations	28
6. On-the-job coaching	27
7. Self-study	24
8. International job rotations	15
9. Mentoring programs	10
10. Assessment centers	10

A 1992 study conducted by ASTD revealed that for middle managers and supervisors, various methods are used:[2]

Method	Percentage of Companies Using Technique for Mid-Level Managers	Percentage of Companies Using Technique for Supervisors
1. Classroom	91%	95%
2. Internal development programs	71	69
3. Individual development plans	60	53
4. On-the-job coaching	58	72

Method	Percentage of Companies Using Technique for Mid-Level Managers	Percentage of Companies Using Technique for Supervisors
5. University development programs	62	17
6. Task forces	56	42
7. Succession planning	44	19
8. Cross-functional job rotations	32	24

ASTD's study further revealed that "for both mid-level managers and supervisors, the projected most important development methods over the next two years are: classroom training and on-the-job coaching."[3]

Our 1992 survey study of MD professionals, all members of ASTD, yielded slightly different results (see Exhibit 6-1). Unlike other researchers, we asked our respondents about the relative effectiveness of methods, too. Note that according to our results, the *most frequently used* method is in-house classroom training. However, planned on-the-job training was cited by our respondents as the *single most effective* method. The reason for the difference between our results and those of ASTD's surveys is probably that our goal was to discover what methods are being used *across all management job categories,* not just in the executive, middle-management, or supervisory ranks. Additionally, our respondents were not concentrated in *Fortune* 500 companies.

The results of our study also differ somewhat from those of a 1987 survey of MD methods in organizations employing at least 1,000 people.[4] Saari, Johnson, McLaughlin, and Zimmerle received 611 returned surveys from 1,000 mailed, so their response rate was 61 percent. Thirty-five percent of their respondents worked in manufacturing companies, 21 percent worked in service firms, and 15 percent worked in wholesale or retail businesses. Thirty-nine percent employed between 1,000 and 4,999 people, and 24 percent employed between 5,000 and 9,999. The researchers found that "as part of overall management training and development, 93 percent of the companies report using on-the-job training, 89 percent report using formal training/education programs, 80 percent indicate using special projects or task forces, 57 percent report the use of mentoring, 40 percent report using job rotation, and 32 percent report using career planning."[5]

Guidelines for Choosing MD Methods

The models appearing in Exhibits 6-2 and 6-3 should help you sort out key issues for consideration when selecting MD methods to meet

Exhibit 6-1. Demographic information from 1992 survey on how often MD methods are used.

Question: What management development practices are used in your organization? For each practice listed in the left column, circle a response in the center column that indicates *how often* the practice is used and then circle a response in the right column that indicates *how effective* you believe the practice to be. Use the following codes in the center column:

1 = Not at all
2 = Seldom
3 = Sometimes
4 = Frequently
5 = With all management employees

Then use the following codes in the right column:

1 = Not at all effective
2 = Seldom effective
3 = Sometimes effective
4 = Frequently effective
5 = Very effective

Management Development Method	How Often Used?		How Effective?	
	Frequency	**Mean**	**Frequency**	**Mean**
In-house classroom courses tailor-made for management-level employees	63	4.14	60	3.83
Planned on-the-job training	60	3.55	56	3.91
In-house classroom courses purchased from outside sources and modified for in-house use	63	3.33	57	3.60
Unplanned on-the-job training	59	3.25	50	3.08
Off-the-job public seminars sponsored by vendors	62	3.24	59	2.85
Off-the-job degree programs sponsored by colleges/universities	61	2.90	55	3.36
Off-the-job public seminars sponsored by universities	62	2.76	55	3.05
Unplanned mentoring programs	58	2.50	51	3.10
Planned job rotation programs	60	2.22	49	3.37

Management Development Method	How Often Used?		How Effective?	
	Frequency	**Mean**	**Frequency**	**Mean**
Unplanned job rotation programs	60	2.15	42	2.86
Planned mentoring programs	59	1.93	44	3.02
On-site degree programs sponsored by colleges/universities	60	1.58	30	2.60
Adventure (outdoor) programs	60	1.32	36	1.89

Source: William J. Rothwell and H. C. Kazanas, "Results of a 1992 Survey on Management Development Practices in the U.S." (Urbana, Ill.: Department of Vocational and Technical Education, 1992, unpublished).

learning needs and implementing an MD curriculum. Review them. Then read the following discussions about them. While not foolproof, these simple models do provide worthwhile guidance for selecting appropriate MD methods to meet organizational, individual, or job-related needs.

Model 1: Group or Individual Needs

Sometimes it is tempting to treat MD as an exercise in "sheep dipping"—providing the same planned learning experiences for everyone. However, such an approach is usually costly and unwise. Indeed, the trend is away from a one-size-fits-all mentality and toward learning experiences geared to addressing *individual* rather than *group* MD needs.[6]

However, there are still numerous occasions when group experiences are highly appropriate. As Exhibit 6-2 indicates, the key question to ask is this: *Is the learning need shared by a group of people?* Group needs may occur under a wide variety of circumstances. Here are some examples:

‣ New laws, rules, or regulations are enacted that affect the organization, and management employees are not familiar with what those legal requirements mean to them.

‣ New organizational policies, procedures, or strategic plans are adopted. They are far-reaching in scope and will be difficult to implement successfully unless everyone is familiar with them.

‣ New, innovative technology is introduced to the organization, and management employees are expected to spearhead its introduction.

Exhibit 6-2. Model for selecting MD methods for groups and individuals.

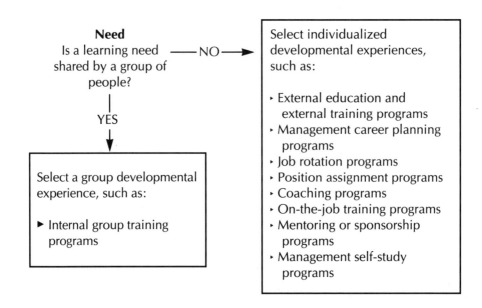

> • Management employees experience changes in their job duties or role expectations due to promotions, downsizing, transfers, or other changes. The job changes are similar enough that group training is more economical than individualized training.[7]

On the other hand, individualized methods are more appropriate when learning needs are not widely shared across many people. A typical example: A newly-promoted supervisor, manager, or executive from a technical background such as accounting, engineering, or data processing has difficulty exercising appropriate interpersonal skills upon promotion to management. Group training is too expensive and inefficient because everyone promoted does not experience this need. Hence, individualized methods are more appropriate. (In cases such as this, some organizations opt to send employees to external educational seminars on human relations.)

Model 2: Types of Needs

Experts on adult development have long contended that learning needs are not all the same; rather, they differ by type.[8] Five types are commonly identified:

1. Cognitive or informational needs
2. Psychomotor or skill needs
3. Affective, feeling, or attitudinal needs
4. Advancement or educational needs
5. Developmental needs

Different instructional methods should be used to meet these needs, as shown in Exhibit 6-3.

Cognitive or informational needs have to do with knowledge. Examples of such needs include definitions and concepts. The provision of cognitive or informational training is perhaps the most common planned learning experience sponsored by organizations for management employees, and most external seminars, such as off-the-job college courses, are focused on meeting cognitive or informational needs. They are especially appropriate for those who have never had any courses in management.

Cognitive or informational training addresses "what" questions and "what" needs—for example, "What is motivation?" and "What methods may be used to delegate work to employees?" It is also used as a means of kicking off a new program, since management employees naturally have to know what a self-directed work team is before they can help establish one or understand what Total Quality Management is before they can introduce such a program.

As the model indicates, if you are trying to meet cognitive needs, you should consider knowledge-based internal group training programs, on-the-job coaching, or on-the-job training. These methods are particularly well-suited to addressing cognitive needs, since they can answer "what" questions particularly well. Knowledge-based training is usually focused on introducing content rather than describing procedures.

Psychomotor or skill needs are frequently associated more with technical than with management employees. Learning experiences designed to meet these needs address "how-to" questions: "How do you fix this machine?" or "How do you prepare a production report?" Note that these questions are directed to technical issues. But it is still possible to design and deliver planned learning experiences based on skill issues to management employees. Indeed, a common complaint among management employees is that they don't receive enough of this training.

As Exhibit 6-3 indicates, psychomotor or skill needs may be met through skill-based internal group training programs or on-the-job coaching/training.

text continues on page 136

Exhibit 6-3. Model for selecting MD methods on the basis of types of needs.

Type of Need

Does the need have to do with transmitting information?	—YES—	Is the information organization-specific?	—YES—	Consider knowl-edge-based internal group training or coaching programs.
NO		NO		Consider external education or management self-study programs.
Does the need have to do with building skills?	—YES—	Are the skills organization-specific?	—YES—	Consider skill-based internal group training, on-the-job train-ing, or coaching programs.
NO		NO		Consider external education or management self-study programs, providing for skill modeling before, during, or after the learning experience.

Source: Henry Ellington, *Producing Teaching Materials: A Handbook for Teachers and Trainers* (London: Kogan Page, 1985).

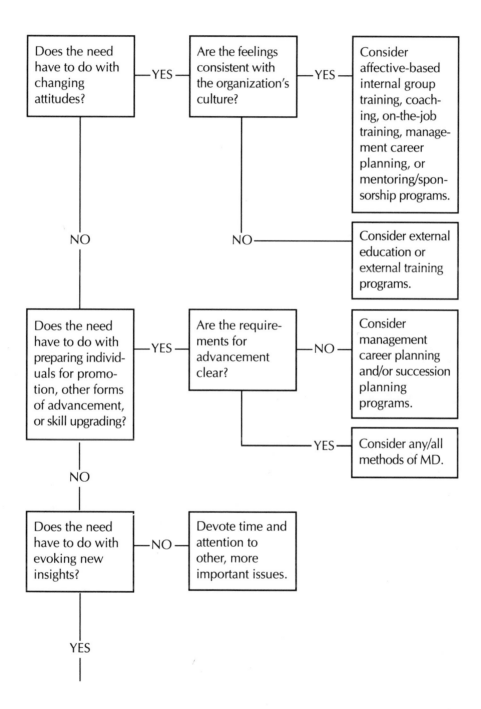

(continues)

Exhibit 6-3 (*continued*).

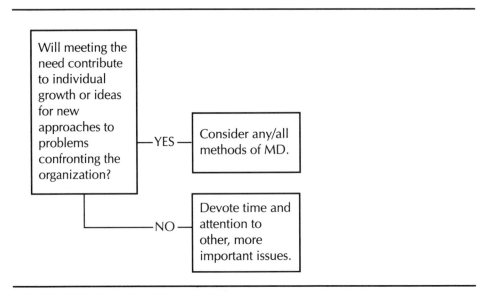

Affective, feeling, or attitudinal needs have to do with establishing new values, life-styles, or philosophies about life, work, management, and people. Short-term planned learning experiences alone rarely produce such sweeping changes in internal beliefs; long-term experiences are usually necessary to do that. Learning experiences of this kind usually focus on "why" questions: "Why should employee participation be valued?" and "Why is Total Quality Management worth pursuing?"

The attitudes of management employees are important, because their opinions exert a strong influence on the job satisfaction of individuals and the morale of employee groups. To employees, their immediate organizational superiors exemplify and embody management; the opinions of their organizational superiors are, they reason, no doubt shared by others in authority.

Many of the challenges facing American organizations center around attitudinal issues. For example, organizations need to:

- Offer exemplary customer service.
- Improve product or service quality.
- Build employee involvement in decision making.
- Address the pervasive cynicism of U.S. workers.
- Deal with a changing work ethic.
- Cope with waning employee loyalty.

Often, however, meeting affective learning needs requires broad-based action extending beyond short-term planned learning experiences, such as one-shot internal group training courses. In fact, it often requires paying attention to all factors influencing performance, including compensation, benefits, recruitment practices, and selection practices, as well as job design and work group structure. Training aimed at changing individuals is inadequate by itself to change organizational culture. The reasons: On-the-job reinforcement is often insufficient following training, and too few people are trained at one time to create a critical mass favoring change.

For these reasons, then, meeting learning needs linked to attitudes or feelings may require increased attention to on-the-job coaching, on-the-job training, individual career planning, and mentoring or sponsorship programs. By paying more attention to these techniques, management can provide individuals with prompt, concrete, and specific feedback about performance or behaviors.

Advancement needs are linked to vertical (promotional) or horizontal (technical) job advancement opportunities. They are closely associated with employee education intended to prepare people for the next job rather than the current job. Management education focused on meeting these needs addresses *future* "what," "how-to" and "why" questions. For example, a supervisor aspiring to a manager position needs to consider these issues: "What should a manager do?" "How should the responsibilities of a manager be met?" and "Why are certain attitudes so important for managers?"

As Exhibit 6-3 indicates, advancement needs can be met effectively only when the organization has clarified and communicated the responsibilities linked to advancement. To that end, management career planning programs and succession planning programs—both methods of clarifying what is needed from the individual and the organization—are essential for clearing up *what* needs to be learned and *how well*.

Once learning needs are clear, many MD methods may be brought to bear on a performance gap between what individuals already know and what they should know to meet future requirements. Short-term methods may be used, such as internal group training, coaching, or on-the-job training programs; long-term methods may also be used, including external education, job rotation (to other functions), position assignment, or management self-study programs.

Developmental needs are linked to organizational growth through individual creativity. They stem from the deep human need to realize one's potential, to be creative. Development focuses on evoking new ideas for the benefit of individuals and their organizations.

MD focused on meeting developmental needs addresses "what's

new" questions. For example, a manager aspiring to an executive position might consider these issues: "How do departments other than my own function?" and "What new methods can be used to address organizational problems in my department or in others?" As Exhibit 6-3 indicates, developmental needs are worth meeting only when some recognizable payoff will be realized. However, the nature of that payoff varies, and the results of developmental experiences are often difficult to quantify. If it is not possible to see any value resulting from the experience—such as sending a management employee off to an Executive Development program, to a basket-weaving or aerobics class, to a community leadership program, or to an adventure learning encounter—then perhaps time, attention, and resources should be devoted to other methods in which the payoffs are more easily identified.

Any MD method may be used to meet developmental needs, thereby broadening individual horizons and stimulating new ideas in an organization. As in management education, developmental experiences may be short-term or long-term. New ideas may come from inside or outside the organization and from such planned learning experiences as internal group training or external educational programs. They may also be elicited through coaching, on-the-job training, job rotation, position assignments, or management self-study programs.

Summary

In this chapter, we used the term *methods* to refer to *modes of delivering planned MD activities*. While it is tempting to select MD methods immediately, we advise you to address questions first about the MD program's purpose, goals, objectives, policy, philosophy, targeted group(s), action plan, curriculum, and administrative support and about the needs to be served. Only then should you pose these questions: *By what methods should learning needs be met?* and *How should the MD curriculum be implemented?*

Chapter 7
Planning and Using Formal Methods

In this chapter we turn to planning and using *formal MD methods*. These approaches to MD are carefully planned and deliberately executed to meet learning needs. They include:

- Succession planning programs
- Management career planning programs
- Internal group training programs
- External group training programs
- External education programs
- Job rotation programs
- Position assignment programs

These MD methods, while seemingly unrelated, all lend themselves to centralized administration and oversight. Formal MD methods may thus be coordinated by an MD director or an MD coordinator.

Succession Planning Programs

Succession planning is an apt starting point for introducing formal MD methods, because it is helpful in identifying gaps between existing and desired management talent.

Succession planning is a systematic approach for identifying, assessing, and developing successors for positions in organizational settings.[1] Successors are typically, but not always, identified from within organizations by their immediate organizational superiors. They are assessed over time spans that may be short or long and are developed so that they are prepared to assume higher-level or more technically sophisticated positions. While most succession plans focus on replacing the incumbents in key positions, succession plans can be extended throughout the management ranks.

The Importance of Succession Planning

Many corporations use some form of succession planning.[2] It is important for:

- Creating a surplus of skills beyond those minimally necessary to ensure organizational survival
- Identifying individuals capable of assuming more responsibility (vertical advancement) or achieving greater technical expertise (horizontal advancement)
- Ensuring continuity of operations in the event of the sudden death, disability, retirement, resignation, or other loss of key management employees
- Identifying individuals as possible replacements for key incumbents in critically important positions
- Pinpointing positions in which no successors have been identified so that contingency plans may be established

When Should Succession Planning Be a Programmatic Focus of MD?

Succession planning is a process, a form of long-term internal recruitment in which decision makers identify possible replacements for incumbents occupying important positions in the organization. The process is *long-term* because few succession plans assume that incumbents must be immediately replaced. It focuses on *possible* replacements because few succession plans assume that identified successors will definitely become permanent successors. Indeed, an actual placement ratio of 60 to 70 percent is indicative of a successful program. Higher ratios make it appear that key replacement decisions are "fixed" or "rigged" to restrict opportunities for members of protected labor groups.

Succession planning should be just one force guiding the organization's planned MD program. But succession planning can pinpoint the need for replacements or successors in management positions. In that sense, it creates an impetus favoring a planned MD program. Since succession planning is a long-term effort, it provides valuable information for charting the long-term direction of a planned MD program.

Carrying Out Succession Planning

In many organizations, a succession planning ritual is carried out at least once a year. There is no one right way to go about that ritual. The most appropriate way to carry out the succession planning process depends on the organization's culture, traditions, and top management philosophies.

With that caveat in mind, we can still describe several key steps that are workable in most settings.

First, top managers should appoint someone to spearhead and coordinate the succession planning program. A good choice is the MD director, MD coordinator, or HR director. The person chosen for this role must be tactful and discreet. Any violation of trust may lead to a complete loss of credibility for the individual and the program. Since the CEO bears ultimate responsibility for organizational succession, he or she should appoint the individual to spearhead the effort. Great care should be taken at the outset to ensure that, if succession matters are to be kept secret, the individual chosen as program coordinator must not learn of succession plans personally affecting him or her.

Second, the MD director or coordinator should work to clarify the purpose, policy, and procedures that will guide succession planning in the organization. The program coordinator should meet with the CEO and with all top managers in the organization, subsidiary, or division to answer such questions as:

- What should be the program's purpose?
- What are the desired results?
- What positions should be included? Should the program focus solely on high-level positions, as is common, or should it extend into the nonexempt ranks to include possible replacements for supervisors or team leaders?
- How often should succession planning be carried out?
- Who should be involved in identifying and developing possible successors? How much say should the job incumbent have in choosing a successor? How much say should others have?
- What forms or other data-gathering methods should be used in the process, and what information should they seek?
- How will confidentiality of the process—and its results—be ensured? What is the organization's philosophy on confidentiality? Who should have access to succession planning results?

Third, the succession planning coordinator should work in consultation with others to draft proposed succession planning policy and procedures and the forms to be used to support them (see the model succession planning policy and procedures in Exhibit 7-1). Forms commonly used in succession planning include:

- A *personal history form* to describe the background of the incum-

Exhibit 7-1. Sample succession planning policy.

Purpose

To ensure replacements for key job incumbents in executive, management, technical, and professional positions in the organization. This policy covers middle-management positions and above in [*name of organization*].

Desired Results

The desired results of the succession planning program are to:

1. Identify high-potential employees capable of rapid advancement to positions of higher responsibility than they presently occupy.
2. Ensure the systematic and long-term development of individuals to replace key job incumbents as need arises due to deaths, disabilities, retirements, and other unexpected losses.
3. Provide a continuous flow of talented people to meet the organization's management needs.
4. Meet the organization's need to exercise social responsibility by providing for the advancement of protected labor groups inside the organization.

Procedures

The succession planning program will be carried out as follows:

1. In January of each year, the MD director will arrange a meeting with the CEO to review results from the previous year's succession planning efforts and to plan for the present year's process.
2. In February, top managers will attend a meeting coordinated by the MD director in which:
   a. The CEO will emphasize the importance of succession planning and review the previous year's results.
   b. The MD director will distribute forms and establish due dates for their completion and return.
   c. The MD director will review the results of a computerized analysis to pinpoint areas of the organization in which predictable turnover, resulting from retirements or other changes, will lead to special needs for management talent.
   d. The results of a computerized analysis will be reviewed to demonstrate how successfully the organization has been attracting protected labor groups into high-level positions and to plot strategies for improving affirmative action practices.
3. In April, the forms will be completed and returned to the MD director. If necessary, a follow-up meeting will be held. In any case, the information

will be deposited in a secure database for retrieval as the need for management talent arises.

4. Throughout the year, the MD director will periodically visit top managers to review progress in developing identified successors throughout their areas of responsibility.

5. As need arises, the database will be accessed as a source of possible successors in the organization.

---

bent in each key position, as well as a *personal history form* to describe the backgrounds of possible successors

‣ A *succession planning chart,* based on the organization chart, highlighting key positions to be filled and individuals identified as possible successors

‣ A *performance appraisal form* for each key job incumbent and each possible successor

‣ A *future potential appraisal form* for each possible successor

‣ An *individual development form* listing developmental steps to be taken to help each designated successor qualify for the position to which he or she has been linked

Sample forms appear in Exhibits 7-2 through 7-6.

Once drafted, the policy, procedures, and forms can be sent out to top managers for comment. This approach minimizes the amount of executive time that must be spent in meetings. If issues emerge that cannot be ironed out in this way, meetings may be held to arrive at consensus.

Fourth, the succession planning coordinator should review procedures regularly so they keep pace with organizational and environmental change. When first unveiled, succession planning procedures should be explained and the importance of the process emphasized. The CEO should unveil the process to dramatize its importance. A brief kick-off meeting led by the CEO can be followed up by briefings or training to describe detailed procedures to the users.

If the MD director has been asked by the CEO to be available to offer one-on-one counseling to senior managers as they plan individual development activities—and such counseling is often advisable—the CEO should say so in the kick-off meeting and encourage the process.

Fifth, the MD director should follow through once forms have been submitted to ensure that progress is being made on individual development plans. For instance, the director may wish to phone key managers or to pay them visits to review succession plans for their areas of

text continues on page 146

Exhibit 7-2. Sample personal history form.

Directions: Please fill in the information requested.

BIOGRAPHICAL INFORMATION

Name: _____

Job Title: _____

Organization: _____

Location: _____

Reports to: _____

Date of birth: _____

Date appointed to present position: _____

Date hired: _____

Salary level: _____

Interests: _____

EDUCATION

Completed Education

Graduation Date	*Degree*	*Major*	*University/College*
_____	_____	_____	_____

Education in Progress

Licenses/Accreditations/Professional Designations

Date Completed	*License/ Accreditation/ Designation*	*Institution*
_____	_____	_____
_____	_____	_____

EMPLOYMENT HISTORY

With Present Employer

Job Titles   *Started*   *Ended*
1.

   Key duties:

2.

   Key duties:

3.

   Key duties:

With Previous Employers

Job Titles   *Started*   *Ended*
1.

   Key duties:

2.

   Key duties:

3.

   Key duties:

SUCCESSION CANDIDATES

Names   *Year Prepared*

Exhibit 7-3. Sample succession planning chart.

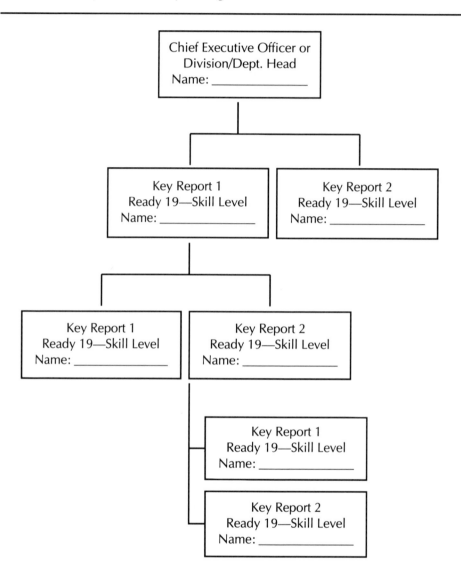

responsibility and to offer them specialized advice about ways to develop management employees. As positions become vacant, the MD director may also be called on to help locate successors by using confidential succession planning information loaded on a personal computer.

Sixth, the MD director or coordinator should establish a procedure to measure program effectiveness as the need for management talent arises. He or she should keep track of positions that were actually filled from within as a result of succession planning. Positive comments about the program from executives should be put in writing so they may be shared as testimonials with skeptics.

Problems Affecting Succession Planning

You may encounter several problems as you develop a succession planning program. To overcome them, keep several points in mind.

The first point is that succession planning is only one part of a comprehensive MD program. It is not the only part. It is not intended to head off all need for external recruiting. Nor is it intended to encourage promotion from within when alternative staffing methods will more effectively infuse new ideas into the organization and prevent inbreeding. But succession planning does encourage the development of internal talent, which may occur less predictably without a succession planning program.

A second point to remember is that no successor is permanently designated as an "heir apparent." Successors may change from year to year. They may also change when external environmental conditions, position demands, or strategic plans change. They should certainly change when individuals designated as possible successors experience dramatic setbacks in performance in their current positions. (Success in the existing job is a critical prerequisite for advancement to more responsible positions.)

A third point is that key policy makers should decide upon a philosophy about candor in the succession planning program. In other words, should designated successors be told of their status? There is no simple answer to this question. Advantages and disadvantages can be cited on both sides of the question. If successors know their status, they may feel advancement is guaranteed and exemplary performance in their present positions does not have to be sustained. However, the reverse can also be true: Designated successors, if told of their status, may approach their present positions with renewed vigor and take an active role in developing themselves for future challenges facing them.

A fourth point to remember: If designated successors are alerted to their status, they should never be queried about what developmental steps they should take to prepare for advancement. The rationale for this general rule is simple enough: They are not positioned to judge what they need. Only position incumbents, top managers, and the MD director should be consulted on this issue. Key position incumbents have a proven track record. They are likely to be valuable resources for identifying strategies to help designated successors narrow the gap

text continues on page 151

Exhibit 7-4. Sample performance appraisal form.

Employee's name: _____

Date of appraisal: _____

Appraiser: _____

PART I
Position Description

Directions: Describe the responsibilities of the individual performing this job. (These responsibilities should be relatively stable and enduring.) State these responsibilities in terms of the most typical activities performed in the position. Use additional paper if necessary.

PART II
Performance Objectives

Directions: In item 1 below, describe specific, measurable objectives that are to be achieved on a continuous and regular basis by the individual in this position. (Base these objectives on the responsibilities set forth in Part I of this Appraisal Form.) In item 2, describe unique, measurable and one-time-only objectives to be achieved over the course of the next appraisal period. Use additional paper if necessary.

1. What specific, measurable responsibilities should the individual achieve in this position on a continual and regular basis?

2. List any unique, measurable, and one-time-only objectives to be achieved during the next appraisal period.

PART III
Review Meetings

Directions: Meet with the individual over the course of the appraisal period to provide guidance and suggestions for achieving requirements of the position and one-time objectives for the year. In the space below, make clear when these discussions occurred and what results or agreements stemmed from the discussions. Use additional paper if necessary, enclosing it in this appraisal booklet. (Enclose separate sheets if you hold more than one review meeting.)

Review Meeting Summary

Date: _____   Time: _____

Results: _____

_____

_____

PART IV
Performance Review

Directions: In the space below, assess how well the individual achieved performance objectives for his or her position during the appraisal period. Compare results at the end of the appraisal period to the position responsibilities and one-time objectives set forth in Parts I and II of this form and established at the beginning of the appraisal period. Base the review on this comparison. Use additional paper as necessary.

(continues)

Exhibit 7-4 (*continued*).

PART V
Management Skills

Directions: For each general management skill listed below, describe the employee's performance over the appraisal period. Appraise management employees only on skill areas applicable to them.

---

1. Planning:

2. Controlling:

3. Organizing:

4. Budgeting:

5. Appraising:

6. Communicating:

7. Developing employees/oneself:

8. Making decisions:

9. Managing projects effectively:

10. Staffing the unit/department:

11. Representing the organization effectively:

12. Influencing others:

13. Making changes:

14. Dealing with changes:

15. Other skills (specify):

Employee comments:

Approvals

Signature of employee: _____   Date: _____

Signature of appraiser: _____   Date: _____

Signature of person authorizing: _____   Date: _____

Effective date: _____

between the knowledge and skills they possess in their present positions and those needed for success in future positions. Top managers should be consulted because they have the best grasp of the organization's strategic plan, including any new performance requirements that may become important in the future. The MD director should also be consulted about possible MD methods that can be used to narrow gaps in knowledge or skill.

Management Career Planning Programs

When used as a formal MD method, a management career planning program is a systematic means of identifying information about management position requirements in an organizational setting, communicating that information to employees, and encouraging them to establish and work toward realistic career goals. In one sense, a management career planning program is a mirror image of a succession planning program because it is driven from the bottom up rather than (like most succession planning programs) from top down. While career

Exhibit 7-5. Sample future performance appraisal form.

Employee's name: _____   Date of hire: _____

Date of appraisal: _____   Date of appointment to present
                                       position: _____

Appraiser: _____   Position level: _____

Part I
Present Position Description/Performance

Directions: In the space below, describe the current responsibilities of this job and how well the job incumbent has been performing those duties over the last year.

Part II
Future Position Description/Performance

Directions: In the space below, describe the responsibilities of this job as you believe they should exist in 5 years if they are consistent with the organization's strategic plan and pressures exerted by external competition. Then describe how well the job incumbent is *presently* equipped to perform those *future* duties.

Part III
Development Needs

Directions: In the space below, describe the job incumbent's development needs by setting forth areas of difference between his or her present position description/performance (Part I) and future position description/performance (Part II).

Part IV
Developmental Plan

Directions: In the spaces below, describe how the individual should be developed to meet the needs outlined in Part III. Center attention on developmental activities that may occur over the next 1 to 3 years.

Need:

How should the need be met?

Notes:

Approvals

Signature of employee: _____   Date: _____

Signature of appraiser: _____   Date: _____

Effective date: _____

---

planning always remains an individual's responsibility,[3] career goal setting can be greatly improved when the organization clarifies position requirements and career paths.

The Importance of Management Career Planning

Few contemporary observers dispute that changes in labor market conditions are occurring more rapidly than ever before. Indeed, labor markets are growing more uncertain as organizations go bankrupt, downsize, relocate, and undergo other changes. It is now estimated that the average person changes careers—not just jobs—between three and five times.[4] Some claim that, in the future, there will be more innovative staffing arrangements than is the norm at present, with temporary management workers and contractors more common than they are today.[5]

Exhibit 7-6. Sample individual development plan.

Employee's Name: _____   Date: _____

Part I
Objectives

1. What are the employee's *learning needs*, and what *learning objectives* will best help meet those needs over the next year?

Part II
Strategies/Methods

2. What *learning strategies or methods* will help the employee achieve the learning objectives outlined in Part I?

Part III
Resources

3. What *resources*—time, money, material, staff, or equipment—does the employee need to achieve the learning objectives listed in Part I by means of the strategies or methods listed in Part II?

Part IV
Evaluation Methods

4. How will the employee's achievement of learning objectives be *measured*? Describe evaluation and measurement methods for each learning objective.

Learning Objective	Evaluation and Measurement Methods
1.	
2.	
3.	

Approvals

Signature of employee: ———————————— Date: —————————

Signature of appraiser: ———————————— Date: —————————

Effective Date: —————————

Against this backdrop, management career planning is becoming more important. Management employees are no longer confident that, as in times past, they can start working for one employer and remain there for a lifetime. To serve their own best interests, they must keep their skills finely honed so that they can compete in the labor market— on a moment's notice, if need be. For this reason, they must plan their careers consistently, incessantly, and even obsessively.

How Do Management Career Planning Programs Differ?

Management career planning programs, like career planning programs geared to other groups, fall into three general categories: (1) *formal programs,* in which the organization takes active steps to encourage career planning and to provide information about position requirements and career paths; (2) *informal programs,* in which individuals are provided with general, but not organization-specific, career planning information and carry out career planning activities on their own; (3) combination programs, in which the organization takes active steps to encourage career planning while individuals take the initiative for their own career planning efforts.

When Should Management Career Planning Be a Programmatic Focus of MD?

Use management career planning as a programmatic focus of MD when it is necessary to increase the participation, involvement, and ownership of individuals in their MD activities. Career planning helps individuals see that MD activities are, in fact, vehicles for helping them realize their career goals. In addition, career planning helps individuals understand that the responsibility for their lives and careers rests with them and not with their immediate organizational superiors, organizations, or co-workers.

*Designing and Implementing
Management Career Planning Programs*

The appropriate steps to take in establishing a management career planning program depend on what kind of program it is—formal, informal, or combination.

A *formal career planning program* is carefully planned. It begins with a few specific questions, such as:

· What should be the program's purpose?
· What job classifications, groups, or functional areas should receive special attention?
· Who should participate in program operations?

Often, the highest priorities are devoted to management groups experiencing higher-than-average turnover and to programs designed to encourage cultural, racial, and sexual diversity in the organization's management ranks.

Subsequent steps in designing and implementing a formal career planning program include identifying organizational needs, selecting target groups, evaluating existing career patterns, selecting appropriate change efforts, effecting appropriate change, and assessing results.[6] Successful programs involve employees, their immediate organizational superiors, and top managers.

A *pilot program* is often a starting point for a formal career planning program. It is a small-scale effort directed at specially targeted departments or occupational groups. Immediate organizational superiors are encouraged to take an active role in program development, are briefed on program particulars, and are encouraged to promote career planning activities among management employees reporting to them. Few organizations choose to direct career planning programs to management employees alone,[7] though some may choose to pilot a career planning program in the management ranks and later extend the program to other groups.

It is common to begin a pilot program by:

Exhibit 7-7. Example of a vertical career path.

Note: The differences in job requirements from one level to the next imply different training, education, and development needs.

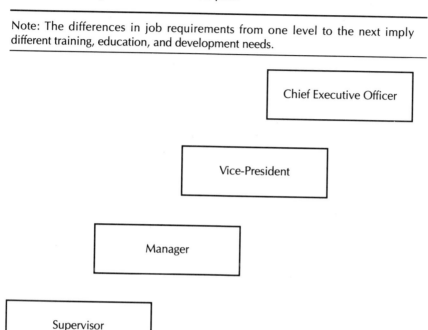

- ‣ Clarifying management position requirements (if position descriptions do not exist or are outdated)
- ‣ Forecasting future management position requirements
- ‣ Clarifying key differences between higher-level and lower-level management positions
- ‣ Establishing vertical career paths showing desirable or typical progressions from lower- to higher-level positions (see Exhibit 7-7)
- ‣ Establishing horizontal career paths showing desirable or typical "position broadening" that can occur within an existing position (see Exhibit 7-8)

Participants in formal career planning programs are frequently trained in career planning methods and furnished with the resources appropriate for setting career goals and taking career action in the context of their organizations (see the sample outline of the training program in Exhibit 7-9). Those who counsel others on career issues may also receive special training on effective career counseling methods.[8]

Exhibit 7-8. Example of a horizontal career path.

Note: The differences in job requirements from one level to the next imply training, education, and development needs.

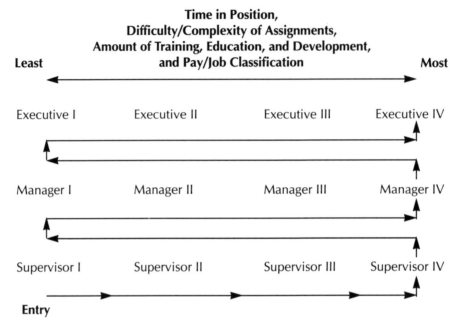

An *informal management career planning program* may also begin with needs assessment. However, the focus is on the individual rather than on the organization. Often, MD directors, MD coordinators, or HR specialists spearhead the effort. Then career planning materials, like those listed in Exhibit 7-10, are gathered and made available. Management employees are able to check out these materials for their own use or for counseling selected individuals on career issues.

In recent years many organizations have experienced considerable success with in-house career planning programs. Of special note are *bottom-up programs,* in which management employees learn to conduct career planning discussions and establish written career plans with their immediate organizational superiors. Unlike performance appraisal discussions that focus on past job performance, career planning discussions focus on future career goals and methods of realizing them.[9] All management levels may be involved in these voluntary programs. Special career planning forms, such as the one shown in Exhibit 7-11, help management employees formulate what career goals to pursue,

text continues on page 161

Exhibit 7-9. Sample training course outline of career planning for management employees.

Purpose

To review key issues and practices in career planning for management employees

Objectives

Upon completing this course, participants should be able to:

1. Define career planning.
2. Explain the importance of career planning.
3. Point out the importance of the current job as it affects career planning.
4. Describe how to assess personal strengths and weaknesses.
5. Identify personal values in career planning.
6. Describe career options in the organization.
7. Chart personal career goals.
8. Draft and communicate a written career plan.

Course Outline

I. Introduction
  A. Describe
    1. The course title
    2. The purpose of the course
    3. The objectives of the course
    4. The structure of the course
  B. Ask participants to summarize their personal goals for the course.
II. What is career planning?
  A. Definition of career planning
  B. Importance of career planning
  C. Importance of taking personal responsibility for career planning
III. How does the present job fit in to career planning?
  A. Surfacing key issues affecting the present job
  B. Surfacing key values
  C. Understanding the importance of the present job as it affects career plans
IV. What about the future?
  A. What are your present strengths and weaknesses?
    1. Definitions of strengths and weaknesses
    2. Methods of identifying strengths and weaknesses
    3. Individual activity
  B. What trends affect career planning?
    1. National trends
    2. Industry trends
    3. Organizational strategy

(continues)

Exhibit 7-9 (*continued*).

    4. Present/future career paths
    5. Effects of strengths/weaknesses on future career prospects
V. How is career planning carried out?
  A. Stating goals
  B. Establishing time frames and choosing methods
  C. Communicating goals and building alliances
  D. Writing down the career plan
VI. Conclusion
  A. Evaluate
    1. Personal career plans
    2. The course
  B. Establish
    1. Methods of self-follow-up
    2. Methods of follow-up with immediate organizational superiors

Exhibit 7-10. Selected list of career planning materials appropriate for management employees.

Books

Michael Arthur, Douglas Hall, and Barbara Lawrence, eds., *Handbook of Career Theory* (New York: Cambridge University Press, 1989).

Duane Brown and Linda Brooks, *Career Choice and Development* (San Francisco: Jossey-Bass, 1990).

Susan Colantuono, *Build Your Career: Getting Ahead Without Getting Out: A How-To Guide for Advancing Within Your Company* (Amherst, Mass.: Human Resource Development Press, 1982).

Daniel Feldman, *Managing Careers in Organizations* (Glenview, Ill.: Scott, Foresman, 1988).

Jerome Kapes and Marjorie Mastie, *Career Assessment Instruments* (Austin, Tex.: Pro-Ed, 1988).

Zandy Leibowitz, Caela Farren, and Beverly Kaye, *Designing Career Development Systems* (San Francisco: Jossey-Bass, 1986).

Professional Careers Sourcebook (Detroit: Gale Research, 1989).

Fred Vondracek, Richard Lerner, and John Schulenberg, *Career Development: A Life-Span Developmental Approach* (Hillsdale, N.J.: Lawrence Erlbaum Associates, 1986).

Sherry Willis and Samuel Dubin, eds., *Maintaining Professional Competence* (San Francisco: Jossey-Bass, 1990).

Elizabeth Yost and M. Anne Corbishley, *Career Counseling: A Psychological Approach* (San Francisco: Jossey-Bass, 1987).

Vernon Zunker, *Career Counseling: Applied Concepts of Life Planning* (San Francisco: Jossey-Bass, 1990).

Periodicals

International Journal of Career Management, MCB University Press, P.O. Box 10812, Birmingham, Ala. 35201 [3 issues/year].

Journal of Career Development, Human Sciences Press, 233 Spring Street, New York, NY [4 issues/year].

Journal of Career Planning and Employment, College Placement Council, 62 Highland Avenue, Bethlehem, PA 18017 [4 issues/year].

---

identify how to achieve those goals, and set the agenda for a meeting to discuss their career goals with their immediate organizational superiors.

Problems Affecting Management Career Planning Programs

No MD method is foolproof. This principle applies as much to management career planning programs as it does to other MD programs.

One problem with management career planning programs is that they rely heavily on the element of trust between employees and their organizational superiors. Employees must be truthful about their career goals and plans. But several issues undermine such truthfulness. For instance, management employees may have their hearts set on career goals *outside* their present employer—for example, they may aspire to become owners of small businesses, independent entrepreneurs, consultants, stay-at-home parents, or caregivers for elderly relatives. Employees may worry that candor about such goals may undermine their career prospects with their present employer. While most employees trust their immediate superiors, a disquieting minority of about 30 percent does not.[10]

Nor is candor a troubling issue for employees alone: Their immediate organizational superiors may face barriers to it as well. For instance, they may be unable to share what they know about the organization's plans to offer early retirement incentives or to eliminate lines of business—all issues that may affect individual career decisions. They may also be prohibited by policy, philosophy, or tradition from sharing what they may know about an individual's prospects for the future as tentatively outlined in succession plans.

There is no simple solution for overcoming these problems. The best advice is to clarify the guidelines for career planning programs. Perhaps individuals can be limited to considering career goals in one organization. A key point may have to be that the program assumes

text continues on page 165

Exhibit 7-11. Sample management career planning form.

Name of employee: Budget center:

_____   _____

Job title: _____

Start date: _____   Date appointed to present position: _____

Immediate supervisor: _____

General instructions to management employees: The purpose of this form is to help you structure your thinking about your career plans. Complete the form, attaching additional paper if necessary. Then forward a copy of this form to your immediate supervisor, and schedule a meeting with him or her to discuss your career plans. It is not mandatory for you to complete this form or to meet with your immediate supervisor about it. If you meet with your immediate supervisor to discuss career issues, please forward a copy of this form to the Human Resources Department for use in identifying company Management Development needs.

Part I
Assessing Personal Career Goals and Interests

What would you like to be doing in this organization in 3 to 5 years?

Part II
Identifying Jobs Within the Organization That Match Up to Personal Career Goals

What jobs in the organization do you feel will help you become what you want to be in the future? How well do you feel they will make use of your special talents and skills? What are those talents/skills? What would you like to know about those jobs?

Part III
Assessing Personal Strengths and Weaknesses
Relative to Necessary Qualifications for the Job

How well qualified do you feel you are at present to do a job you would like to do in the future in this organization? In what ways do you feel especially well prepared now to do this job? In what ways do you feel less than well prepared?

Part IV
Expressing Interest in Promotion or Transfer or in Increasing Technical
Competence to the Supervisor and to the Human Resources Department

What career advice would you especially like to get from your immediate organizational superior? from the HR department? What information would help you establish clear career goals and work toward preparing yourself for the future?

Part V
Identifying Conditions Inside or Outside the Organization That May Change
Necessary Minimum Job Qualifications

How might changing conditions inside or outside the organization affect what you need to know or do to achieve your career goals? How might changing organizational policies, procedures, work methods, or organizational conditions affect what you need to know or do to prepare for meeting your career goals in the organization?

(continues)

Exhibit 7-11 (*continued*).

Part VI
Preparing a Personal Action Plan to Narrow Gaps Between Present Knowledge, Skills, and Experience and Those That Are Necessary to Meet the Minimum Qualifications for the Job

What can you do over the next year to equip yourself with the knowledge, skills, and experiences you need to prepare for achieving your long-term career goals? Consider such activities as forming a mentoring relationship with someone who is doing what you want to do or who is familiar with how to advance in a given occupational field; seeking approval from your supervisor to work on short-term assignments that are related to your career goals; seeking long-term work assignments on your present job that are related to your long-term career goals; seeking a lateral transfer, temporarily or permanently, to provide experience in line with long-term career goals; seeking approval from your immediate supervisor to do work similar to what you would like to be doing (job enlargement); seeking approval from your immediate supervisor to take on additional duties that require more responsibility (job enrichment); preparing an independent study plan to learn more about a new subject, occupation, or discipline (career diversification); identifying meetings, seminars, conferences, workshops, or other organized events where you can learn new skills or knowledge pertinent to your career goals in the organization; teaching seminars, presenting at conferences, or otherwise learning by doing the work. Meet with your immediate supervisor, and list specific objectives for the next year in the space below.

Part VII
Follow-Up

How well do you feel you have been progressing toward your career goals in the organization? What significant strides have you made?

Approvals

Signature of employee: _____   Date: _____

Signature of employee's supervisor: _____   Date: _____

Effective date: _____

"all other things being equal"—meaning that there will be no major changes in the organization's or the individual's plans.

A second problem with management career planning programs is that they can create legal liability or build unrealistic employee expectations unless they are carefully handled. Employees' immediate organizational superiors must be trained to avoid making oral or written promises that they cannot keep. Top-performing employees may grow disenchanted if they feel betrayed on promises of promotions. Such promises may also be construed as legally binding contractual agreements. Managers should avoid statements such as:

"If you do all the things we have discussed, then you will be promoted."

"You can't be fired here."

"If you maintain good performance in this organization, the chance is zero that you will be laid off."

"Don't worry about your future. I'll see to it that you receive the next promotion."

Instead of making sweeping and dangerous statements like these, managers should instead emphasize the tentative nature of organizational goals and plans, explaining that they are always subject to change because of the effects of a dynamic competitive environment. Immediate organizational superiors should promise only what they are certain they can deliver.

Internal Group Training Programs

Businesses in the United States spend roughly $10 billion annually on supervisory, management, and executive training.[11] According to a 1991 *Training Magazine* survey, 72 percent of the responding organizations provide supervisory training, 77 percent provide management training, 57 percent provide senior management training, and 65 percent provide executive training.[12] (See Exhibit 7-12.) A substantial portion of this training is provided by in-house staff only: 26 percent of supervisory training, 19 percent of manager training, 14 percent of senior manager training, and 8 percent of executive training derive from this source.[13] In many cases, in-house staff teams up with outside vendors in joint training ventures. *Training Magazine* indicates that such joint ventures account for 68 percent of supervisory training, 73 percent of manager training, 49 percent of senior manager training, and 62 percent of executive training.[14]

Exhibit 7-12. Who gets the training?

Job Category	Organizations Training (%)[1]	Average Number of Individuals Trained[2]	Projected Number of Individuals Trained (in millions)[3]	Average Number of Hours Delivered[4]	Projected Total Hours of Training Delivered (in millions)[5]
First-line supervisors	72%	33	3.7	34	125.2
Middle managers	77	24	2.8	33	93.4
Senior managers	57	12	1.1	33	35.1
Executives	65	8	0.8	33	25.7

[1]All U.S. organizations with 100 or more employees that provide formal training to people in these categories.
[2]Average number of individuals trained per organization based only on those organizations that provide some training.
[3]Total number of people trained in all organizations (in millions).
[4]Average hours of training provided per individual.
[5]Total hours of training (in millions) delivered by all organizations to employees in these categories. (One person receiving training for one hour equals one "hour of training.")
Source: Chris Lee, "Who Gets Trained in What." Reprinted with permission from *Training Magazine,* 28:10 (1991), p. 48, Lakewood Publications, Minneapolis, Minn. All rights reserved.

Many topics treated by in-house training staffs focus on supervisory and management issues (see Exhibit 7-13). The most common training courses offered in-house center on performance appraisals, leadership, hiring/selection, interpersonal skills, team building, delegation skills, and employee training methods (train-the-trainer). Each year other internal group training programs are offered on topical issues or trends. For example, many organizations offer internal group training on customer service, total quality management (TQM), and team building. Our 1992 survey of MD specialists revealed a prioritized list of the ten major trends affecting planned MD programs (see Exhibit 7-14)—and these trends decidedly affect the most topical internal group training experiences.

Defining Internal Group Training

Internal group training is often planned, designed, delivered, and followed up systematically to narrow the gap between what individuals

text continues on page 169

Figure 7-13. Specific types of training.

Types of Training	Percentage Providing[1]	In-House Only (%)[2]	Outside Only (%)[3]	Both (%)[4]
New employees orientation	82%	76%	0.3%	7%
Performance appraisals	76	53	3.3	20
Leadership	69	16	13	40
Hiring/selection process	65	31	7	27
Interpersonal skills	64	19	8	37
Word processing	63	24	12	28
New equipment orientation	62	34	4	25
Team building	61	16	10	34
Delegation skills	60	18	12	29
Listening skills	59	22	8	30
Time management	59	15	14	30
Train-the-trainer	59	18	15	26
Product knowledge	58	40	2	16
Goal setting	58	21	8	30
Personal computer applications	57	17	7	33
Motivation	57	15	9	33

[1]Percentage providing this type of training.
[2]Percentage saying all training of this type is designed and delivered by in-house staff.
[3]Percentage saying all training of this type is designed and delivered by outside consultants or suppliers.
[4]Percentage saying all training of this type is designed and delivered by a combination of in-house staff and outside suppliers.
Source: Chris Lee, "Who Gets Trained in What." Reprinted with permission from *Training Magazine,* 28:10 (1991), p. 48, Lakewood Publications, Minneapolis, Minn. All rights reserved.

(continues)

Exhibit 7-13 (*continued*).

Types of Training	Percentage Providing[1]	In-House Only (%)[2]	Outside Only (%)[3]	Both (%)[4]
Decision making	56	16	11	29
Safety	56	25	2	29
Stress management	54	14	15	26
Computer programming	54	10	15	29
Problem solving	53	16	7	30
Quality improvement	50	17	3	30
Managing change	50	17	3	30
Conducting meetings	48	23	7	18
Writing skills	47	13	15	20
Public speaking/ presentation	47	14	11	22
Planning	46	18	3	25
Data processing	45	13	9	22
Negotiating skills	43	11	12	21
MIS	43	8	10	25
Substance abuse	42	11	11	20
Finance	41	13	11	18
Smoking cessation	39	9	18	12
Strategic planning	38	11	8	12
Ethics	37	18	4	19
Marketing	37	10	8	19
Outplacement/ retirement planning	36	19	8	9
Purchasing	29	11	7	11

Types of Training	Percentage Providing[1]	In-House Only (%)[2]	Outside Only (%)[3]	Both (%)[4]
Creativity	27	8	5	14
Reading skills	20	6	7	8
Foreign language	16	5	8	4
Other (topics not listed)	6	3	0.5	2

know or do and what they should know or do. Such training is useful when employees face similar changes in the workplace, such as:

> ‣ Preparing for changes in their jobs or responsibilities
> ‣ Qualifying for vertical or horizontal advancement in management
> ‣ Orienting themselves to new work roles after promotion
> ‣ Keeping their knowledge or skills up-to-date

It is *systematic* because there is a direct tie-in linking the processes of identifying performance problems, assessing training needs, writing performance objectives, selecting training methods, delivering training, and choosing evaluation approaches.

Internal group training for management employees is prepared and/or conducted by members of the organization—often by the MD director, MD coordinator, or internal training and development specialists. Its chief advantage is that it can be uniquely geared—in a way that is difficult, time-consuming, and expensive for external training vendors—to the organization's culture, philosophy, work requirements, and procedures to increase the possibility that what is learned will be applied on the participants' jobs.

However, recent writers on MD have pointed out that much of the substantial investment businesses make in internal group management training each year is of questionable value.[15] One reason: Its on-the-job results are often difficult to see or measure. Another reason: It is difficult to ensure that the on-the-job work environment supports and allows for application of what is learned.

When Should Internal Group Training Be a Programmatic Focus of MD?

Use internal group training as a solution only when performance problems stem from deficiencies of knowledge, skill, or attitude. Internal group training is an appropriate focus for MD when:

Exhibit 7-14. Trends affecting MD.

Question: Management is undergoing dramatic changes as a result of unfolding trends. For each trend listed in the left column, circle a response in the center column that indicates how important you feel it is and then check a response in the right column that indicates whether you are modifying the planned Management Development program of your organization to address the trend. Use the following codes in the center column:

1 = Not at all important
2 = Not very important
3 = Somewhat important
4 = Important
5 = Very important

	How important?		Is your organization modifying the management development program to address the trend?*	
			Yes (✓)	**No** (✓)
Trend**	**Frequency**	**Mean**	**Frequency**	**Frequency**
1. Increased emphasis on quality and service	58	4.55	52	4
2. Accelerated rate of change	57	4.09	40	14
3. Increased pressure to measure productivity	58	3.93	30	26
4. Increased expectations for more participation from all levels of the work force	57	3.84	38	17
5. Increased use of flatter, more flexible organization designs	59	3.71	30	27
6. Increased need for worker commitment	59	3.69	37	19
7. Reduced staff	58	3.67	31	26

*Not all respondents to the survey checked every item; not all respondents indicated whether or not their organizations are modifying the MD program to address the trend. Therefore, frequencies do not add up.
**This list of trends was adapted from Patricia A. McLagan and Debra Suhadolnik, *Models for HRD Practice.* Copyright 1989, American Society for Training and Development, Alexandria, Va. All rights reserved.
Source: William J. Rothwell and H. C. Kazanas, "Results of a 1992 Survey on Management Development Practices in the U.S." (Urbana, Ill.: Department of Vocational and Technical Education, 1992, unpublished).

| Trend** | How important? | | Is your organization modifying the management development program to address the trend?* | |
| | | | Yes (√) | No (√) |
	Frequency	Mean	Frequency	Frequency
8. Business strategies that concentrate more on human resource issues	57	3.60	35	21
9. Increased diversity of the work force	59	3.58	31	26
10. Increased use of systematic approaches to Management Development	56	3.43	32	24

‣ The organization is large enough to have a steady stream of individuals entering and progressing through the management ranks
‣ Groups of people share common (macro) learning needs
‣ On-the-job training is not likely to produce desired results at all or else is not likely to produce those results quickly enough
‣ Consistency of training content across learners is important

Internal group training takes advantage of economies of scale. It reduces the time and effort necessary to train individuals on similar issues or organizational policies, procedures, or requirements. Its advantages are its (presumed) consistency in training groups of people and its efficiency in training them in a shorter time than would typically be necessary if they were trained individually.

But internal group training is not appropriate when performance problems stem from causes other than deficiencies of knowledge, skill, or attitude. Nor is it appropriate if the organization is too small to warrant internal group training, if individuals experience widely diverse learning needs, if on-the-job training would be more cost-effective, or if methods other than internal group training would be less expensive and still achieve the desired changes in individual performance.[16]

Planning Internal Group Training

Of all MD methods, internal group training lends itself best to systematic instructional planning. As we stated in Chapter 4, theories of *curriculum design*—that is, approaches to planning instruction or learning—vary widely. A management training curriculum is essentially an instructional plan that helps individuals make transitions into, through, or out of the management ranks. Some subject-centered curricula are too rigid, forcing all learners to participate in the same experiences. Like the sequence of course titles in Exhibit 7-15, they imply a one-size-fits-all mentality that is increasingly eschewed by writers on MD because it is at odds with a trend toward increasingly individualized workplace learning. Other approaches to curriculum design produce more flexible learning plans that allow for individualization of planned learning experiences and accommodate individual learning styles. Such instruction is more effectively planned through individualized development plans.

Often, MD specialists aim to strike a balance between standardized (rigid) and individualized (flexible) training. After all, everyone who is promoted, transferred, or hired into a new position shares certain common learning needs. But they also experience uniquely individualized or job-specific learning needs. What is necessary, then, is a plan for group instruction to satisfy macro learning needs *and* a plan for individual instruction to satisfy micro learning needs.

While there are various ways to plan internal group training experiences depending on the approach to curriculum design that is selected, one ambitious approach is to follow a twelve-step instructional systems design model for management training.[17]

1. *Distinguish between issues appropriate for training and issues more appropriate for other methods.* To that end, start out by asking these questions:

- Is the problem caused, in whole or in part, by a learning need?
- Does a group of management employees share a learning need?
- Is the learning need likely to persist over time as new people enter—and progress through—the management ranks?
- Does the organization have the time, money, and expertise to offer internal group training to address the learning need?

If the answer to question 1 is "no," then some method other than

Exhibit 7-15. Sample MD curriculum.

Job Class	Course Title	Length
Presupervisor/ supervisor	• Orientation to the Role of Supervisor	1 day
	• General Principles of Supervision	1 day
	• Principles of Labor Relations	1 day
	• Setting Performance Objectives	1 day
	• Conducting Performance Appraisals	1 day
	• Facilitating Health, Wellness, and Safety	1 day
	• Handling Stress	1 day
	• Leading Meetings	1 day
	• Managing Conflict	1 day
	• Listening Skills	1 day
	• Written Communication Skills	1 day
	• Interviewing Skills	1 day
	• Dealing With Employee Performance Problems	1 day
	• Understanding the Supervisor's Role in Strategic Plans	1 day
Premanager/ manager	• Orientation to the Role of Manager	1 day
	• Managing People	1 day
	• Managing Quality	1 day
	• Establishing and Managing Work Teams	1 day
	• Managing Time	1 day
	• Solving Problems and Creative Thinking	1 day
	• The Manager as Career Coach and Career Counselor	1 day
	• Strategic Thinking, Planning, and Managing	1 day
Preexecutive/ executive	• Orientation to the Role of Executive	1 day
	• Annual Briefing on Legal Trends Affecting the Industry	1 day
	• Annual Briefing on Strategic Thinking, Planning, and Managing	1 day
	• Annual Briefing on Industry Trends	1 day

internal group training should be used to meet the need (see Exhibit 3-1). If the answer to question 2 is "no," then group training is inappropriate; individualized training is called for. If the answer to question 3 is "no," the learning need is a one-time occurrence that may be met more cost-effectively by sending people outside the organization. If the answer to question 4 is "no," then internal group training is again not likely to work. An external vendor may have to be used, or management employees may have to be sent outside the organization for external training.

If the answers to all the questions are "yes," however, then internal group training is appropriate.

2. *Assess the learning needs of management employees.* This issue was treated in Chapter 3.

3. *Assess relevant learner characteristics.* Before designing internal group training, you must know something about the learners. Typical areas to investigate are these:

- Who are the learners?
- What do they already know about the issue?
- What problems are they facing?
- How much do they want to learn about the issue?
- What are their individual learning styles?

Just as products or services should be geared to meet the needs of an identifiable market, internal group training should be tailored to meet the learning needs of an identifiable group of targeted learners. The learners' characteristics should influence the way that learning experiences are designed.

4. *Assess the work setting(s) in which the learning will be subsequently applied.* Before designing internal group training, find out about the work setting. It's important to answer these questions:

- What conditions in the work setting may impede management employees from applying what they learn in internal group training?
- What conditions in the work setting will encourage management employees to apply what they have learned in internal group training?
- Are sufficient time, money, staff, and other resources available to permit learners to apply what they learn?

Just as products or services should be positioned so they can be sold and should be designed to meet the requirements of the users, so too should internal group training be tailored to fit the conditions in which the learners will perform. If a problem exists with the work setting, then separate action should be taken to correct the problem.

5. *Analyze the work performed.* Before designing internal group training, you must know about the work performed by the targeted learners. Points to consider include:

- What do the targeted learners do?
- How do they perform the work?
- How is the subject of the training related to the work, work methods, work procedures, and problems confronting those performing the work?
- What knowledge and skills are needed now to perform the work?
- What knowledge and skills will be needed to perform the work competently in the future?

Management training should be tied to the present and/or future work performed by the targeted learners.

6. *Prepare performance objectives and measurement methods.* A *performance objective,* synonymous with *instructional* or *learning objective,* is perhaps best understood as a statement of the results desired; when a performance objective is met, a training need is satisfied. Objectives are thus designed to narrow or close a gap between existing and desired performance. A *measurement method* is a means of assessing a performance objective. It answers this question: "How well was the performance objective achieved by the learner?"

Start the process of designing internal group training by transforming statements of needs into performance objectives. With the results of a needs assessment in hand, begin drafting performance objectives to clarify what participants in training should know, do, or feel at the end of the learning experience. Stated another way, think of a performance objective as a description of what people should know at the completion of training. Typical objectives define:

- *What* trainees should be able to do when they get up and leave the room after completing an internal group training experience
- *How well* they should be able to do it
- *Under what conditions* or *with what resources* they should be able to perform

Perhaps an example will help to clarify these issues. You are designing an internal group training course on job interviewing for supervisors. Begin course preparation by first investigating how supervisors conduct interviews and how they should conduct them. Pinpoint the gap between what is presently being done and what should be done. Then prepare performance objectives and measurement methods to describe and measure what the targeted learners should know or do when they complete the training.

State performance objectives in this way:

"Upon completing this training, participants should be able to. . . ." [*Begin with a verb and clarify the conditions in which the task will be performed, what the learner should be able to do, and the means by which success will be measured.*]

Some writers on instructional design suggest that pre- and posttest items should be developed directly from performance objectives before training materials are selected, prepared, and, if necessary, modified.[18] While most people think of test items as written questions posed in a true-false, multiple-choice, essay, or other format, they may also take the form of role plays, simulations, or practically oriented work demonstrations.

7. *Clarify the training delivery techniques to be used.* At this writing, over 600 management training delivery techniques have been identified.[19] According to the 1991 *Training Magazine* study, the most popular training delivery techniques are (in order of use):[20]

1. Videotapes
2. Lectures
3. One-on-one instruction
4. Role plays
5. Audiotapes
6. Games/simulations
7. Slides
8. Films
9. Case studies
10. Self-assessment and self-testing instruments
11. Noncomputerized self-study programs
12. Video teleconferencing
13. Teleconferencing (audio only)
14. Computer conferencing

Exhibit 7-16 lists these techniques, explains when they are appropriate, and summarizes their key advantages and disadvantages. Some techniques may be used by themselves for individualized training, but often many techniques are combined when delivering internal group training. The most popular combination is video and lecture.

8. *Select, design, and, if necessary, modify internal group training materials.* Once performance objectives have been stated and delivery methods have been chosen, it is time to select, design, or modify instructional materials. We use the term *select* to mean sourcing from existing printed, published, distributed, or otherwise available mate-

text continues on page 180

Exhibit 7-16. Techniques for delivering internal group training.

Method	Appropriate Uses	Key Advantages and Disadvantages
Videotape	‣ Meeting learning objectives tied to visual identification ‣ Highlighting ideas and simulating behaviors	‣ *Advantage:* Captures attention through the senses of sight and sound ‣ *Disadvantage:* Does not work well for introducing complex theories or for giving hands-on practice
Lecture	‣ Meeting learning objectives tied to facts or theories	‣ *Advantages:* Efficient method for communicating information; familiar to most people from their school experiences ‣ *Disadvantages:* Depends heavily on skills of presenter; can be boring; listeners can hear faster than speakers can talk
One-on-one instruction	‣ Meeting learning objectives tied to comprehending and applying facts, theories, principles, and motor skills	‣ *Advantages:* Permits immediate feedback; transfer of learning is not a problem because the learner is usually positioned at the work site ‣ *Disadvantage:* Can be disorganized and unstructured
Role play	‣ Meeting learning objectives tied to comprehending and applying facts, theories, principles, and motor skills	‣ *Advantages:* Builds learner involvement; provides means by which learners can practice what they learn ‣ *Disadvantage:* May be difficult for learners to engage themselves in

(continues)

Exhibit 7-16 *(continued)*.

Method	Appropriate Uses	Key Advantages and Disadvantages
		artificial roles and experiences
Audiotape	‣ Meeting learning objectives tied to facts and theories	‣ *Advantages:* Relatively inexpensive to produce; lends itself well to use in automobiles during long commutes ‣ *Disadvantages:* difficult to use as a stand-alone medium because learners' attention will wander
Games/simulation	‣ Meeting learning objectives tied to comprehending and applying facts, theories, principles, and motor skills	‣ *Advantages:* Build learner involvement; provide means by which learners can practice what they learn ‣ *Disadvantages:* May be difficult for learners to act within the rules of games or to live up to the spirit of simulations
Slides	‣ Meeting learning objectives tied to visual identification	‣ *Advantages:* Easy, inexpensive to prepare when computer software assistance is used; eye-popping colors intensify visual stimulation. ‣ *Disadvantages:* Cannot be used effectively without special equipment or a darkened room
Film	‣ Meeting learning objectives tied to visual identification ‣ Highlighting ideas and simulating behaviors	‣ *Advantage:* Captures attention through sense of sight and sound ‣ *Disadvantages:* Does not work well for intro-

Method	Appropriate Uses	Key Advantages and Disadvantages
		ducing complex theories or for giving hands-on practice; increasingly obsolete when compared to more convenient videotapes
Case study	‣ Meeting learning objectives tied to comprehending and applying facts, theories, principles, and motor skills	‣ *Advantages:* Builds learner involvement; provides means by which learners can practice what they learn ‣ *Disadvantages:* May be difficult for learners to identify and/or solve problems without more details than are typically provided in most case studies
Self-assessment and self-testing instruments	‣ Meeting learning objectives tied to self-discovery and affective (feeling-oriented) issues	‣ *Advantages:* Provoke individual insight; motivate people to learn ‣ *Disadvantages:* Expensive; difficult to validate
Noncomputerized self-study programs	‣ Meeting learning objectives tied to facts, theories, or principles	‣ *Advantages:* Easy to use; easy to distribute ‣ *Disadvantages:* Difficult to write; difficult to keep current
Video teleconferencing	‣ Meeting learning objectives tied to visual identification ‣ Highlighting ideas and simulating behaviors	‣ *Advantage:* Captures attention through the senses of sight and sound ‣ *Disadvantage:* Does not work well for introducing complex theories or for giving hands-on practice

(continues)

Exhibit 7-16 (*continued*).

Method	Appropriate Uses	Key Advantages and Disadvantages
Teleconferencing (audio only)	‣ Meeting learning objectives tied to facts and theories	‣ *Advantages:* Relatively inexpensive to present ‣ *Disadvantages:* Difficult to use as a stand-alone medium because the attention of learners wanders
Computer-conferencing self-study programs	‣ Meeting learning objectives tied to facts, theories, or principles	‣ *Advantages:* Easy to use; fast ‣ *Disadvantages:* Hard to keep learners interested; may be unstructured and poorly organized; require special equipment to use

rial; we use the term *design* to mean preparing instructional materials from scratch for internal use; and we use the term *modify* to mean revising existing materials to suit the unique needs of one organization or one group of learners.

Using existing materials is more common now than it was a decade ago because management training material—so-called *off-the-shelf material*—is readily available for purchase from many commercial publishers, video distributors, and other sources. For instance, the American Management Association catalog contains many self-study management courses that can be adapted for group delivery or used, as intended, for self-study. Published books and articles can also be made into training materials, although copyright restrictions should be scrupulously observed.

MD specialists looking for materials to use in training should rely on their performance objectives as a guide for undertaking a search. They should start out with two key questions: (1) What are learners supposed to do, and (2) what materials or activities will help them achieve the objectives? MD specialists can then undertake a search for existing books, articles, videotapes, audiotapes, research, and learning activities to help achieve the performance objectives.

Designing original materials, while costly and time-consuming, is a second popular alternative. It is appropriate when the training content is to center around unique practices of one organization and when it is important to use actual forms, procedures, or methods from the organization. For instance, MD specialists may tailor training to suit one organization's policies and procedures regarding employee performance appraisals, employment interviews, or progressive discipline.

To design internal group training materials, MD specialists usually begin with an outline called a *syllabus*. Each performance objective becomes the basis for a part of the syllabus. The outline can stand alone as a *lesson plan* to guide subject matter specialists who serve as instructors, or it can become the basis for a detailed lesson plan to guide prospective instructors who are not experts on the subject. A detailed lesson plan is advantageous because it ensures consistency in training across groups. It can also become the basis for video or audio scripting—or it can be used in other media.[21] A sample lesson plan format appears in Exhibit 7-17.

Modifying existing materials, the third option, is the middle ground between selecting and designing instructional materials. First, MD specialists must locate materials from inside or outside the organization. Then they must modify the materials for instructional use to ensure they will help achieve identified performance objectives. Finally, they should have the materials reviewed by subject matter experts (SMEs) from inside or outside the organization to ensure they are accurate, current, and appropriate.

9. *Plan and monitor the instructional design process.* Few MD specialists advise leaping directly from preparing training materials to delivering the training, though novices may be tempted to do just that. It is better to test and revise materials before offering the training. Instructional materials may be tested in several ways. (Strategies for testing materials are described in Chapter 10.)

10. *Conduct the training.* Few MD specialists can dispute the importance of delivery, since all previous steps in planning instruction come together at that time. Effective classroom delivery is a more complex subject than it appears to be. Many books have been written on the subject. Here are a few useful tips for conducting successful internal group training sessions:

- Plan and rehearse the session carefully beforehand.
- Arrange the facilities in a way appropriate to the experience.
- Make sure you have the right number of handouts.
- Arrange to have needed equipment on hand, checking well before a training session begins to make sure the equipment is in working order.
- Start the session by giving the title of the course, reviewing its

Exhibit 7-17. Sample lesson plan format.

Procedures	Lesson Outline
▶ Hand out an *attendance sheet*. ▶ Display V-1, The Purpose of the Course.	Give the course title, The Career Counseling Workshop Explain the purpose of the course: **Course Purpose** To introduce supervisors, managers, and executives to effective career counseling methods
▶ Display V-2, The Objectives of the Course.	Explain the objectives of the course: **Course Objectives** Upon completing this course, participants should be able to: 1. Define *career counseling*. 2. Explain the value of career counseling. 3. Describe key steps in a model of the career counseling process. 4. Demonstrate each step in the model of career counseling. 5. Identify personal values in career planning.

purpose, describing the performance objectives, and summarizing what topics will be treated in the session.

▸ Provide information about needs assessment results so participants will understand the gap between *what is* and *what should be*.

▸ Introduce yourself, and ask participants to introduce themselves when they do not already know each other.

▸ Provide an opportunity for participants to surface issues of importance to them, perhaps by going around the room and asking them, "What do you hope to learn about today, and why?"

‣ Ask questions frequently—one every two or three minutes.
‣ Maintain effective eye contact with the participants.
‣ Vary your voice tone.
‣ Move out with participants, rather than lurking behind a podium.
‣ Avoid disputes with argumentative participants so you do not dampen group spirit and thereby reduce participation.
‣ Provide a forum to discuss obstacles that keep participants from applying on the job what they learn in training.
‣ Ask participants to surface suggestions or strategies for overcoming obstacles that keep them from applying what they learn.
‣ Ask participants to offer suggestions for improving the training session—and take their advice.

11. *Evaluate training results.* There are four levels of evaluation: *participant reactions, participant learning, participant performance,* and *organizational results.*[22] Evaluation is covered at greater length in Chapter 10.

12. *Follow up to ensure that what is learned in training is applied by learners on the job.* After all, off-the-job learning will be of minimal value in improving performance if people do not apply what they learn. We have chosen to give *transfer of learning*—sometimes called *transfer of training*—special emphasis, although it is really part of evaluation. The reasons: It is critically important and is too often neglected. If genuine improvement is to flow from internal group training, the change effort must not cease when a classroom course adjourns; rather, the change effort begins then. At every stage in designing and delivering internal group training, MD specialists should be thinking about what they (and others) can do to encourage the transfer of learning from the training environment to the job environment. A few methods that can be helpful for this purpose are provided in Exhibit 7-18. Refer to that list, noting what methods are already being used in your organization and what additional methods could be used to increase the likelihood of learning transfer.

Problems Affecting Internal Group Training

Several special problems are common when planning and assessing internal group training for management employees.

One problem is that internal group training is sometimes designed and offered inappropriately. For that reason, MD specialists should resist pressure to chase the latest fads. Whenever a new training course is proposed, always ask these questions:

Exhibit 7-18. Methods for improving transfer of learning from internal group training to the job.

Before Training Delivery

1. Involve targeted participants and their immediate organizational superiors in the instructional design process.
2. Feed needs assessment results back to prospective participants and their immediate organizational superiors to stimulate interest and to create an impetus for change.
3. Visit the work site, and identify obstacles that will prevent transfer of learning.
4. Plan incentives for transfer of learning.

During Training Delivery

1. Ask the immediate organizational superiors of targeted participants to speak on the importance of the topic during the training session.
2. Ask learners to surface barriers to transfer of learning, and devise strategies to overcome them.
3. Ask the learners' immediate organizational superiors to attend training to increase the learners' accountability for applying what they learn.

After Training Delivery

1. Build measures of application into job descriptions and performance appraisals to encourage transfer of learning.
2. Visit the work site of past participants in training, and ask them how well they have been applying what they learned.
3. Send written surveys to learners in order to ask them how well they have applied what they learned—and what obstacles to application they encountered.
4. Send written surveys to the immediate organizational superiors and/or subordinates of the learners about six months after participation in a planned learning experience in order to assess how much change they perceive in the learner.

Source: D. Georgenson, "The Problem of Transfer Calls for Partnership," *Training and Development,* 36:10 (1982), pp. 75–87.

‣ What performance problem will the training solve?
‣ How is the training related to the organization's strategic plan?
‣ What will happen if the training is *not* designed and delivered?

Weigh the answers carefully.

A second problem is that internal group training may be neglected because of time and staffing constraints. In recent years, downsizing and layoffs have produced massive restructuring in the white-collar and middle-management ranks. One result is that fewer people remain to do the existing work than there were formerly. This reality has led to reduced flexibility in staffing schedules. MD specialists may find it difficult to induce prospective management participants to attend internal group training even when it is needed and appropriate. To overcome this problem, use two strategies: First, appeal directly to the immediate organizational superiors of prospective participants to enlist their support; second, make training available in multiple formats—such as self-study, video, and audio—so that extremely busy learners can take the training material home (if need be) rather than take time out during the hectic workday to attend class.

A third problem is that needs assessment is often handled improperly. Research continues to show that far too few organizations take steps to distinguish learning from nonlearning needs and to identify what learners really must know, do, or feel at the end of their learning experiences.[23] As a result, much time and money are wasted in delivering misdirected training.

The best way to overcome this problem is to make a concerted effort to assess needs for internal group training. Avoid shortcuts. Instead, make a real effort to bring a return on investments of time and money.

A fourth problem is that management training is not always tied, as it should be, to the organization's strategic plan or to its identifiable business needs. To solve this problem, double-check every proposed internal group training course against the organization's strategic plan. If the training cannot be justified, then it should not be offered. Twelve specific methods have already been identified to link up planned learning efforts with strategic plans, and these methods can be applied to MD.[24]

External Group Training Programs

External group training is instruction that is planned, designed, delivered, and evaluated by external vendors, university faculty, or community college staff. It is not tied to the degree requirements of a university and is not uniquely geared to change or to modify one organization's culture, philosophy, work requirements, or procedures. Its purpose is to broaden individuals by exposing them to new viewpoints.

Examples of external group training include seminars offered off-site by professional associations, industry groups, nonprofit organizations, and for-profit consulting firms. Some community colleges offer "individual enrichment seminars" but do not grant college credit to participants. Seminars of this kind are widely and frequently adver-

tised through newspapers, direct-mail brochures, radio announcements, and direct-phone solicitation.

When Should External Group Training
Be a Programmatic Focus of MD?

There are specific circumstances in which it is appropriate to use
external group training. These include the following:

- The organization is too small to have a steady stream of individ-
  uals entering and progressing through the management ranks.
- Groups of people do not share common learning needs.
- Internal group training is not likely to produce desired results
  quickly enough.
- The organization's management employees need exposure to new
  ideas.
- Individuals have unique learning needs that are best met outside
  the organization.
- Consistency of training content is not important.

External group training is advantageous for meeting short-term
individual learning needs or for rectifying individual performance
problems. But it is generally not appropriate when the organization is
large enough to warrant internal group training, when more than a
few individuals experience similar learning needs, when on-the-job
training would be more cost-effective, or when alternative methods
would be less expensive.

Planning External Group Training

Although MD specialists often think of a management training curriculum as limited to internal programs, it can also include external
programs. For example, some organizations send all newly promoted or
about-to-be-promoted individuals to special seminars sponsored by industry associations, professional associations, or universities.

To plan and execute external group training, MD specialists may
choose to follow a six-step model.

1. *Distinguish issues appropriate for external group training from
those more appropriate for other methods.* For instance, external group
training should not be chosen as an alternative to disciplining wayward
management employees who are neglecting their responsibilities. Nor
should it be used as a vehicle to clarify work expectations when

immediate organizational superiors have neglected their responsibility to do so. External group training is also inappropriate as a means for rewarding exemplary performers by giving them fancy vacations in exotic locations.

2. *Assess training needs of management employees.* Use external group training to broaden individual horizons and to give management employees the opportunity to meet new people, share ideas with people from outside their organization, or experience new insights. Be sure what the management employee "needs" before researching and selecting an appropriate seminar.

3. *Research external seminars and sponsors or contract to have seminars developed.* Literally thousands of seminars are offered each year; roughly 32 percent of the entire U.S. population participates in one such seminar each year.[25] Some organizations rely on them increasingly, substituting them for internal group training. But finding one to meet the unique needs of one management employee can pose a real challenge for those unaware of where or how to look.

Assuming that the learning needs of management employees have been identified, you can use the sources listed in Exhibit 7-19 to track down external seminars that may be appropriate. (As one alternative, subscribe to the American Society for Training and Development's TRAINET data base, which lists thousands of seminars.)

Once you have identified the titles of seminars that *appear* to meet the unique individual or group learning needs of management employ-

Exhibit 7-19. Sources of information for management training.

ASTD Buyer's Guide and Consultant Directory (Alexandria, Va.: American Society for Training and Development, 1991).

Nancy Harris and Douglas Mackey, *The Corporate University Guide to Short Management Seminars 1991 Edition* (Fairfield, Iowa: The Corporate University, 1990).

Harper Moulton, *The Evaluation Guide to Executive Programs*, 7th ed. (Fairfield, Iowa: The Corporate University, 1990).

Seminars Directory (Detroit: Gale Research, 1988).

Seminars: Directory of Professional and Continuing Education Programs (Madison, Wis.: Creative Communications, 1992).

SIS Workbook (Irvine, Calif.: Seminar Information Service, 1991).

Training Business Directory (Rochester, N.Y.: Hope Reports, no date).

Judith Wood, ed., *Bricker's International Directory of University Executive Programs* (Princeton, N.J.: Peterson Publications, 1991).

Judith Wood, ed., *Bricker's Short-Term Executive Programs* (Princeton, N.J.: Peterson Publications, 1991).

---

ees in your organization, contact vendors to request detailed information, such as performance objectives, topic outlines, evaluation results, names and addresses of past participants who can be contacted directly for references, and a biosketch listing the instructor's credentials. Then compare this information to the learning needs of management employees in your organization. Assess how well the seminar matches up to the needs. If in doubt, send only one or two people to the first seminar—or attend yourself—and use that experience to decide whether others should be sent.

You may wish to use the same basic approach to research a vendor to design a program for internal group training. You can obtain information about consultants offering training on specialized topics by using *The ASTD Buyer's Guide and Consultant Directory* or *Training: Marketplace Directory* (Minneapolis: Lakewood Publications, 1991). Once qualified vendors are identified, contact them for more information about the training they offer and about their credentials. If possible, watch them in action. If that is not feasible, at least call your counterparts in other organizations to find out what the vendors did and what results were obtained from their efforts. Then compare what you hear to what your organization needs.

Always prepare a written contract to specify exactly what you expect the vendors to do when they come in-house to deliver training. Spell out everything you expect. Be sure to make clear what penalties will be imposed on vendors who miss deadlines or do not meet other project requirements. Then have a competent lawyer review the contract before it is executed.

4. *Select participants and send them off-site as appropriate to meet identified needs.* In short, identify and prioritize who should attend the external seminar. As you do so, realize that many external seminars are designed to tempt a spur-of-the-moment response. If an attractive direct-mail brochure lands on the desks of management employe experiencing an immediate learning need, they will often behave like compulsive and less-than-critical consumers. Many assume that any seminar will be better than none.

But few organizations can afford the luxury of sending their management employees trekking off to parts unknown, often at significant expense, without being sure that the learning experiences will genuinely benefit them. One way to solve this problem is to check the references of a seminar's sponsoring organization to obtain detailed information about training content before investing time, enrollment fees, and travel expenses.

5. *Ensure that participants are clear about why they have been selected to attend seminars, are willing to take initiative to learn, and*

are held accountable for results upon their return. To ensure a real payoff from external group training, be sure that participants meet with their immediate organizational superiors before they attend. That meeting should clarify why they are being sent and what they should learn. If accountability is established first, participants can aggressively press seminar instructors to ensure that their learning needs are met. When the participants return to their organizations, they can then be debriefed to determine what they can be held accountable for applying on their jobs.

The aim should be to establish a basis of accountability so that the organization's investment in external seminars has a payoff. Above all, management employees should *not* be sent to attend external seminars in glamorous locations as a form of vacation or as a reward for work well done. If they are, the value and credibility of external seminars are diminished and scarce organizational resources are squandered.

6. *Evaluate the results.* Once management employees have returned from attending external group training, they should be asked to evaluate the results. In this way, the organization can determine what benefits—if any—were realized.

There is no one best approach for evaluating the results of external group training. Many methods are used. Some organizations require participants to write and circulate an essay about what they learned; some organizations require participants to complete a written questionnaire, similar to the questionnaires handed out at the end of internal group training sessions; some organizations require participants to train others about what they learned. Any one of these approaches can be helpful, depending on the desired results.

Problems Affecting External Group Training

Of all MD methods, external group training lends itself least effectively to systematic planning. There is one major reason for this: External seminars—what those in the training trade call *public seminars*—are rarely designed to meet the unique learning needs of one individual, group, or organization. In many cases their value is suspect because the information they provide is not necessarily compatible with a particular organization's culture, philosophy, competitive conditions, or work expectations.

One partial solution to this problem: MD specialists should establish a means of evaluating public seminars before management employees attend them. Another partial solution: Require prospective participants to meet before and after the seminar with their immediate organizational superiors. The preattendance meeting should focus on clarifying why individuals are being sent and what they are expected to learn; the postattendance meeting should clarify what they learned and how they can apply it to their jobs.

External Education Programs

External education is directly tied to the degree or certification requirements of a high school, adult educational institution, university, or college. Like external group training, external education is usually conducted off-site—though external educational experiences can sometimes be brought on-site before working hours, during lunchtime, or after hours by special arrangement with educational institutions. Such education is not uniquely designed to change or to modify one organization's strategic plan, culture, business philosophy, work requirements, or procedures. Nor is it designed, delivered, or evaluated by the MD director, MD coordinator, or MD staff.

The purpose of external education is to broaden individual horizons by exposing people to new ideas from outside their organizations. In this respect it is similar to external group training. But it is also generally more effective in helping individuals realize their career goals by helping them qualify to advance in a present occupation, change occupations, or prepare for outplacement. A major difference between external group training and external education is that training focuses on helping individuals qualify for jobs with one employer, but education focuses on the general betterment of individuals. By giving individuals educational credentials such as degrees, external education may provide a means to make individuals occupationally mobile across employers.

Examples of external education include courses taught through educational institutions, executive M.B.A. programs, night school programs, correspondence study, or "university without walls" programs. Often publicized through catalogs and schedules published by educational institutions, job-related courses typically qualify for employer reimbursement through educational assistance programs—a common employee benefit in many organizations.

When Should External Education Be a Programmatic Focus of MD?

External education is appropriate for MD when:

- The organization is too small to have a steady stream of individuals entering and progressing through management ranks.

- The prospect of earning a degree increases motivation to learn.
- Individuals have unique learning needs that are best met outside the organization.
- Long-term individual skill development is desirable.
- The organization's management employees need to broaden their horizons by coming in contact with new ideas from other organizations, industries, or cultures.
- Maintaining consistency across training or educational content is not essential.

External education is particularly advantageous for meeting long-term individual needs. Like external group training, however, it is generally not appropriate as a substitute for internal group training in these circumstances:

- The organization is large enough to make internal group training worthwhile.
- Individuals experience similar learning needs.
- The need exists to use learning experiences to change or to modify the organization's strategic plan, culture, business philosophy, work requirements, or procedures.
- On-the-job training would be more cost-effective.
- Other approaches to performance improvement would be less expensive or more appropriate for achieving desired individual changes.

Unique exceptions are tailor-made MBA programs, common in some European countries, and internal group training programs that meet the requirements for recommended college credit in the United States through the Program on Noncollegiate Sponsored Instruction (American Council on Education, One Dupont Circle, N.W., Washington, DC 20036; telephone 202-939-9430).

Planning External Education

When planning external education for management employees, MD specialists confront three key questions: First, should external education be tied to other programs? Second, should external education be tied to succession plans to help prepare talent to meet the organization's needs? Third, should external education be tied to management career planning programs in a way designed to help individuals realize their career goals? Depending on the answers to these questions, methods of planning external education may vary.

If external education is treated as a stand-alone program, then a policy on organizational tuition reimbursement or prepayment should be prepared and communicated to employees. This policy should describe the purpose of the tuition reimbursement or prepayment program, stipulate allowable charges (tuition, fees, books), provide a means by which to distinguish between job-related and nonjob-related courses, clarify how employees apply for tuition reimbursement or prepayment, establish yearly or lifetime limits on tuition reimbursements or prepayments available to individuals, and clarify criteria for obtaining tuition reimbursement (such as a minimum grade of C or better in courses). The policy should also explain whether the employer will permit course attendance or study during work hours, how the employer will handle tuition reimbursement or prepayment if the employee terminates in the middle of a course, how educational achievement will affect the employer's decisions regarding promotions, transfers, or salary increases, and what academic counseling services (if any) the employer will offer.

Some employers distinguish between two types of educational programs: those requested by employees and those requested by the employer. Those requested by employees are *voluntary,* or *discretionary;* those requested by the employer are *involuntary,* or *mandatory.* Voluntary courses are taken for individual improvement, are attended on the employee's own time, and are subject to minimum grade requirements for tuition reimbursement. In contrast, involuntary courses are taken to help satisfy job requirements or to rectify identified performance deficiencies. Employees may attend involuntary courses on the employer's time. They may also be considered necessary for continued employment. Tuition for these courses is often prepaid, and participants receive complete reimbursement for all necessary and contingent expenses.

If external education is tied to a succession planning program, a possible starting point is preparation of an individual development plan (see Exhibit 7-6) designed to narrow the gap between what prospective successors already know and what they should know to qualify for advancement. In this respect, external education becomes a vehicle by which to meet future position requirements. However, since external educational experiences rarely take into account one organization's strategic plan, culture, business philosophy, work requirements, or procedures, they must often be supplemented with planned learning experiences designed in-house to help individuals qualify for advancement.

If external education is tied to a management career planning program and is intended to help individuals identify and meet their career goals, then a typical starting point is the preparation of a written career plan (see Exhibit 7-11) that links career goals to individual learning needs. In this respect, external education becomes a vehicle to help individuals realize their career aspirations.

Problems Affecting External Education

Keeping people from leaving an organization is difficult. But many top managers and MD specialists worry that the substantial costs of external education will increase the occupational mobility of management employees but produce no payoffs in job performance to the employer who subsidized the education.

To address this issue, some employers institute a payback policy. Management employees who benefit from substantial educational benefits—such as expensive Ivy League or Big Ten Executive M.B.A. programs—are asked to reimburse their employers for educational subsidies if they terminate their employment before a specified time following completion of their studies. However, legal authorities disagree on whether these agreements are enforceable. Can a payback agreement be enforced as a contract? If terminating employees refuse to pay back funds, what recourse does the employer have? Can the employer sue or turn the account over to a collection agency? These and similar issues make employee eduation programs difficult to administer.

Another problem with educational programs has to do with tax issues. For years Congress has played an annoying game with the tax deduction available for educational reimbursements. Each year the deduction lapses, and a political firestorm rages. It is reinstated only at the last minute after strong lobbying by business and education groups. Congressional leaders vowed to decide the issue once and for all in 1992. That did not happen. The tax deduction for educational reimbursement remains a political football. Most employers and HR authorities agree that repeal of the tax deduction is a shortsighted, naive, and politically expedient attempt to increase government revenue. It is true that isolated abuses, such as vendors offering a few seminars to travelers on ocean liners to make glamorous cruises tax-deductible, are widely publicized. But it is also true that repeal of the tax deduction for educational reimbursements could seriously erode the incentive for employees to participate in work-related education at precisely the time when human, rather than financial, capital is playing an increasingly important role in the international competitiveness of American business.

Job Rotation Programs

A management job rotation (MJR) program is a planned effort to develop management trainees, supervisors, managers, or executives by placing them in new jobs and work settings under the guidance of new organizational superiors for extended time spans. Job rotations have been widely used to develop management employees. A 1987 survey conducted by Saari, Johnson, McLaughlin and Zimmerle of 1,000 organizations—611 questionnaires were returned—revealed that "40 percent [of the responding organizations] report using job rotation."[26]

The aim of management job rotations is to help individuals increase their portfolio of knowledge and skills. Since learning occurs on the job, the transfer of learning does not pose the same looming concern that it does for off-the-job learning experiences such as internal group training, external group training, and external education. Job rotation programs may also be combined with other forms of training and education.

When Should Management Job Rotation Be a Programmatic Focus of MD?

Job rotation is perhaps the best-suited of any formal MD method to increase the organization-specific knowledge of management employees. After all, it gives them firsthand experience with different functions, operations, people, and situations. It is highly appropriate in organizations seeking to:

   • Broaden individuals' experience, giving them in-depth exposure to areas outside the functions or occupational specialties for which they were originally hired and in which they have advanced. As best-selling authors John Naisbitt and Patricia Auburdene note, one way to reinvent the corporation is to "move people laterally to develop well-roundedness."[27] That is what job rotation is all about.

   • Build the credibility of future leaders. As James Kouzes and Barry Posner write, "People are more likely to follow you if they have confidence that you understand their area, the organization, and the industry."[28] Job rotation builds that credibility.

   • Alleviate career burnout. As Leonard and Zeace Nadler explain, "some good employees find that after several years of doing the same job, they lose their interest and motivation, and though they are not interested in leaving the organization, they are seeking different job challenges within the organization."[29] Job rotation can create a new challenge to stimulate individuals.

‣ Test how well high-potential management employees (HiPos) adapt to change, solve problems, and learn how to learn. By rotating management employees through different positions, decision makers gain insight about how flexible HiPos are and how well they perform under different conditions.

‣ Give management employees exposure to new cultures and ways of doing business. Many large international corporations find that, by rotating their management employees internationally, they enable the employees to develop crucial sensitivity to the unique cultural and business conditions that affect corporate operations outside the United States.

‣ Give management employees exposure to new models of effective leadership and different management styles. Management employees who rotate gain firsthand experience with different management styles and are able to observe firsthand the effects of these styles.

In a survey study on management job rotation programs we conducted—117 of 500 questionnaires were completed and returned, making the overall response rate 24.3 percent—we found that organizations sponsoring a planned MJR program do so primarily for the following reasons, listed in order of importance:[30]

1. Developing individuals for increased responsibility
2. Increasing the pool of promotable management talent
3. Improving the organization's ability to respond to technological change
4. Helping individuals realize their career plans within the organization.

These reasons were ranked by respondents as slightly more important than such other reasons as increasing the productivity of management employees, contributing to effective implementation of the organization's strategic plan, improving the organization's ability to respond to environmental change, providing general training to individuals inside the organization, and improving the morale of management employees.

Planning and Carrying Out Management Job Rotation Programs

You can plan a job rotation program by following a six-step model, as follows:

1. *Determine the program's purpose and scope, and select a method for choosing participants.* By *purpose* we mean what the program is

intended to achieve. By *scope* we mean what areas of the organization are to be included and/or excluded. By *methods of selection* we mean how individuals are chosen to participate.

Management employees should not be rotated if decision makers have not clarified the program's purpose. After all, rotations can be anxiety-producing for participants, their spouses, and children, especially when international travel is involved. Moreover, rotations can be expensive if the organization pays all relocation fees, ensures participants do not assume the burden of higher housing costs in the new location, assists participants in selling their current homes, and provides employment assistance for working spouses.

The scope of the program is also important. Some division or department managers institute *limited-scope* rotation programs restricted to their own management employees. The purpose is usually to ensure cross-training and development across management employees in one part of the organization only. On the other hand, decision makers in some organizations institute *broad-scope* rotation programs, encompassing some or all management employees throughout the organization. The aim is to ensure management development on a larger scale, help realize succession plans, and improve the selection process for management employees aspiring to more responsible positions.

Finally, the method of selecting participants is also important. In some organizations rotation programs are purely *voluntary*. When a vacancy occurs at a management level, management employees are given an opportunity to rotate. They may even choose assignments. In other organizations, rotation programs are *mandatory,* and individual choice is thus restricted. Management employees are told to rotate. They have little choice to refuse if they wish to keep their jobs. Finally, rotations may be *competitive*—high-potential employees compete on the basis of their abilities, and "winners" receive organizational investments of time, money, and effort.

In our survey of management job rotation programs, we found that voluntary and competitive rotation programs are used by organizations slightly more often than mandatory programs.[31] Voluntary rotation programs are advantageous because participants are by definition willing to rotate to increase their opportunities in the organization and to take on greater or newer challenges. Unfortunately, a disadvantage is that they do not always attract those who can benefit most from rotation. Mandatory rotation programs avoid that problem but risk the loss of otherwise promising employees when working spouses or school-age children oppose being uprooted.

    2. Identify functions and activities that individuals will learn through rotations. It doesn't make much sense to rotate management employees without having a good idea about what they should learn through their moves. For this reason, it is important to establish performance (learning) objectives for *each* rotation. The objectives may simply take the form of the functions, activities, duties, or responsibilities performed by the present job incumbent, or they may include new, one-time objectives unique to rotating employees only.

To establish performance objectives for a rotation, start by preparing an up-to-date position description listing all the major responsibilities of the job incumbent. Show the description to the job incumbent— or else ask the incumbent to write it. Then compare the description to the responsibilities previously performed by the rotating employee. Identify responsibilities new to the rotating employee, establishing them as the performance objectives for the rotation. In this way, rotation leads to gradually increasing knowledge and experience for participants, presenting them with new challenges to broaden their horizons.

3. *Enlist the support of participants and affected employees.* When establishing a management job rotation program, you must grapple with several issues, including these:

   ‣ How can the support of participants be enlisted and maintained?
   ‣ How can the support of affected employees—especially those reporting to rotating management employees—be established and maintained?
   ‣ What problems or difficulties with rotations can be foreseen and overcome?

Participant support is most important to establish in mandatory rotation programs, since voluntary and competitive rotation programs assume that support from the participant already exists. Three methods may be used, separately or in combination, to build that support: (1) an incentive program geared to encourage participation; (2) moral suasion; and (3) a support program.

In our 1990 survey of management job rotation programs, we found that relatively few special incentives are offered to management employees on rotation.[32] For instance, not one survey respondent indicated that his or her organization makes it a policy to offer special leave, before or during rotations, as an incentive; only a few respondents indicated that management employees on rotation in their organizations are given a special leave after the rotation or are awarded a one-time bonus; and fewer than one-fourth of our respondents cited as routine the practice of promoting managers on rotation upon arrival at their new work sites. However, the survey respondents did indicate that more than half of management employees on rotation receive some incentive, such as:

- Assurance of possible promotion if the rotation is successfully completed (100 percent of respondents agreed that this practice affects high percentages of management employees on rotation in their organizations).
- Assurance that the rotation will be viewed favorably when an appropriate position becomes available (83.3 percent of respondents agreed that this practice affects high percentages of management employees on rotation in their organizations).
- Assurance of possible salary consideration (66.6 percent of respondents agreed that this practice affects high percentages of management employees on rotation in their organizations).
- A special one-time salary increase (50 percent of respondents agreed that this practice affects high percentages of management employees on rotation in their organizations).[33]

The responses thus seem to indicate that employees bear the burden of demonstrating their ability on rotation, after which they may become eligible for rewards. Incentives offered before or during rotation are less uncommon than are rewards bestowed afterward for proven, successful performance.

Persuasion is a second way to encourage participation in management job rotations. Individuals to be rotated meet with their immediate organizational superiors, who offer persuasive career advice. Without making legally binding promises or offering false assurances, an immediate organizational superior explains the purpose of the rotation, what the employee is intended to learn from it, how long the rotation will last, where the rotation will be geographically located, who is employed at that location, why interaction with those people may be useful to the employee's development, when the rotation should begin, why the employee was chosen for the rotation, and how the employee will be trained, coached, or otherwise guided before and during the rotation.

At this meeting the management employee should also be informed about what assistance, if any, the organization will provide to (1) support a geographical move, (2) deal with problems created by uprooting spouse and family, (3) help with learning a new culture or language (if an international assignment), and (4) assist with other issues of importance to the employee. In some cases it may be appropriate to establish several meetings: the first between employee and immediate organizational superior, and the second including spouse and children. If the rotation will not require extensive travel, the employee's new organizational superior—the person to whom the management employee will report while on rotation—may be included in these discussions as well.

A third way to encourage participation in management job rotations is through a support program, meaning an organized and systematic effort to address the concerns of the person—and, indeed, the family—affected by a management rotation. Components of such a support program may include any or all of the following:

- Training to help the rotating employee adjust to new job responsibilities
- Training to help the employee adjust to a new work environment
- Training to help the employee adjust to new immediate organizational superiors
- Assistance in finding a comparable home in the new location
- Assistance in selling the family home
- Training to help the employee and his or her family learn about a new culture
- Assistance to uprooted spouses seeking employment in a new location
- Assistance in helping children make the transition
- Assistance in caring for elderly parents[34]

4. *Prepare learning contracts for each rotation.* Adult learning theorist Malcolm Knowles has been an outspoken advocate of contract learning.[35] A learning contract is an action plan to guide the learning of one individual or group. At minimum it should set forth:

- *Performance objectives.* What should the person know or be able to do upon completion of a planned learning experience?
- *Instructional methods.* How should the learning experience be carried out?
- *Evaluation techniques.* How should the learner's achievement of instructional objectives be measured?

A sample learning plan, used in conjunction with succession planning, was provided in Exhibit 7-6. The same form can be modified to serve as a learning contract for a management job rotation. A learning contract provides an excellent starting point for a management job rotation. It establishes accountabilities, clarifying what the learner is to know or do upon completion of the rotation.

In our research study of management job rotation programs, we found that individual learning contracts are prepared for all rotating management employees by 30 percent of all organizations with management job rotation programs.[36] Moreover, 17.4 percent of the organizations take steps to make these contracts mutually agreeable to employees and their immediate organizational superiors.

5. *Provide training and coaching to support individuals and work groups affected by a job rotation program.* Preparing for a rotation is important, but supporting and coaching employees on rotation is vital to success. After rotations begin, management employees on rotation should receive training to help them learn new job duties, receive coaching on how to deal with difficult but predictable problems arising on the new job, and receive frequent feedback at predictable intervals so they are kept apprised of how they are doing.

Some method should also be established to foster acceptance of management employees on rotation by their peers and their new work group. People naturally feel anxious when they start to work for a new immediate organizational superior, since they are unsure how his or her expectations will match up with those to which they have become accustomed. It is for this reason that changes in leadership are sometimes viewed as a way to introduce change itself.[37] To ease the natural concerns of employees about the switch in leadership, management employees on rotation should meet right away with their work groups and review their basic expectations. They should also meet individually with the highest performing and most seasoned veterans of the work group to ask for their advice, suggestions, and support. Such approaches, if followed, will garner support and ease the transition.

6. *Evaluate the effectiveness of management job rotation programs and the performance of individual participants.* In our research study, most respondents agreed with the statement that "an individual performance evaluation is prepared after each rotation."[38] Respondents from sixteen of twenty-three organizations sponsoring management job rotation programs indicated that such evaluations are conducted with 51 to 100 percent of management employees on rotations.

Two separate issues may be subject to evaluation on rotations: *developmental issues* and *performance issues*. Developmental issues have to do with how well individuals satisfy the performance objectives of their rotations; performance issues have to do with how well individuals satisfy the requirements of the jobs into which they rotate.

Some organizations make no distinction between a standardized performance appraisal conducted at regular intervals with all management employees and a special rotation appraisal conducted at the middle or the end of a management job rotation. But it is possible to make that distinction. Special rotation appraisals may be filled out on forms specifically designed for this purpose. Often, the forms are quite simple (see Exhibit 7-20). But they do provide a means by which to give individuals feedback on their performance, stimulating their further development and providing the organization with a valuable record of how well the individuals have been performing. To improve the likelihood of further development from this feedback, some MD specialists prefer to ask rotating employees to *self-evaluate*. The employees' evaluations can then be compared to—and coupled with—the appraisal performed by their immediate organizational superiors during the rotation. (See the sample self-evaluation form in Exhibit 7-21.)

Problems Affecting Management Job Rotations

Rotation programs go awry when they are not adequately planned. If management employees are just shifted around without explanation, then they quickly become disenchanted, since moves are anxiety-producing for them and for their families. Likewise, if the purpose of a rotation program is not clearly spelled out, then it is not clear to participants—or to their immediate organizational superiors—why it's worthwhile for them to invest time in the program. And if no time is devoted to training, coaching, and evaluating the rotated employees, then the developmental value of the rotations will not be great.

To overcome these problems, then, it is important to follow the steps outlined in this chapter in order to establish the rotation program on a sound footing. Of chief importance is determining and communicating the program's purpose, scope, and methods of selecting participants. It can also help to sensitize the immediate organizational superiors of management employees on rotation to the importance of providing regular feedback and coaching to their subordinates.

Position Assignment Programs

A *position assignment program* is designed to increase the knowledge or skills—or to change the work attitudes—of management employees through short-term, on-the-job assignments. Individuals are exposed to new work duties, responsibilities, tasks, projects, or people for short time spans. In this respect position assignment programs differ from

Exhibit 7-20. Sample performance evaluation form for a management job rotation program.

Name of employee: _____

Budget center: _____ Job title: _____

Start date: _____ Date appointed to present position: _____

Immediate supervisor: _____

Directions: Use this form to evaluate an individual's performance and development while on a management job rotation. Answer the questions appearing in each part. Then share the completed evaluation with the employee, and schedule a meeting with him or her. When you are finished, forward the original copy of the evaluation to the HR department for inclusion in the employee's HR file. Attach more paper, if necessary.

PART I
Rotation Objectives

What were the learning or job performance objectives of this rotation? (*Attach a copy of the Learning Plan, if it spells out the objectives. Otherwise, describe them below.*)

PART II
Areas of Strength

What strengths did the employee demonstrate during this rotation? Describe them below. Be as specific as possible, citing examples when appropriate.

Strengths   *Example*

PART III
Areas for Improvement

What areas for improvement did the employee demonstrate while on this rotation? Describe them below. Be as specific as possible, citing examples when appropriate.

Areas for Improvement   *Example*

Approvals

Signature of employee: _____   Date: _____

Signature of employee's supervisor: _____   Date: _____

Effective date: _____

---

job rotations in which individuals move into new positions with new duties, new co-workers, and a new supervisor.

Position assignments may stand alone or may be paired with succession planning programs, management career planning programs, internal group training programs, external group training programs, external education programs, or job rotation programs. A position assignment helps others judge how well individuals may function in other positions for which they are being considered or groomed, as in the case of assigning individuals to "fill in" for vacationing job incumbents whose responsibilities are at a higher level than those of the employees temporarily taking their places.

When Should Position Assignments Be a Programmatic Focus of MD?

Position assignments may serve a number of goals. They may be used to:

- Recruit or select new talent by trying out individuals on carefully chosen, critical activities that are part of a possible future job.
- Cross-train supervisors, managers, or executives in activities in other parts of an organization, division, or department.
- Prepare individuals for advancement to more technically complex duties in the same job (*horizontal advancement*) or in a more responsible job (*vertical advancement*).
- Develop individuals by helping them cultivate new insights or improve working relationships across an organization.

What are some examples of position assignments? To list a few:

Exhibit 7-21. Sample self-evaluation form for a management job rotation program.

Name of employee: _____

Budget center: _____   Job title: _____

Start date: _____   Date appointed to present position: _____

Immediate supervisor: _____

Directions: Use this form to evaluate your own performance and development while on a management job rotation. Answer the questions appearing in each part. Then share the completed evaluation with your immediate organizational superior, and schedule a meeting with him or her. When you are finished, forward a copy to the HR department for inclusion in your HR file. Attach more paper, if necessary.

PART I
Rotation Objectives

What were the learning or job performance objectives of this rotation? (*Attach a copy of the Learning Plan, if it spells out the objectives. Otherwise, describe them below.*)

PART II
Areas of Strength

What strengths did you feel you demonstrated on this rotation? Describe them below. Be as specific as possible, citing examples when appropriate.

Strengths   *Example*

PART III
Areas for Improvement

What areas for improvement did you recognize from this rotation? Describe them below. Be as specific as possible, citing examples when appropriate.

Areas for Improvement   *Example*

Approvals

Signature of employee: _____   Date _____

Signature of employee's supervisor: _____   Date: _____

Effective date: _____

- Asking nonexempt employees to fill in for vacationing exempt employees
- Asking exempt employees to serve as backups or stand-ins for their immediate organizational superiors during vacations or other periods of absence
- Trading duties across exempt or nonexempt incumbents in a work unit, department, or division to spread knowledge and skills
- Delegating some high-level duties, on a short-term basis, to individuals in lower-level positions for a developmental purpose
- Giving individuals special projects on new areas of the organization, new product lines, new equipment, or new people to assess— or build—their skills
- Sending individuals on field trips to collect information from competitors or organizations renowned for their effective practices
- Having individuals serve as organizational representatives to suppliers, distributors, customers, or other stakeholders
- Sending individuals on college or technical recruiting trips

As many as eighty-eight such assignments have been linked to managerial success.[39]

Planning Position Assignments

More than one way may be used to plan a position assignment program. The right approach depends on the program's purpose. (Of course, a program may have more than one purpose.)

If the aim of the program is to cross-train management talent, you should start by identifying all management responsibilities in an organization, division, department, or work unit. You might think of this process as akin to writing a job description for an entire unit, department, division, or organization. Then link the activities and responsibilities to people already performing them. Finally, schedule times so those who do not customarily perform them may gain exposure to them through observation, participation, or firsthand experience. Exhibit 7-22 is an example of a worksheet for planning departmental management cross-training or cross-exposure.

Exhibit 7-22. Worksheet for planning departmental management cross-training or cross-exposure.

Directions: Use this worksheet to plan management cross-training or cross-exposure in *one* department. In column 1, list the responsibilities peformed by management employees. (If necessary, simply list all duties appearing on position descriptions for management employees in the department.) In column 2, list the names and titles of individuals *not* presently performing the duties. In column 3, describe how and when the management employees listed in column 2 will be cross-trained or cross-exposed to these tasks or duties. (Leave column 3 blank if it is decided not to cross-train or cross-expose an individual to a task or duty.) In column 4, make notes about the results of the cross-training or cross-exposure experiences. Add paper as necessary.

Column 1	Column 2	Column 3	Column 4
What duties and responsibilities are performed by all management employees in the department?	Who does *not* perform the duty?	When and how will employees listed in column 2 be cross-trained or cross-exposed to tasks or duties they are not presently performing?	What were the results of the cross-training or cross-exposure experience?

If the aim is to educate one individual in preparation for promotion, modify the approach to make it more specific to the position for which the employee is being groomed. Prepare a current job description for the position. Verify it with the incumbent to ensure that all duties, activities, and responsibilities listed on the description are actually performed. Interview the incumbent's immediate organizational superior to determine whether any *changes* are contemplated in those duties and activities. If so, list them. Group together related activities or duties and prioritize them from most to least important. In this context, *important* may mean *critical to job success* or *most often performed.* Then assess how well the individual who is being groomed for advancement is *currently* able to perform each duty listed. Handle this assessment process like a performance appraisal, even though the individual is not presently doing the job. Finally, prioritize areas in which the individual requires development, identifying appropriate position assignments that can help the person to meet the responsibilities of the new position, by using a worksheet such as the one shown in Exhibit 7-23.

If the aim is simply to educate or develop individuals through short-term assignments, apply the same approach described in the preceding paragraph, with one important modification. Instead of focusing on "duties to be performed in the next position," focus instead on "new insights" to which the individual should be exposed.

Problems Affecting Position Assignments

Position assignments go awry when they are not adequately linked to future needs or when they are not planned.

Managers who prize development may enjoy giving people assignments designed to "stretch" (broaden) them. But those assignments will not be useful or helpful if they are not related to future organizational or individual needs. Position assignments should not be given for their own sake; rather, they should be linked to identifiable needs.

Poor planning can also torpedo the best-intentioned position assignments. Before the position assignment begins, the employee's immediate organizational superior should clearly formulate what the management employee should know, do, or feel by the end of the assignment, how he or she will learn during the assignment, and how success or failure will be evaluated. Without planning and direction, results will be uncertain.

To overcome these problems, it is important to take these steps:

1. *Identify the purpose of the position assignment and the needs it*

Exhibit 7-23. Worksheet for preparing an individual for promotion using short-term work assignments.

Directions: Use this worksheet to help you prepare an individual for promotion using short-term and on-the-job work assignments. In column 1, list the tasks, duties, or responsibilities of the targeted position for which the individual is being prepared (make any anticipated changes in the duties of the position, as necessary). In column 2, check whether the individual is already prepared to perform the task, duty, or responsibility. In column 3, focus attention only on those tasks, duties, or responsibilities for which the individual needs to be prepared. Describe when and how the individual should be prepared using short-term position assignments linked to the tasks, duties, or responsibilities. Add paper as necessary.

Column 1	Column 2		Column 3
What tasks, duties, or responsibilities are performed in the targeted position?	Prepared Now?		When and how should the individual be prepared for tasks, duties, or responsibilities for which he or she has not already been prepared?
	Yes	No	
1.			
2.			
3.			
4.			

   is intended to meet. What is it that individuals should learn from the assignment?
2. *Spell out the desired outcomes.* Establish performance objectives for position assignments to clarify what people should know or do upon completion.
3. *Communicate expectations.* Be sure that immediate organizational superiors meet with management employees before a position assignment begins, to explain why the assignment is

being given and what lessons they should strive to learn. Then be sure that follow-up meetings are later held to double-check that desired results are being achieved.

Summary

In this chapter we reviewed the following *formal MD methods*:

- Succession planning programs
- Management career planning programs
- Internal group training programs
- External group training programs
- External education programs
- Job rotation programs
- Position assignment programs

These MD methods, while seemingly unrelated, all lend themselves to centralized planning, administration, and oversight.

Chapter 8

Planning and Using Informal Methods

Informal MD methods grow out of the daily interaction between management employees and their immediate organizational superiors. The methods are often spontaneous and are tailored to meet unique individual needs in a way that is not true of formal MD methods.

In this chapter we turn to such informal MD methods as:

- On-the-job management training
- On-the-job management coaching
- Management mentoring or sponsorship
- Management self-development
- Management self-study

These methods are similar in that they do not lend themselves to centralized planning, administration, or oversight; rather, they are better handled at the work site and overseen by the learners, their immediate organizational superiors, or their co-workers. Informal MD methods are mainstays of MD, and they have existed in one form or another for many years.

However, informal MD methods are not always as fully utilized as they could be. There are many reasons why this is true. One reason is that management employees are promoted from within but are only rarely trained on how to train, educate, or develop those reporting to them. As a result, they lack a belief in the value of MD. Moreover, they have no skills to carry it out. A second reason: Supervisors, managers, and executives are not necessarily rewarded for training, educating, or developing others. Often, getting the work out is judged to be the only priority. One predictable result is that, as needs for management talent surface, it is apparent that nobody has been gradually and systematically prepared to assume the new responsibilities posed by predictable—let alone unpredictable—changes. Then decision makers are faced with limited options: developing individuals on a short-term basis, hiring from outside, transferring from inside, or thrusting ill-prepared people into the jobs. These problems can be avoided if management employees are better trained to use, apply, or encourage such informal MD methods as on-the-job management training, on-the-job management coaching, management mentoring or sponsorship, management self-development, or management self-study.

On-the-Job Management Training

On-the-job management training (OJT) is an apt starting point for discussing informal MD methods. OJT is frequently used in many organizations, regardless of industry. At least one authority, some years ago, estimated that 95 percent or more of a management employee's development occurs on the job.[1] OJT is often preferred because it is fast and inexpensive. Moreover, it can be easily individualized.

Defining On-the-Job Management Training

On-the-job management training (OJT) occurs on or near the work site. It is the most common form of training offered to employees—management or otherwise—in organizations today. Indeed, the American Society for Training and Development estimates that employers spend between three and six times more on OJT each year than they spend on internal group training.[2] OJT is important because it has the potential to reduce the unproductive breaking-in period for newly hired, newly transferred, or newly promoted management employees.

The terminology associated with OJT is not consistent. But it is helpful to distinguish between two types of OJT: *unstructured* and *structured*.[3]

Unstructured OJT means *unplanned training at the work site*. As problems arise on the job, employees are given quick instructions and shorthand guidance about how to handle them. After many months or years of encountering problems and receiving guidance, management employees are eventually able to handle most problems as effectively as their immediate organizational superiors, who frequently function as their trainers.

Unstructured OJT is not systematically planned to meet learner needs; rather, it is organized around day-to-day experience. This approach is a leisurely one in which management employees take many years to be trained. It is increasingly ineffective in light of the rapidly changing conditions in modern organizations, but it has been used for time eternal. We have elsewhere called it *learning by osmosis*,[4] linking it to the process of osmosis, by which single-cell entities ingest food through a permeable membrane. Similarly, in learning by osmosis, people are expected to absorb knowledge, skills, or attitudes simply by being exposed to them.

Structured OJT means *planned training at the work site*. Employees are given planned instruction designed to:

- Clarify what they are supposed to do and/or what results they are expected to achieve.
- Introduce them systematically to important policies, procedures, laws, and regulations affecting what they do.
- Brief them about employees, working conditions, equipment, and other important matters in the area they are to oversee as supervisors, managers, or executives.

Structured OJT is akin to *job instruction training* (JIT), an approach first devised during World War I to increase the effectiveness of training given to shipbuilders. Unlike unstructured OJT, JIT is formally planned and organized in the work setting and makes use of lesson plans or outlines, training schedules, and planned feedback to learners about their performance. It is appropriately conducted on the work site so that problems of transfer of learning are minimized. A chief advantage of structured OJT is that the learning and the working environments are similar, facilitating transfer of learning and speedy application of what is learned. Another advantage is that, when management employees are trained by their immediate organizational superiors, they can be held accountable for applying on the job what they learned in training. That is not always easy or possible when others do the training or when the training occurs off the job.[5]

When Should On-the-Job Management Training Be a Programmatic Focus of MD?

Structured OJT should be used when an organization's management is willing to:

- Commit the time to carry out training properly.
- Devote the resources of time, money, staff, and equipment to it.
- Assign knowledgeable, experienced, and competent people to carry it out.
- Minimize the daily distractions of the work environment so employees have sufficient time to be trained.

‣ Train people in the principles of structured OJT so they know how to carry it out.[6]

On the other hand, OJT should not be used when these conditions cannot be met *or* when training will:

‣ Pose a hazard to employees or other people.
‣ Undercut the credibility of those being trained.

Planning and Delivering On-the-Job Management Training

Structured OJT is usually not approached as a program sponsored by an organization; rather, it is planned and delivered at the work site, one on one, between a management employee and his or her immediate organizational superior. However, a centralized MD function can facilitate the process by training management employees in how to be effective trainers for their employees.

A ten-step model may be followed when planning and delivering structured OJT for management employees:

1. *Ask the immediate organizational superiors to conduct a thorough job analysis or job breakdown.* That is the traditional starting point for structured OJT in technical jobs; it also works for training in management or professional jobs. However, special approaches may have to be used for management job analysis. After all, the activities and work outputs of managers differ markedly from those of technical workers. See Exhibit 8-1 for a description of how to carry out a management job analysis in compliance with the Americans with Disabilities Act.

One result of a thorough job analysis or job breakdown should be an updated job description. It provides information about the major purpose of the job; essential functions and the estimated time devoted to these functions; nonessential functions and the estimated time devoted to those functions; knowledge and skills required to perform the job effectively; and special working conditions, if any.

2. *Prepare an individualized training schedule to make management employees productive in their work as quickly as possible.* Without a plan of some kind, training will take a backseat to the daily pressures of getting the work out. One way to avoid this problem is to use the updated job description as a starting point for developing an individualized training schedule. Immediate organizational superiors should

text continues on page 216

Exhibit 8-1. Form for conducting job analysis for management positions in compliance with the Americans with Disabilities Act.

Job analysis is the process of determining job activities, tasks, and responsibilities. Effective July 26, 1992, employers with 50 or more employees must comply with the requirements of the Americans with Disabilities Act (ADA). ADA prohibits discrimination against the disabled. To conduct a job analysis for management positions in compliance with ADA, take the following steps by answering the questions posed in the boxes appearing in the left column below.

> **Step 1**
>
> What is the key purpose of the job?

Start the job analysis by determining why the job exists in the organization. Prepare a summary of the job's purpose. *Example:* The MD director oversees, coordinates, and facilitates the planned MD program for the corporation.

> **Step 2**
>
> What are the functions of the job?

Continue the job analysis by preparing a list of the job's functions. (A *function* is a duty, activity, or responsibility.) Be sure to describe the function in terms of *results to be achieved*, if possible.

> **Step 3**
>
> What are the essential and nonessential functions of the job?

Use the list of major functions prepared in step 2 as a starting point to distinguish *essential* from *nonessential* functions. An *essential* function *must* be performed by an individual doing the job. It can be distinguished from functions that are only "desirable" or that are tangential to the job's key purpose.

Distinguish *essential* from *nonessential job functions* by posing the following questions to *each* function in the list identified in step 2:

— Do those presently performing the job carry out the function?

— Have those performing the job carried out this function in the past? Was it ever listed on the job description, or is it still being performed even if not presently listed on a job description?

Step 3	— Would seriously negative consequences affect the individual, work group, department, division, or organization if this function were not performed?

Step 3
(continued).

What are the essential and nonessential functions of the job?

— Would seriously negative consequences affect the individual, work group, department, division, or organization if this function were not performed?
— Is it impossible to transfer this function permanently to other employees in the work group, department, division, or organization?
— Would the job be dramatically changed if the function were not performed?
— Does the job exist solely to perform this function, as indicated in the job's summary (statement of purpose) identified in step 1?
— Does the function require specialized knowledge, skill, or education?

List *essential functions* in one section of the job description.

List *nonessential functions* in one section of the job description.

Step 4
What are the key skills required of the job?

Using the list of essential functions in step 3, identify the key skills required for the job and list them on the job description.

Step 5
What are the working conditions of the job?

Describe any special working conditions for the job—such as outdoor work or work around special equipment.

Step 6
Do job incumbents agree with the job description?

Show the draft job description to employees presently performing the job, and ask them if it accurately reflects:

— The purpose of the job
— Essential job functions
— Nonessential job functions
— Skills required to perform the job
— Special working conditions

first group together related functions of the job. They should then prioritize the functions for training.

The schedule should include information on:

- How employees will be trained for each responsibility/duty
- By whom employees will be trained
- When each step of on-the-job training will be completed
- How training results or outcomes will be measured so that the employees' levels of ability can be assessed

The worksheet in Exhibit 8-2 can be used as an aid for this purpose.

3. *Explain the training schedule to management employees so that they understand the desired results to be achieved from the training and the sequence of training events.* When adults enter new jobs or undertake new duties, they frequently experience anxiety. They are unsure of what the change will mean to them, and they are usually reluctant to appear foolish. For these reasons, then, it is often wise to begin their training with a brief overview of what they can expect. This approach builds learners' self-confidence and self-esteem. Moreover, gestalt learning theorists suggest that people learn most effectively from the whole to the part, beginning with an overview (a map of everything to be learned) and proceeding to a detailed examination (a step-by-step description of each part of the map).[7]

Begin the training, then, by giving the learners an overview of what they are expected to learn and how the training will proceed.

4. *Provide a detailed explanation of each key duty, activity, or desired outcome of the management job—or, at least, point the learners to sources from which they can receive detailed explanations.* The management employees' immediate organizational superiors, who often serve as the trainers, should implement the training schedule by going through it in an organized fashion, preferably treating related activities at the same time so that learners can structure what they hear and take notes as necessary. The trainers should begin by explaining each key duty, activity, or outcome, always making clear *why* it is important. (If immediate organizational superiors do not have the time to conduct the training personally, they should assign knowledgeable people to substitute for them.)

Learners should never be treated as mere passive receivers of information. Indeed, they can be assigned to investigate a duty, activity, or issue on their own so they take an active part in their own learning. What is learned through investigation is usually remembered better than what is merely explained. To use this approach, pose a series of questions about an issue for the learners to investigate and direct them to the right sources to find the answers. Then ask them to report back for follow-up when they have found the answers.

5. *Identify and provide instructions about applicable organizational or governmental policies, procedures, regulations, or other mandates that influence how the duty or activity is to be carried out.* Many management duties and activities are affected by organizational policies or procedures and by government laws or regulations. As management employees receive structured OJT, they should be familiarized with these policies, laws, and regulations.

6. *Explain detailed points related to each activity or duty.* Management employees' immediate organizational superiors should explain, in detail, each activity or duty the management employee is to perform. The individualized training schedule should indicate what activities to discuss.

7. *Show management employees how to perform the duty or activity—or pair them up with those already successfully performing.* In management work, some activities lend themselves to demonstrations; others do not. For instance, if management employees must use a computer, they can certainly be given a demonstration of the required procedures. But if they are to conduct job interviews or carry out disciplinary interviews, they may have to learn by watching experienced people carry out those activities. Nor do all tasks lend themselves to demonstrations. An example is decision making. Management employees may have to ask questions to find out the steps taken by managers in reaching a decision. See Exhibit 8-3 for a list of questions that can help surface the reasons or mental steps by which a decision is reached.

8. *Let management employees perform the duty.* However, trainers must also watch the results. The true test of structured OJT is how well learners can perform afterwards. After explaining the duty and demonstrating it, the employees' immediate organizational superiors should then let the learners perform the duty or task—but should also watch the results.

9. *Provide detailed feedback about how well management employees perform, praising what is properly done and offering encouragement for what should be improved.*

10. *Put management employees on their own to perform what they have learned.* However, they should receive concrete feedback at regular intervals so they know how well they are doing.

text continues on page 221

Exhibit 8-2. Worksheet for planning structured on-the-job training for management employees.

Directions: Use this worksheet for planning structured on-the-job training for management employees. In the activities column, list all essential job functions for which the employee is to be trained. Indicate the training priority on the line to the left of the activity. Then describe how, by whom, and when the on-the-job training should be done. Finally, indicate how training results or outcomes will be measured so that the employee's level of ability can be assessed. Add paper to this worksheet as necessary.

Priority	**Activities**

_____   1. _____

                    _____

                    ‣ How will training be done?

                    ‣ Who will perform the training?

                    ‣ When should the training be completed?

                    ‣ How will results be assessed?

_____   2. _____

                    _____

                    ‣ How will training be done?

                    ‣ Who will perform the training?

                    ‣ When should the training be completed?

Priority	Activities

> ‣ How will results be assessed?

——————   3. ————————————————————

——————————————————————

> ‣ How will training be done?

> ‣ Who will perform the training?

> ‣ When should the training be completed?

> ‣ How will results be assessed?

——————   4. ————————————————————

——————————————————————

> ‣ How will training be done?

> ‣ Who will perform the training?

> ‣ When should the training be completed?

> ‣ How will results be assessed?

Exhibit 8-3. Worksheet for answering questions about decision making.

Directions: Use this list of questions to help you learn how to go through the mental steps of a process. Pose the questions to one or more people who are widely recognized in the organization as excellent performers in the area of decision making. Record the answers to the questions for future reference and for comparison with answers provided by other excellent performers.

---

1. Today I would like to ask you some questions about how you go about deciding [*describe topic*]. I'd like you to think back to the last time you had to make a decision on this issue. Begin by describing for me the circumstances of that situation. How did you go about reaching the decision you reached? Explain the steps in reaching the decision.

   Description of situation:

   Step-by-step description of reaching decision:

2. What issues are most important to keep in mind when reaching a decision in a situation like the one you described?

3. How would I know when it is appropriate to make a decision on this issue? In other words, how do I recognize when the steps you described should be used?

   Cues to the need for decision making:

4. In your opinion, what mistakes in decision making would be the easiest for a novice to make? How could these mistakes be avoided?

   Most likely mistakes:

Ways to avoid mistakes:

Problems Affecting On-the-Job Management Training

The major problems with OJT concern management attitudes and managers' lack of training in performing OJT properly.

Management attitudes are a source of problems because some managers do not believe that structured OJT is worthwhile. They favor a sink-or-swim approach. Because they suffered through that experience, they believe others should, too.

There is no simple solution to that problem. Attitudes are difficult to change. But, with time and proper incentives, employees' immediate organizational superiors can learn that it is worthwhile to devote time to structuring OJT.

Another problem is lack of training. Knowing how to train does not come naturally. It requires knowledge and skill in its own right. In a survey we performed, we identified the most common topics treated in training on how to conduct structured OJT. These topics, listed in Exhibit 8-4, can be helpful as a starting point for developing internal group training for management employees on the subject of structured OJT.

On-the-Job Management Coaching

The American Heritage Dictionary defines a *coach* as "a person who trains athletes or athletic teams; a person who gives private instruction, as in singing or acting; a private tutor employed to prepare a student for an examination."[8] The same definition carries over to business settings. A coach is one who provides on-the-spot guidance, instruction, and feedback.

On-the-job coaching and *on-the-job training* are closely related terms. In practice they often overlap. Sometimes they are used synonymously.

However, we use the term *on-the-job management coaching* to mean guidance, feedback, and counseling provided in the work setting to management employees, typically by their peers or immediate organi-

Exhibit 8-4. Topics treated in classroom training on how to conduct structured on-the-job training.

Topic	Percentage of Organizations Treating the Topic (N = 52)
Showing learners how to perform the task	96.2%
Having learners perform the task with the trainer observing	96.2
Putting learners at ease	94.3
Providing feedback to learners on how well they are performing a task or procedure	94.1
Demonstrating all steps of effective OJT	92.3
Emphasizing key points for learners to remember	90.6
Analyzing work tasks or procedures	90.4
Motivating learners to learn	90.4
Telling learners how to perform a task	90.4
Applying adult learning theory to OJT	88.5
Questioning learners on key points about what they are learning	88.5
Clarifying the learners' performance standards	86.8
Placing learners in the correct work setting to learn the task	86.5
Showing learners how to correct errors they make	84.3
Finding out what learners already know about the task	80.8
Documenting training progress	79.6
Modifying OJT methods based on individual learning styles	65.4
Modifying OJT methods to deal with learning disabilities	52.0

Source: William J. Rothwell and H. C. Kazanas, "Structured On-the-Job Training (SOJT) as Perceived by HRD Professionals," *Performance Improvement Quarterly,* 3:3 (1990), p. 21. Copyright 1990 by the Learning Systems Institute, 919 West College, R-19, Florida State University, Tallahassee, FL 32306. Reprinted by permission from *Performance Improvement Quarterly.*

zational superiors. It ranges from simple advice to mandated direction and is chiefly used to stimulate individual creativity or improve on-the-job performance. It may be unplanned or planned.

When Should On-the-Job Management Coaching Be a Programmatic Focus of MD?

Use on-the-job management coaching when:

‣ There is need to improve the job performance of management employees.
‣ Management employees feel it is their responsibility to develop those reporting to them.

Planning and Delivering On-the-Job Management Coaching

Few management employees receive training on how to coach others effectively. But mounting interest in self-directed work teams and employee involvement programs has produced a groundswell of interest in the role of coach, counselor, and facilitator. Indeed, the skills that a management employee needs in participative or empowering organizations differ dramatically from those needed in authoritarian organizations.

Various models of coaching have been proposed.[9] While differing in complexity, they share common characteristics. Perhaps the best way to distinguish them is by the amount of planning each involves.

Oral coaching is usually spontaneous. It occurs on the spot, immediately before or after action is taken. Oral coaching requires the immediate organizational superior to pay close attention to what an employee is about to do (or has done) and to make a deliberate effort to offer useful comments on it. For instance, the employee's immediate organizational superior praises what is done right and ignores—or issues mild reprimands about—what is done wrong. More attention is paid to finding people performing properly than finding them performing improperly.[10]

To praise orally on the spot and thereby reinforce good performance, the employee's immediate organizational superior should follow a simple model. We present the model in the context of a simple example.

Coaching Model for Issuing Praise	*Application of the Model*
1. Describe briefly what the employee did.	"I have noticed that you have been working overtime on that project."
2. Praise the employee's efforts, expressing gratitude.	"I really appreciate your efforts."

(continues)

Coaching Model for Issuing Praise	*Application of the Model*
3. Emphasize the importance of the employee's efforts.	"I'm sure you realize that, if we do not receive the business that this project means for us, our profits will suffer this year."
4. Summarize the positive conse- quences of the employee's efforts in terms of what they mean to the or- ganization, the immediate organi- zational superior, or the work group.	"Your efforts will mean our owners will be pleased with our performance this year, and that could mean a bonus for all of us!"

Note that *personal* expressions of gratitude or praise, like the one shown in the example, are more powerful than *impersonal* ones. An example of a personal expression of gratitude is this: "I really appreci- ate what you are doing. Thank you." Such a simple comment can have a powerful effect, reinforcing good performance. In contrast, an imper- sonal expression of praise takes this form: "Everyone really appreciates your effort!" This comment could be heard as distant, cold, and re- moved. It may have minimal effect—or even a negative effect.

To correct a worker orally on the spot, the employee's immediate organizational superior should follow a different model.

Coaching Model for Correcting Problem Performance	*Application of the Model*
1. Describe clearly what the employee should improve.	"I have noticed that you have not been working overtime on the project that is behind deadline."
2. Emphasize the importance of the employee's efforts.	"I'm sure you realize that if we do not receive the business that the project means for us, our profits will suffer this year."
3. Summarize the consequences of the employee's efforts.	"More vigorous effort will mean that our owners will be pleased with our profit performance this year, and that could mean a bonus for all of us!"
4. Express confidence in the employ- ee's ability to "do it right."	"I am confident of your willingness to pitch in, doing whatever it takes to get that project back on track."

Note that this approach does not attack the person; rather, it focuses on what needs to be done to achieve desired results. It preserves harmonious working relationships between employees and their immediate organizational superiors while helping employees understand what to do to improve performance. In this respect, coaching becomes a method of offering advice, direction, and counseling.

But oral coaching does not always work. Some people are unwilling or unable to listen, experiencing difficulty in accepting compliments or in taking criticism. In these cases, oral coaching may eventually have to be followed up by written coaching.

Written coaching is planned. It requires very close attention to the details of what the employee has been doing. Indeed, the employee's immediate organizational superior should collect specific examples of what the employee has been doing right—or wrong.

To praise employees in writing and thereby reinforce good performance, their immediate organizational superiors should use the same basic approach as the one that is used in oral coaching. On the other hand, a written reprimand should adhere to the organization's disciplinary policies and procedures. While there are various philosophies and approaches to discipline, most share common characteristics: First, individuals are warned orally; second, they receive written documentation; third, they are suspended; fourth and finally, they are discharged.

Written documentation typically answers seven specific questions:

1. What has the employee been doing?
2. What should the employee be doing?
3. Why is the gap between *what is* and *what should be* important?
4. What are the consequences of the gap?
5. What advice can the employee's immediate organizational superior offer to help the employee narrow or close the gap?
6. How long will the employee's immediate organizational superior allow for the employee to narrow or close the gap?
7. What future disciplinary action will be taken if the employee's performance or behavior does not improve by the date agreed upon or if the behavior does not cease?

We have found that many employers are reluctant to take these steps—even when warranted—because they dislike emotional confrontations with people. But if these questions are answered in writing and provided to a management employee, they can often have a profoundly positive effect on performance.

An appropriate way to approach problem performance is to prepare written documentation first, answering the questions just listed. Then share the documentation with the employee, asking him or her to go to a quiet place to read it. Then reconvene after ten to thirty minutes, and ask the employee for opinions. (Give the employee the opportunity to respond in writing, attaching comments to the documentation if necessary.) Above all, follow up as planned to coach the employee, making every effort to help the person improve.

Problems Affecting On-the-Job Management Coaching

Few people can dispute that an employee's immediate organizational superior exercises significant influence over individual development. What employees' immediate organizational superiors say can—and does—exert tremendous influence over what employees say and do. It is through the power of this interaction that coaching works.

But the status of employees' immediate organizational superiors can influence the value of coaching. If the immediate organizational superior is a high-potential, high-performing employee, then individual coaching carries substantial weight and credibility and can influence perceptions throughout the organization. The reverse is also true: If the immediate organizational superior is a low-potential or plateaued performer, then individual coaching may be less useful or effective.

Management Mentoring or Sponsorship

The term *mentor* first appeared in Homer's *Odyssey*. A mentor is a teacher whose primary goal is to prepare another person for a successful life or career.

In modern organizational settings, mentors offer advice to others about career, work, or personal issues. Unlike coaches, who are usually the immediate organizational superiors of those they coach, mentors need not be. Indeed, employees choose their own mentors based on traits they admire or wish to emulate. Research has revealed that outstanding performers share one trait on common: Most can point to one or more mentors who helped shape them personally or professionally.[11]

A *sponsor* is different from a mentor. Sponsors are positioned one or more levels above their *protégés* on the organization's chain of command. Sponsors protect their protégés and advertise their achievements. Sponsors also challenge their protégés by seeing that they receive choice assignments to showcase their talents.

Mentoring and sponsorship take two forms in organizations: *infor-*

mal and *formal*. Informal mentoring or sponsorship is not administered by the organization; rather, individuals seek out people they admire and ask for their advice or help. A special chemistry exists between two people. Each gains from the relationship: The mentor satisfies a deep-felt need to help and develop others; and the protégé benefits from the advice of one who is more experienced, more politically savvy, and more acutely aware of competitive or organizational conditions.

Formal mentoring or sponsorship programs are administered by the organization. A human resources department representative or an MD specialist links mentor or sponsor and protégé, usually on the basis of their personalities, areas of interest, or experiences. Their first meeting is by appointment. Mentors or sponsors may even be given special training on how to fulfill their roles and provided with suggested questions to use as icebreakers with their protégés. Thereafter, they may continue their relationship, though they are not forced to do so.

When Should Mentoring or Sponsoring Be a Programmatic Focus of MD?

Use mentoring or sponsorship to supplement other MD methods. Mentoring and sponsorship can be most effective when tied to:

- Succession planning programs as a tool for developing management employees as replacements for key positions
- Management career planning programs as a means of providing management employees with personalized career counseling from those who have already climbed the career ladder successfully
- Internal group training programs, external group training programs, and external education programs to help people learn how to apply on the job what they learned off the job
- Job rotation programs as a means of exploring new approaches to be used on new jobs with new people and new problems
- Position assignment programs as a means of exploring approaches to use in handling special problems, situations, or people

Planning and Implementing Mentoring and Sponsorship Programs

By definition, most mentoring and sponsorship occur spontaneously and are thus unplanned and informal. To improve the mentoring or sponsorship capabilities of management employees in organizational settings, however, organizations can offer internal group training on these subjects and encourage management employees to become mentors. Effective mentors and sponsors share certain characteristics; successful protégés also have distinctive characteristics (see Exhibit 8-5). Training can enhance these characteristics (see Exhibit 8-6).

Problems Affecting Mentoring and Sponsorship Programs

Three special problems may arise with mentoring and sponsorship.

One nettlesome problem has to do with mentoring or sponsorship between individuals of different sexes. Mentoring and sponsorship relationships are often intimate ones. When such relationships exist between two people of different sexes, people may assume that more exists in the relationship than mere friendship or mentoring. This problem is sometimes called the *development dilemma*.[12]

There is no simple solution to this problem. One approach is to encourage mentoring and sponsoring relationships between same-sex individuals only. Another, perhaps better, approach is to train management employees on mentoring and sponsorship. As part of this training, they should learn about ethical issues in same-sex and different-sex mentoring and sponsorship relationships. Through training, people can learn to overcome preconceptions, misconceptions, and prejudice.

A second problem has to do with dependence in mentoring or sponsoring relationships. As people gain experience, they eventually outgrow their mentors and sponsors. They may pick new ones. In some cases, the protégé's success eventually eclipses the mentor's, posing a unique problem for their relationship. They must learn to part on amicable terms.

Exhibit 8-5. Characteristics of effective mentors, sponsors, and protégés.

Mentors should be:	Sponsors should be:	Protégés should be:
‣ Skilled listeners	‣ Skilled listeners	‣ Skilled listeners
‣ Interested in the development of people	‣ Several organizational levels removed from the protégé	‣ Willing to seek out advice assertively
‣ Experienced on the issue about which they advise others	‣ Experienced on the issue about which they advise others	‣ Willing to take advice
‣ Knowledgeable about people, products, and the organization	‣ Knowledgeable about people, products, and the organization	‣ Able to tell when an approach that worked in the past will not work—or would have to be modified—if used now or in the future

Exhibit 8-6. Sample training course outline of techniques for effective mentoring and sponsorship.

Purpose

To introduce supervisors, managers, and executives to effective mentoring or sponsorship techniques.

Objectives

Upon completing this course, participants should be able to:

1. Define *mentor*.
2. Define *sponsor*.
3. Explain the value of mentoring and sponsorship.
4. Describe key steps in a model of the mentoring and sponsorship process.
5. Demonstrate each step in the model.
6. Identify personal values.

Course Outline

I. Introduction
  A. Describe
   1. The course title
   2. The purpose of the course
   3. The objectives of the course
   4. The structure of the course
  B. Ask participants to summarize their personal goals for the course.
II. What are mentoring and sponsorship?
  A. Definitions
  B. Importance of mentoring and sponsorship
  C. The role of the immediate organizational superior in mentoring and sponsorship
III. What skills are needed for effective mentoring and sponsorship?
  A. Supporting mentoring and sponsorship relationships
  B. Encouraging individuals to approach others for advice and help
  C. What are the skills of a mentor or sponsor?
   1. Description of skills
   2. Role plays
  D. Valuing diversity: same-sex and different-sex mentoring/sponsorship
   1. Description of key issues
   2. Role plays
   3. Discussion, follow-up, and debriefing
IV. Conclusion
  A. Evaluate
   1. Participants' mentoring and sponsorship skills
   2. The course
  B. Establish plans to improve and practice mentoring and sponsorship skills

---

A third problem has to do with preparing for the future. Mentors and sponsors rely heavily on what they have learned from their experience. That is as it should be. But the past in which they developed posed unique challenges, different from those the future holds in store. Protégés must learn that mentors and sponsors can be helpful, reflecting their own experience and their own values. But mentors and sponsors are not always helpful in predicting the future and suggesting strategies to address the new, unique challenges posed by it.

For this reason, protégés must recognize that there are limits to the value of mentoring and sponsorship arrangements. The past is not always a predictor of the future. Protégés must make their own efforts to predict, and grapple with, future challenges.

Management Self-Development

To a considerable extent, all MD is self-development. After all, individuals are the final arbiters of their own learning needs. And without individual motivation, no learning will occur.

Self-development refers to independent efforts undertaken by adults to improve themselves and to grapple with the work-related and life-related challenges they confront. Research by Cyril Houle in the 1950s revealed that adult learners can be classified into three groups:

1. *Goal-oriented learners,* who set out to achieve predefined objectives from their learning activities
2. *Activity-oriented learners,* who set out to increase their social contact through learning
3. *Learning-oriented learners,* who seek personal challenge and growth[13]

Houle's student Allen Tough extended the investigation of learning, finding that adults are typically motivated to learn by problems confronting them in their work or their lives. Learning is organized around "projects . . . defined as a series of related episodes, adding up to at least seven hours. In each episode more than half of the person's total motivation is to gain and retain fairly clear knowledge and skill, or to produce some other lasting change in himself."[14] Tough found that most adults spend more time than they realize on learning projects of this kind: "Almost everyone undertakes at least one or two major learning efforts a year, and some individuals undertake as many as fifteen or twenty. . . . It is common for a man or woman to spend 700 hours a year at learning projects."[15]

More recent studies of self-development and self-initiated learning have focused on *learning style* or *cognitive style,* meaning the way that individuals approach learning and learning situations. Individuals vary in their learning styles. While descriptions of learning styles vary, one well-known scheme was devised by David A. Kolb. According to Kolb, individuals may be categorized into four dominant categories:

1. *Convergers,* whose learning style focuses on technical, but not interpersonal, issues
2. *Divergers,* whose chief sensitivity is to values, meanings, and feelings
3. *Assimilators,* whose strength is devising abstract models
4. *Accommodators,* who thrive on action, risks, and adapting to situations[16]

If individuals are aware of their learning styles, they can take advantage of their learning abilities to master new situations and develop themselves effectively.

When Should Self-Development Be a Programmatic Focus of MD?

Self-development should always be a programmatic focus of MD. If it is not, individuals will not be truly committed to learning, expecting others to take responsibility for their development—and perhaps their lives and careers as well. Unfortunately, too many people expect their employers and their immediate organizational superiors to take that responsibility.

Planning and Carrying Out Self-Development Activities

By encouraging the use of individual development plans, organizations can help individuals plan and carry out self-development activities. Using that approach, management employees negotiate work-related learning projects or learning episodes each year with their immediate organizational superiors. In this way it is possible to achieve a marriage of interests between the organization and the individual.

To use this approach, an MD specialist can simply make available a learning contract form like the one appearing in Exhibit 7-6. It is then up to employees and their immediate organizational superiors to set aside time for planning learning projects. The process can stand alone, or it can be directly tied to such activities as management performance appraisal, succession planning, or work planning.

Alternatively, the process can be entirely voluntary. Employees may complete an individual development plan in conjunction with a career planning form like the one shown in Exhibit 7-11. In this way, learning is linked to career plans, prompting individuals to undertake learning activities designed to turn their career goals into realities.

If employees and their immediate organizational superiors agree to send copies of completed learning contracts to the MD director or MD coordinator, the contracts of many employees can be evaluated to identify common learning needs. Then the MD director or MD coordinator can function as a resource person and an enabling agent to help meet those needs.

Exhibit 8-7 lists numerous self-development activities. Read over the list for ideas about how to approach self-development or how to advise others to approach it.

Exhibit 8-7. Examples of self-development activities.

- Read about new topics.
- Go to trade shows.
- Tackle a tough problem.
- Think over different approaches to implementing a solution.
- Lead a charity drive or a civic or religious group.
- Take a self-assessment test.
- Talk to a child about a complex subject.
- Write an article.
- Write a book.
- Use your library regularly.
- Talk to a person from another culture.
- Examine your boss's job description, and assess what parts of it you can and cannot do.
- Talk to a parent about your childhood.
- Talk to a parent about your life.
- Write a letter to yourself about areas of your life that you could improve.
- Seek out people who are experts on a subject of interest to you and talk to them about it.
- Read a literary classic and critique it.
- Take a course at a local school on a subject of interest to you.
- Attend a music recital.
- Attend lectures.
- Talk to other people about unfamiliar topics.
- Talk to people at different levels of experience about what they have learned.
- Teach or train others about something you know.
- Paint a picture.
- Write a poem.
- Write a memo.
- Learn new software.
- Take a walk in a scenic location.
- Take a trip to another country.
- Talk to your spouse about areas in which you could stand to improve.
- Attend a play, and write a critique.
- Fill out a performance appraisal on yourself.
- Watch someone do something you have always wanted to do.
- Delegate a difficult job task, coaching another person how to do it.
- Seek out someone in another organization doing the same job you do, and talk to him or her about how to deal with job problems.

Problems Affecting Self-Development

Self-development is heavily influenced by *current* or *pending* problems confronting learners. For instance, people who are about to go to Spain are highly motivated to learn about that country. Likewise, couples soon to become parents are highly motivated to learn about babies, and an individual about to be promoted becomes highly motivated to learn about the new job.

Learning of this kind is decidedly *problem-driven*. It is affected by *recency bias,* the tendency to focus on recent or pending problems or issues. Longer-term matters are too often deemphasized.

It is this short-term emphasis that can lead self-development astray. If learners take no time to reflect on the long term, they will not be able to establish and work toward meeting long-term career goals. They become compulsive consumers of learning activities, rather than thoughtful, analytical pursuers of continuous individual improvement and growth.

Perhaps the best way to avoid this negative side effect of self-development is to establish a means of checking signals about learning projects with others, such as immediate organizational superiors, mentors, sponsors, coaches, MD specialists, or other knowledgeable people. If learners cannot explain how specific learning projects are tied to their career goals or work-related performance improvement goals, then the value of these projects can be examined to ensure that the learners are not neglecting other projects with greater potential for long-term payoff.

Management Self-Study

There are many ways to undertake learning. Individuals may initiate their own self-development learning projects, prompted by immediate problems they are encountering. In a related manner, they may choose to learn through organized methods, such as pursuing correspondence study, reading job-related or career-related materials, viewing videotapes, or listening to audiotapes.

Learning materials abound. For the motivated person, it is only a matter of finding the time to locate and use them.

Self-study refers to efforts made by individuals to improve themselves by organized study and to grapple with the work-related and life-related challenges they confront.

When Should Self-Study Be a Programmatic Focus of MD?

Self-study is appropriate for management employees who are:

- Motivated to learn on their own
- Patient enough to take the time to research materials to help them meet their needs
- Interested in learning a subject in depth, rather than remaining comfortable with a shallow understanding sufficient just to get by
- Comfortable with structured learning material, such as correspondence study, that probably does not directly answer pressing questions or solve pressing problems
- Creative and capable of coming up with their own solutions to problems rather than relying uncritically on what others think
- Capable of devoting time to researching materials and studying them

Self-study is rarely appropriate when any or all these conditions cannot be met.

Planning and Carrying Out Self-Study Activities

Since self-study is usually individually initiated and individually implemented, the role of the organization must necessarily be supportive rather than directive. If a decision is made to pursue self-study as a programmatic focus of MD efforts, then MD directors or MD coordinators can take several steps to support the efforts. They may:

- Survey or interview individuals about self-study activities of interest or value to them, making sure to determine the underlying reasons for this interest.
- Identify common needs across individuals, when they exist, to provide economical approaches to meeting self-study needs.
- Identify materials and activities to support self-study efforts.
- Provide administrative support, such as completing and turning in paperwork for correspondence courses, helping individuals enroll, and interfacing with sponsors of courses or other materials.
- Help individuals evaluate the value of their self-study efforts and assess how they may apply to their jobs what they have learned.

Use the worksheet in Exhibit 8-8 to identify self-study activities; use

Exhibit 8-8. Worksheet for identifying self-study activities.

Directions: Give this worksheet to a management employee, and ask him or her to use it as a starting point for a discussion between the employee and his or her immediate organizational superior about self-study activities that could be particularly valuable for the employee. (These activities can range from those conducted during working hours to those conducted outside working hours.) Ask the management employee to take notes on the answers to the questions posed on this worksheet.

Questions to be posed by the management employee and answered by the management employee's immediate organizational superior:

1. What learning activities were particularly helpful to you in preparing you for your present job? Include *any* activity of value to you—not necessarily training, education or development activities sponsored by the organization, but also such others as leading a civic or religious group, serving on the board of directors of a local charity, working with a local school, or raising children. Try to confine your answer to only one or two learning activities that were *most* helpful to you.

2. What learning experiences would you suggest for me? Please make some suggestions, explain why you believe they would be helpful to me form the organization's perspective, and offer advice about what I should try to learn from them.

---

the list in Exhibit 8-9 to source self-study materials; and, finally, read the case study in Exhibit 8-10 to see how one organization successfully used two different self-study methods for MD.

Problems Affecting Self-Study

The same key problem that affects self-development affects self-study: Learning becomes *problem-driven* and is affected by *recency bias,* with the possible result that learners take no time to reflect on the long term. The approach used to overcome this problem with self-development may also be used with self-study: A means of cross-checking self-

Exhibit 8-9. Sourcing self-study materials.

Sources of Audiotapes

American Management Association, 9 Galen Street, Watertown, Mass. 02172; telephone: 800-225-3215.

Nightengale-Conant Corporation, 7300 North LeHigh Avenue, Chicago, Ill. 60648; telephone: 800-323-5552 (in Illinois 312-647-0300).

Sources of Videotapes

American Management Association, 9 Galen Street, Watertown, Mass. 02172; telephone: 800-225-3215.

American Media, 1454 30th St., West Des Moines, Iowa 50265; telephone: 800-262-2557.

Britannica Training & Development, 310 S. Michigan Avenue, Chicago, Ill. 60604; telephone: 800-554-9862.

Coronet/MTI, 108 Wilmot Road, Deerfield, Ill. 60015; telephone: 800-621-2131 (in Illinois 312-940-1260).

CRM/McGraw-Hill Films, 2233 Faraday Avenue, Carlsbad, Calif. 92008; telephone: 800-421-0833.

Dartnell, 4660 Ravenswood Avenue, Chicago, Ill. 60640; telephone: 800-621-5463 (in Illinois 312-561-4000).

Films, Inc., 5547 N. Ravenswood Avenue, Chicago, Ill. 60640; telephone: 800-323-4222, Ext. 44 (in Illinois 312-878-2600, Ext. 44).

Salenger Films/Videos, Inc., 1635 12th St., Santa Monica, Calif. 90404; telephone: 213-450-1300.

United Training Media, 6633 W. Howard St., Niles, Ill. 60648; telephone: 800-558-9015 (in Illinois 312-647-0600).

Video Arts, Inc., 4088 Commercial Avenue, Northbrook, Ill. 60062; telephone: 800-553-0091 (in Illinois 312-291-1008).

Video Publishing House, Four Woodfield Lake, 930 N. State Parkway, Ste. 505, Schaumburg, Ill. 60173; telephone: 800-824-8889.

Note: This list is neither an endorsement of vendors nor a testament to the quality of their material; rather, it is intended only as a list of sources for management self-study materials.

study learning projects should be established with organizational superiors, mentors, sponsors, coaches, MD specialists, or other knowledgeable people. In this way, the payoffs from these efforts may be considered at the outset before substantial investments of time or money have been committed to them.

Exhibit 8-10. Case study of successful use of self-study in MD.

Todd Lendquist is the MD director at Ace Office Supplies, a manufacturer and distributor of office products. Ace employs over 1,500 people—approximately 350 of them are management employees—at its corporate headquarters in Duluth, Minnesota. Ace is not unionized.

Two years ago, Todd was in a quandary. Whenever he issued a schedule of management training classes, many people signed up to attend. But few actually showed up for the classes. Todd felt that, while the perceived need for the classes was high, the corporation's downsizing effort had made it exceedingly difficult for company team leaders, supervisors, managers, and executives to find time during working hours to attend internal group training.

So Todd decided to try something different: He would make the learning efforts more geared to self-study than to group study. To that end, he conducted a needs assessment survey and used the results to identify and prioritize topics of perceived value to management employees. He then scheduled a large meeting room for his use, on a long-term basis, about one-half hour before working hours began. Todd rented videotapes, none longer than 20 minutes, on topics of interest identified through the survey. He also ordered breakfast to be brought into the meeting room. Todd called this series "The Great Brown Bag Breakfast Management Video Training Effort."

Todd prepared handouts before the meeting, showed the video, and then held a brief discussion after the video. The first 10 minutes consisted of an introduction and an opportunity for networking among participants. The next 20 minutes consisted of the video showing. The final 30 minutes consisted of discussion, a question-and-answer period, and an occasional simple exercise. Every session ended with a simple activity for participants to take back to their jobs and apply. Todd decided that no session would last longer than 60 minutes. The first 30 minutes were held on the individual's time; the last 30 minutes were held on company time.

The survey results revealed that the most important topics were perceived to be total quality management (TQM), employee involvement, and on-the-job training. Todd then sent out a schedule of sessions on these topics by electronic mail and office carrier. He notified all team leaders, supervisors, managers, and executives of the schedule—and all topics that he would cover.

Todd was astounded by the results. On the first showing, 300 of the company's 350 management employees signed up to attend—and 120 showed up. Todd decided to make "The Great Brown Bag Breakfast Management Video Training Effort" a long-term program. He also planned to use its sessions to build interest in longer classroom sessions he offers.

After a year of these sessions, Todd began to notice that the same people attended every week. One day he set aside some time in a session to ask them about others who never attended. Using the information he learned from their remarks, Todd established "The Great Management Training Library Check-Out and Take-Home Store." Todd purchased the most popular videos he had shown at the Brown Bag Breakfasts and made them available to management employees to check out,

(continues)

Exhibit 8-10 (*continued*).

take home, and watch on their own time. He also purchased audiotapes, books, self-assessment questionnaires, and computer software on the same topics.

Again, Todd was astounded by the results. Many people who never attended a Brown Bag Breakfast contacted Todd so they could check out material for the 2-week loan period.

Using these two simple methods—Brown Bag Breakfasts and a video check-out library—Todd increased the amount of training offered to management employees by several hundred percent.

Summary

In this chapter we reviewed the following *informal MD methods*:

- On-the-job management training
- On-the-job management coaching
- Management mentoring or sponsorship
- Management self-development
- Management self-study

These methods share one important similarity: They do not lend themselves well to centralized planning, administration, or oversight. Rather, they are better handled at the work site and overseen by the learners, by their immediate organizational superiors, or by their co-workers.

Chapter 9

Planning and Using Special Methods

Special MD methods are neither formal nor informal. They may be planned or unplanned. But they are distinctive because they are cutting-edge or controversial methods. In this chapter we turn to three of them:

1. Adventure learning
2. New Age Training (NAT)
3. Action learning

Adventure Learning

Sometimes called *outdoor learning, adventure learning* is a popular and trendy method that traces its origins to the personal fitness craze, to increased interest in the outdoors, and to the ecology movement. However, it is not a uniformly accepted MD method. Indeed, some "critics charge that outdoor management training is nothing more than an excuse for busy managers to take 'vacations' on company time."[1]

But adventure learning can be more than an excuse for getting away from the maddening job pressures of the 1990s. Its appeal does not appear to be short-lived, as might be expected of a flash-in-the-pan fad. It poses an exciting alternative to learning in stuffy classrooms or hectic workplaces. It is also truly *experiential* because it is decidedly short on theory but long on application.

Defining Adventure Learning

Adventure learning is set in the outdoors or in a wilderness. Its aim is to lead individuals to examine their values and to lead group members

239

to reach new conclusions about how they work together and depend on each other.

Adventure learning experiences can be divided into three categories: (1) *short-term*, (2) *intermediate-term*, and (3) *long-term*. They can also be further divided according to their focus: *individual* change or *group/team* change.

A *short-term adventure learning experience* is a mere outdoor jaunt. It lasts only a few minutes. MD specialists use it much like a role play, simulation, or case study to break monotony and reinforce a lesson begun in a classroom session. It need not be set in a wilderness; rather, it can be set in other outdoor locations, such as in a municipal park, on a tennis court, next to a tree, by a streetlight, or even in a parking lot. Descriptions of short-term adventure learning experiences of this kind appear in Exhibit 9-1.

An *intermediate-term adventure learning experience* ranges in length from several days to a week. There are two kinds: (1) *the stand-alone program*; and (2) *the management retreat*.

In a *stand-alone program* the learning experience is not tied to background readings or to introductory lectures; rather, participants begin and end their learning experience outdoors. For instance, they take a camping trip together. Learning experiences specifically designed to evoke new ideas have been planned, however. These experiences may use ropes, logs, or rafts.

Stand-alone programs are frequented more often by supervisors and nonexempt workers than by middle managers or executives. The participants are usually part of the same work unit, work group, or work team. At this writing, the costs range from $300 to $2,800 per participant and are usually set in a local park rather than in a wilderness.

A *management retreat* is a special subcategory of the intermediate-term adventure learning experience. Retreats are held in such pastoral settings as resorts or parks. Participants may be *individuals, stranger groups, family groups,* or *work groups. Stranger groups* consist of people who have never met before and will never meet again; *family groups* consist of spouses and possibly their children; *work groups* consist of a manager—often a top manager—and all those reporting to him or her. Individuals attend to learn about themselves; in stranger groups, participants learn about themselves and how they relate to others (group dynamics); in family groups, which are akin to marriage encounters, people learn how they interact with significant people outside the workplace; and in work groups, they learn how they interact with significant people in their workplaces.

Learning activities during stand-alone programs vary widely.

Exhibit 9-1. Short-term adventure learning experiences.

Activity 1

Objective:
   To reflect on the status of a group

Materials required:
   A long piece of rope or twine; scissors or penknife; tape

Time required:
   Allow 10–20 minutes.

Setting:
   Move from an indoor setting (such as a classroom) to an outdoor setting (such as a sidewalk, parking lot, or municipal park).

Procedure:
   1. When discussing teamwork, suggest that a small group can learn best by doing something together.
   2. Ask group members to create small groups by counting off in threes or fours, and appoint a spokesperson. Leave the work setting or classroom, and go outdoors.
   3. Ask each group to illustrate how the group interacts by depicting the group as it appears to them. Tell each group to use a piece of rope for that illustration. Make the scissors, penknife, or tape available to each group, as needed.

Discussion questions:
   ‣ Ask the spokesperson of each group to explain what the group's illustration means. How has the group depicted itself, and why has the interaction been illustrated in the way it was?
   ‣ Ask members of each group to describe how they believe the group *should* appear. (Allow them a few minutes to repeat the activity.)
   ‣ Ask participants *how* they may *change* their groups (or themselves) so that the group appears as they believe it *should* appear in response to item 3 above.

Activity 2

Objective:
   To build camaraderie and team spirit

Materials required:
   Wiffle ball, plastic bat, catchers' mitts

Time required:
   Allow 60 minutes.

(continues)

Exhibit 9-1 (*continued*).

Setting:
   Move from an indoor setting (such as a classroom) to the nearest baseball diamond. (If no baseball diamond is available, secure permission to use a parking lot or other open space available nearby.)

Procedure:
   1. When discussing teamwork, suggest that people can gain insight about how well they interact by playing a team sport.
   2. Ask the group to break into two groups. Leave the work setting or classroom, and go outdoors. Ask the groups to play baseball (or wiffle ball) together.

Discussion questions:
   ‣ After the game is over, ask the members of the winning team what their impression is about what it feels like to lose.
   ‣ Ask the members of the losing team how they feel.
   ‣ Ask the two groups to compare how they interacted during the game and how they interact at work. What similarities do they note? What differences do they note?

They may include group meetings in a lodge or less formal activities such as gardening, wood chopping, yoga, meditation, massages, hot baths, saunas, and swimming.[2]

A *long-term adventure learning experience* lasts a week or more. Participants camp outdoors, usually in the wilderness. Learning experiences have *not* necessarily been planned. As participants partake of all the excitement and dangers of life in the wilderness—such as white-water rafting, mountain climbing, sailing, and other hazardous ventures—they learn about themselves and their group. The aim is to lead a group to develop strong cohesiveness and camaraderie. Experiences of this kind are frequented more often by executives or middle managers than by supervisors or nonexempt workers. The costs at this writing also range from $300 to $2,800 per participant.

When Should Adventure Learning
Be a Programmatic Focus of MD?

Adventure learning is not for the fainthearted. The most rigorous adventure learning experiences pose hazards to participants that are seldom cause for concern in learning experiences centered in classrooms or work sites. After all, in what other learning experiences do MD specialists have to worry about participants falling off a mountain, drowning in a babbling brook, or getting lost in the woods?

Adventure learning is uniquely suited to meeting *affective* (feeling-centered) learning objectives. It can also be used to support more than one programmatic focus of MD. For individuals, it helps to:

- Clarify problems, concerns, or desires.
- Reveal how individuals relate to groups (generally) or family members or co-workers (specifically).
- Foster reflection about personal or career problems.

For groups it helps to:

- Intensify cohesiveness and feelings of interconnectedness.
- Reveal group dynamics stripped of the (sometimes shallow) courtesy found in workplaces.
- Build camaraderie.
- Spur new insights into more effective ways of working together.

Generally, however, adventure learning is not appropriate for meeting *cognitive* (knowledge-centered) objectives. Nor is it appropriate for helping people increase their technical knowledge.

Planning and Offering Adventure Learning

Short-term adventure learning experiences can be readily planned and offered to supplement internal group training and on-the-job training. Activities similar to those described in Exhibit 9-1 may be readily adapted for many uses. If managed effectively, they are usually greeted enthusiastically by participants.

But intermediate-term and long-term adventure learning experiences are another matter. Rarely will an MD director, MD coordinator, or MD specialist be qualified to plan and deliver them. (An exception, of course, is the MD director who has previously managed such programs for a consulting firm.) An external vendor will be needed to design, operate, and follow up the adventure. Many vendors specialize in adventure learning. That external vendor becomes the *trip facilitator*.

Always approach a prospective external vendor with clear-cut performance objectives for adventure learning in mind. If you don't, you will probably waste valuable time—and perhaps incur additional expense—figuring out what results should stem from the adventure learning experience. Be sure that the activities planned match up to the identified learning needs. If they don't, the experience will probably turn into nothing more than a pleasure trip. Decision makers will later shake their heads, wondering what returns the organization received for its substantial investment. The credibility of the MD function may also suffer as a result.

A better approach is to begin by considering these questions:

- What should participants feel at the end of the experience?
- Who should participate?
- How will adventure learning contribute to meeting participants' needs?
- Why is adventure learning preferable to other MD methods for meeting those needs?

Once these questions have been answered (you can use the worksheet in Exhibit 9-2 to sort out key issues), approach consulting firms specializing in adventure learning. Ask for advice about the best adventure learning design to meet the identified needs and to achieve the specified learning outcomes. To help in this process, use an evaluation form like the one shown in Exhibit 9-3 for vendors of adventure learning experiences.

Before an intermediate-term or long-term adventure learning experience begins, identify the participants. Hold a briefing session for them. If possible, have them complete an expectations activity like the one in Exhibit 9-4 as an aid in planning the experience. Finally, have them sign a release form, reviewed and approved in advance by the organization's legal counsel, to absolve the organization of liability stemming from injuries or fatalities that may occur during the experience. Update emergency information about the participants so that appropriate people may be contacted as necessary.

As the adventure learning experience begins, the trip facilitator should explain its purpose, desired outcomes, and any special responsibilities of the participants. Be sure, too, that the role of the trip facilitator or scout is clarified. It should not be assumed that everyone understands the purpose of the trip, the objectives to be achieved, or the role of the group leader(s).

If the adventure learning experience includes such specific challenges as logrolling, rope climbing, or white-water rafting, the trip facilitator should be sure to debrief participants after *each* experience in order to catch them in a teachable moment. Learners should be asked to *process their feelings*, meaning they should describe what they feel before they have recovered from the intensity of the moment. They should be asked to clarify what they have learned from the experience about themselves, other individuals in the group, or the group as a whole. The trip facilitator should allow them to learn from each other, intervening only when one person attacks another. Personal attacks only undermine group cohesiveness and should not be tolerated for long.

After the trip is concluded, the trip facilitator should hold a debriefing session with participants. They should be asked to share what they feel they learned. Those insights should be recorded for future playback. If necessary, experiences of previous groups may also be shared. Participants should be asked to address questions like these:

- What did you learn?
- How do you feel about yourselves and others in the group?
- In your opinion, how did the adventure learning experience contribute to helping you meet your learning needs?

The participants should then be asked to record their insights on a videotape segment or in a letter, indicating how they can apply on the job what they learned from the experience.

Problems Affecting Adventure Learning

Adventure learning presents unique challenges. Not everyone feels comfortable participating in such experiences. Some people do not find the outdoors particularly appealing; some have family or personal commitments that complicate their ability to participate; some fear the dangers implicit in mountain climbing, rafting, or other hazardous ventures. Participants' spouses may be uncomfortable if male and female co-workers camp outdoors for some time.

There is no simple way to meet these challenges. But here are a few suggestions:

- Consider the need for an adventure learning experience carefully.
- Do *not* pressure individuals who have qualms about participating. Let dissenters opt out.
- Take care to avoid making it appear that the learning experience is geared to one group, individual, or sex—or is designed to exclude anyone.
- Take care to discuss the idea with your organization's legal counsel well ahead of time, clearing it so that liability issues can be minimized. If they cannot be minimized, then don't proceed with the adventure learning experience.

New Age Training

Think of crystals, astrology, Far Eastern philosophy, ESP, UFOs, meditation, and yoga. As you do, you enter the realm of the *New Age*.

Exhibit 9-2. Worksheet for planning adventure learning experiences.

Directions: Use this worksheet to help you structure your thinking about the objectives of an adventure learning experience before participants take part in it.

---

1. What is the purpose of the experience? Why do you feel that an adventure learning experience is the best way to achieve that purpose?

2. What should participants feel or appreciate more upon their return from the experience? (State objectives.)

3. Describe precisely what activities will best achieve the objectives described in question 2. Examples of possible activities might include: logrolling, backpacking, mountain climbing, rafting, sailing, boating, rope climbing, hiking, jogging, camping, fishing, or hunting. Describe the events in any special sequence you feel they should follow.

   Date/time:

   Activities:

   *How activities are
   related to the objectives:*

4. How should the adventure learning experience be evaluated?

5. How should the lessons learned by the participants in the adventure learning experience be transferred back to their jobs? By what means can the likelihood of such transfer of learning be increased?

Critics charge that so-called New Age methods are silly or even potentially dangerous because they mislead gullible people.[3] Adherents point to the large number of true believers who give credence to horoscopes, UFOs, and ESP.

Defining New Age Training

New Age Training (NAT) is the application of New Age beliefs and approaches to MD. NAT uses many methods to help individuals or groups undergo change and learning. Among the most widely accepted for MD are neurolinguistic programming (NLP), suggestology, visioning, meditation, yoga, and imaging. Least accepted and most controversial for MD: crystals, astrology, ESP, UFOs, certain abstruse Far Eastern philosophies of leadership, and instruction based on religion in the workplace.

When Should New Age Training Be a Programmatic Focus of MD?

Try to avoid the least acceptable NAT methods (which we do not discuss in this book). A more prudent course of action is to combine accepted NAT methods with other MD methods. For example, use visioning, meditation, yoga or imaging methods to punctuate traditional classroom activities. That approach can be quite effective—and it minimizes possible controversy.

Planning and Offering New Age Training

If NAT methods are used in combination with more traditional methods, then planning and offering them are relatively simple.

> • Identify occasions when they may be appropriate. For example, visioning activities work well in creativity training, team-building

text continues on page 250

Exhibit 9-3. Evaluation form for vendors of adventure learning programs.

Vendor's name: _____   Date: _____

Ranking: _____   Evaluator(s) _____

_____

Directions: Use this form to evaluate vendors of adventure learning programs. Use one form per vendor. Fill out the vendor's name, the date, and the name(s) of those evaluating the vendors' program(s). For each question posed check (√) *yes* or *no*. Then comment on the response—or the vendor—in the space below the question. Finally, rank the vendor in comparison with others, and enter the score below the vendor's name on page 1 of the evaluation form. Use 1 to designate the most desirable vendor. Use higher numbers to designate less desirable vendors.

	Yes	No
1. Has the vendor stated the purpose of the adventure learning experience? *Comments*:	☐	☐
2. Has the vendor stated the perfomance objectives of the adventure learning experience? *Comments*:	☐	☐
3. Has the vendor adequately described what will occur on the adventure learning experience? *Comments*:	☐	☐
4. Has the vendor supplied a rationale for the adventure learning experiences proposed for the client organization? *Comments*:	☐	☐
5. Has the vendor provided a lesson plan or other description of events that will happen during the adventure learning experience? *Comments*:	☐	☐
6. Do the activities recommended by the vendor appear to match up to the performance objectives of the client organization? *Comments*:	☐	☐

	Yes	No
7. Has the vendor identified where the trip will be held? *Comments*:	☐	☐
8. Does the location appear to be appropriate for meeting the performance objectives of the adventure learning experience? *Comments*:	☐	☐
9. Is it clear who the trip facilitator will be? *Comments*:	☐	☐
10. Is the trip facilitator qualified by appropriate credentials in psychology or related disciplines to conduct an adventure learning experience? *Comments*:	☐	☐
11. Does the vendor have a proven track record of facilitating adventure learning experiences? *Comments*:	☐	☐
12. Is the vendor's accident rate low? *Comments*:	☐	☐
13. Has the vendor adequately described safety precautions? *Comments*:	☐	☐
14. Is the vendor able to supply testimonials from satisfied clients? *Comments*:	☐	☐
15. Do the vendor's references check out? *Comments*:	☐	☐

(continues)

Exhibit 9-3 (*continued*).

	Yes	No
16. Has the vendor taken adequate precautions to minimize legal liability? *Comments:*	☐	☐
17. Has the vendor provided a realistic estimate of all costs associated with the trip? *Comments:*	☐	☐
18. Is the vendor's price competitive? *Comments:*	☐	☐

sessions, or strategic planning meetings; imaging works well with creativity training; and yoga or meditation works particularly well at the beginning or ending of a group session by establishing a relaxed but alert climate.

· At the outset of the experience, explain its purpose and how it relates to what participants have learned or will learn.

· Give step-by-step instructions to participate. Do not assume they will know what to do.

· Follow up the experience with a brief discussion to clarify the results and to reinforce how the method relates to what participants have learned or will learn.

See Exhibit 9-5 for examples of two NAT methods that may be effectively used in MD.

Problems Affecting New Age Training Methods

Like adventure learning and other cutting-edge approaches, NAT methods are by no means a panacea for MD. To cite two common problems:

1. Some people may not wish to participate in the least accepted NAT methods on religious grounds.
2. Some participants—or their families—fear brainwashing by

controversial NAT methods, which means that the use of these methods may create a public relations nightmare and an enormous potential legal liability for the organization.

We do not recommend mixing MD with the least accepted New Age techniques because we feel that religion in all its forms is a very personal matter that is ill-suited to the workplace. But if you feel pressured by influential managers to use extreme measures, be sure to review the techniques you plan to use with the organization's legal counsel and alert supporters to potential risks beforehand.

Action Learning

Historically, MD specialists have focused their attention on what might be called *content-oriented MD methods*, designed to communicate information, build skills, or change the attitudes of individual managers. Content-oriented MD methods are intended to improve efficiency ("doing things right"). One key assumption is that management employees will improve performance if trained in what they are expected to do and how well they are expected to do it. Another common assumption is that the best, most reliable information about management comes from academic theories and research about management.

But increasing attention is being devoted to *action learning*.[4] Intended to improve effectiveness ("doing the right things"), action learning is designed to *discover* new ideas and approaches for application in unique cultures or organizational settings. It unleashes the creative abilities of individuals, groups, or organizations, making planned learning experiences a competitive weapon to uncover utterly new ways to address complex organizational problems. It assumes that participants in a planned MD program should learn from organization-specific and job-specific problems confronting them.

When Should Action Learning Be a Programmatic Focus of MD?

Most organizations use some action learning methods. Usually it is a question of how often—or how well—they are used. Organizations pursuing Total Quality Management (TQM) or employee involvement typically devote more time and effort to action learning, since it is particularly well-attuned to participative management. Moreover, TQM focuses on continuous improvement—what the Japanese call *kaizen*—in a way consistent with the assumption of action learning adherents that the world is dynamic and constantly changing.

Exhibit 9-4. Expectations activity for adventure learning experiences.

Directions: Use this worksheet to assess the expectations of prospective participants in an adventure learning experience. Before they embark upon the experience, administer these questions to gauge their expectations.

---

1. What do you feel is the purpose of this experience? Why is your employer sponsoring this experience?

2. What do you want to learn from this experience?

3. How supportive of this experience is your spouse or significant other? (*Mark an X above the point on the scale below that best represents his or her level of support.*)

Actively op-poses the experience.	*Is somewhat opposed.*	*Neutral/is not aware of it.*	*Is somewhat supportive.*	*Strongly supports the experience.*

4. Indicate what activities you are and are not willing to participate in during the adventure learning experience. (*Mark an X in the appropriate boxes.*)

Willing to participate	*Activity*	*Unwilling to participate*
☐	Backpacking	☐
☐	Boating	☐
☐	Camping	☐
☐	Canoeing	☐
☐	Fishing	☐
☐	Gardening	☐
☐	Hiking	☐
☐	Hot-bathing	☐
☐	Hunting	☐
☐	Jogging	☐
☐	Mountain climbing	☐

Willing to participate	Activity	Unwilling to participate
☐	Rafting	☐
☐	Rope climbing	☐
☐	Sailing	☐
☐	Swimming	☐
☐	Woodchopping	☐
☐	Yoga	☐
☐	Other	☐

5. How should this experience be evaluated? How will you define success?

Using Action Learning

Content-oriented MD methods traditionally rely on historical information, such as management theories, and are not necessarily tied to unique conditions in one organizational setting. Nor do they rely on learning materials adapted from problems confronting learners; rather, they may rely heavily on learning materials, purchased externally, about management.

Action learning methods are different. They use problems or issues affecting an organization, group, job, or individual as the basis for learning experiences. Management competencies are inferred, in part or in whole, from information gathered from *outside* the organization through benchmarking, customer surveys, or similar data-gathering methods. Customers, suppliers, distributing wholesalers, and competitors become key sources of information about *what should be*. That information is then compared to what already exists in the organization (*what is*). The difference between *what is* and *what should be* creates a performance gap that can be narrowed or closed by management training, education, or development. The targeted participants of an MD program are actively involved in planning their own learning activities and seeking out new knowledge, skills, and attitudes important for organizational and/or personal success.

Two models may guide the use of action learning. One is the *situation-specific* model; the second is the *comprehensive* model. The situation-specific model emphasizes small-group learning; the compre-

Exhibit 9-5. New Age activities.

Visioning Activity

Objective:
To help members of a group establish a unified vision of an idealized future they wish to realize

Materials Required:
Flipchart paper; flipchart stand; marking pens; masking tape

Time Required:
Allow 30 minutes.

Procedure:
Create small groups of 3 or 4 people each. Ask each group to:
1. Set up a flipchart.
2. Elect a spokesperson.
3. Work together to answer this question:
   "Envision the *ideal future*. What would it look like in this organization, division, department, work group, or team?"
4. Describe the characteristics of that ideal future in short, descriptive phrases, and record them on the flipchart. As flipchart sheets are filled, tear them off the pad and use masking tape to affix them to the wall.
5. Avoid critical statements or disagreements; rather, work together quickly in listing adjectives to describe the future, even if they seem to conflict.
6. Summarize key points of agreement in your description, prioritizing what you most desire for the future.

Discussion Questions:
1. Ask each group spokesperson: What were the key points of agreement?
2. Ask each group spokesperson: What priorities did your group decide on? What was the reasoning for those priorities?

Imaging Activity

Objective:
To help members of a group relax and increase their collective creativity

Materials Required:
None

Time Required:
Allow 10–15 minutes.

Setting Required
Meeting room or classroom.

Procedure:

Ask participants to:

1. Remain seated.
2. Close their eyes.
3. Envision a pastoral setting.
4. Imagine that, as the facilitator counts backward from 10, they are entering the pastoral setting. They can feel wind at their backs, see water lapping on the banks of a lake, and feel the heat from a soft, golden sun.
5. Listen as the facilitator counts backward, beginning at 10.

When the facilitator reaches 1, tell the participants that they are entering the setting and will remain there for a few minutes.

Discussion Questions:

1. Ask participants: Did you actually feel the wind, see the lake, and feel the heat of sunshine?
2. How many fell asleep during the imaging session? (Ask for a show of hands.) Explain that sleep indicates complete relaxation.
3. How might imaging help you relieve stress you face during the workday?

---

hensive model encourages ambitious, large-scale change and learning throughout an organization.

To use the situation-specific model, take the following steps:

1. Identify a problem confronting a group or team.
2. Call together management employees—and, potentially, others—who are affected by the problem, who are knowledgeable about it, or who have a stake in solving it.
3. Ask the group to work together to analyze the problem, develop solutions, and create an action plan for improvement.

The central idea is to surface information about problems and to have the people affected by them arrive at an action plan to solve them. Group problem solving is thus coupled with group action planning.

On the other hand, a six-step model is helpful in guiding comprehensive action learning that unleashes employee involvement and learning throughout the organization:

1. *Gather information from outside the organization through benchmarking, customer-oriented research, or environmental scanning.* MD specialists and line managers ask competitors what they are doing. They ask customers, suppliers, distributing wholesalers, and other stakeholders what the organization should be doing. Then they pose

Exhibit 9-6. Sample plan for a customer focus group.

Objective:
  To elicit information about ways to improve customer service and quality through improved management practices

Materials required:
  Flipchart pad; flipchart stand; marking pens; masking tape

Time required:
  Allow ½ to 1 day.

Procedure:

1. Select between 5 and 20 customers or constituents of your organization at random and pay their way to a central location. Explain that the purpose of the focus group is to improve customer service and quality through improved management practices.
2. At the beginning of the session, ask the participants to introduce themselves and say a few words about the business they do with your organization.
3. Then provide a description of your organization. Be sure to cover at least:

   • The history of the organization
   • Key external trends or regulatory issues affecting the industry and organization
   • The structure of the organization
   • The financial condition of the organization
   • The organization's future prospects and plans (as reported in annual reports and other public documents)
   • The organization's philosophy of doing business

4. Take a break. Then ask group members to count off to create 3 to 5 small groups. Furnish the groups with flipchart pads, flipchart stands, masking tape, and marking pens. Ask each group to appoint a spokesperson. Then ask each group to answer the three key questions that follow, and to list the answers on flipchart sheets. Have them tear off sheets as they are filled, tape them to a wall, and be prepared to discuss the answers.

Discussion questions:

   • From the collective experience of the group members as customers, what are the key strengths of the organization? (List them on the flipchart in order of importance; 1 = most important.)
   • From the collective experience of the group as customers, what are the key areas in which the organization could improve? (List them on the flipchart in order of importance; 1 = most important.)
   • Assume that management bears complete responsibility for the organization's key strengths and key areas for improvement. In what areas do you believe management employees in this organization need better training, education, and development? (List them on the flipchart in order of importance; 1 = most important.)

5. Ask the small groups to report on their prioritized lists. Appoint someone to take complete notes from all small groups.
6. At the end of the session, thank all the groups for their help. Explain briefly who will receive the results and what will be done with them.
7. Thank the focus group participants for their help. (A modest gift for each participant is appropriate.)
8. Then, when the results are used in the organization, send a letter to the participants to point out how their input was used. Describe exactly what use was made of it and what improvements in customer service, quality, or management development resulted from it.

---

questions about management's role in solving problems or taking action.

Many methods may be used to gather information from customers, competitors, and other stakeholders, including customer surveys and focus groups. (A sample focus group plan is presented in Exhibit 9-6.) Benchmarking information about practices in other organizations may also be gathered by phone surveys, written surveys, and field trips. (The value of benchmarking as a tool in needs assessment is briefly described in Chapter 3.)

2. *Gather information about the organization.* In one approach, MD specialists emphasize strategic plans as a starting point to guide MD learning activities; in another approach, MD specialists and managers harness the power of employee involvement by surveying exempt and nonexempt employees about new ideas and/or the existing strengths and weaknesses of the organization's management talent. To this end, many data-gathering methods may be used. Among them are attitude surveys, upward performance appraisals, idea teams, and employee focus groups. This data-gathering effort should yield results that may be compared with externally collected benchmarking information.

3. *Compare what is to what should be.* A committee consisting of a top manager, a middle manager, a supervisor, and others is formed to interpret the results of steps 1 and 2. The committee is a tool for involving people in the decision-making process. Visible top management support for this effort should be demonstrated by involving a key top manager, such as the CEO or the COO, on the committee.

4. *Identify performance improvement methods appropriate to narrowing the gap between what is and what should be.* Committee members focus their attention on this question: how can management performance be improved and developed continuously in the organization?

text continues on page 260

Exhibit 9-7. Action learning methods and techniques.

Approach and its Purpose	Procedures
Survey feedback To surface problems or issues that interfere with effective management performance and to focus attention on solving them	1. Draft or buy an attitude survey, economizing on items so as to zero in on the most important issues only. 2. Set up the survey so that information will be collected by division or work group. 3. Send out the survey (ideally), having secured top management approval and support beforehand. 4. Compile results. 5. Feed a summary of the results back to top management, emphasizing the 3 or 4 most important issues identified. 6. Feed the detailed results back to management employees in charge of each work group. 7. Facilitate feedback and joint action planning in each work group. 8. Facilitate action planning for the management employee in charge of the work group. 9. Follow up on the action planned and results subsequently achieved.
Process consultation To focus on barriers to effective one-on-one or interpersonal interactions	1. Identify a management employee who is the target of complaints about belligerence or poor interpersonal skills—or, alternatively, any manager who would like to improve his or her interpersonal skills. 2. Meet with the management employee, explaining that his or her interpersonal skills could be improved if he or she is willing to learn. 3. "Shadow" the manager—that is, follow him or her around—to group or one-on-one meetings with subordinates, peers, or superordinates. 4. Take notes on the manager's inter-

Approach and its Purpose	Procedures
	actions with others during meetings or other interpersonal interactions—specifically, on how he or she: a. Interrupts others. b. Uses eye contact. c. Asks questions. d. Makes statements. e. Solicits and treats information about alternative, even dissenting, points of view. f. Solicits and treats information about the feelings of other people. g. Handles conflict. 5. Provide immediate, concrete feedback to the manager about what he or she does in each meeting. 6. Solicit the manager's ideas on improving his or her methods of interacting with others. 7. Monitor and praise progress.
Organization mirroring To surface perceptions about one organizational unit and its interactions with others	1. Identify a work group, team, department, or division that is negatively perceived by others in the organization—or, alternatively, simply wishes to improve its image. 2. Draft a survey to solicit information about: a. The greatest strengths and weaknesses of the work group, team, department, or division. b. Any special strengths or weaknesses perceived about the leader of the work group, team, department, or divison. 3. Conduct the survey a. Inside the work group, team, department, or division. b. Outside the work group, team, department, or division with other target groups—particularly those believed to have percep-

(continues)

Exhibit 9-7 (*continued*).

Approach and its Purpose	Procedures

	tions of the work group, team, department, or division that are sharply at odds with the group's.
	4. Feed the results back to:
	  a. The work group.
	  b. The leader of the work group.
	5. Use the results to establish action plans for improvement.

Third-party peacemaking To mediate interpersonal conflict constructively	1. Identify 2 or more management employees who are having difficulty getting along—or simply wish to improve how well they interact. 2. Meet with the management employees, explaining that their interpersonal skills could be improved and thereby potentially improve the interaction of their employees. 3. Ask them separately what issues are leading to conflict between them or have created problems for each of them in the past. 4. Bring the management employees back together, summarizing the problems or issues they individually surfaced. 5. Encourage the management employees to establish specific goals to improve their interaction. 6. Gain a commitment from each management employee to focus on issues, not personalities, in the future.

5. *Design planned learning experiences with the active involvement of the targeted participants.* One way to do that is to use the *action research model*, the basis of Organization Development, to guide instructional development and to harness the power of group decision making. To apply that model, the learning facilitator or MD specialist should take these steps:

1. Surface perceptions of problems (such as those uncovered in steps 1 through 3).
2. Establish a means to gather information about the problems from group members and diagnose those problems.
3. Feed back the information about the problems to group members.
4. Validate the information about the problems with group members.
5. Guide group members through the process of highly participative problem solving.
6. Facilitate efforts of the group to establish objectives for change (what corrective action to take) and to devise strategies for achieving the objectives (how to take the action).
7. Facilitate group action on problems.
8. Monitor the effectiveness of the action taken by the group and collect information about effectiveness from other sources.
9. Provide feedback to the group about the effectiveness of the action taken.
10. Facilitate group efforts to improve the corrective action and to ensure continuous improvement by returning to step 1 of this process and starting over.[5]

6. *Select MD methods and techniques to identify new knowledge, skills, and attitudes.* In recent years many methods and techniques have emerged to assist groups in joint decision making and problem solving. Most lend themselves effectively to helping teams or groups surface problems and possible solutions.[6] They can also be used to assess future conditions or to pinpoint emerging trends affecting the work. They are thus well-suited to action learning. Exhibit 9-7 summarizes several action learning techniques that have been used in Organization Development change efforts.

Problems Affecting Action Learning

Action learning methods are highly appropriate for generating energy and for unleashing employee involvement. But they can be threatening to the standard-bearers of the status quo, who feel they erode the traditional power and decision-making authority of management. To work effectively, action learning methods must be supported by top managers.

Summary

In this chapter we reviewed three special MD methods—adventure learning, New Age Training (NAT), and action learning. They may be planned or unplanned. They are distinctive because they are on the cutting edge of practice or are controversial.

Part IV

Evaluating Management Development Methods and Programs

Introduction to Part IV

This concluding part focuses on evaluating MD. We introduce Chapter 10 by defining evaluation. We also describe different types of evaluation, key obstacles to evaluation, methods for overcoming those obstacles, and a step-by-step approach for conducting a program evaluation.

Chapter 10

Evaluating Methods and Programs

If you asked MD directors to identify one area of their planned MD programs that could stand significant improvement, you would be likely to hear answers like these:

> "Evaluation. We have trouble demonstrating that real changes resulted from MD programs. And we have no compelling way to show how MD efforts are affecting the organization's 'bottom line' or strategic plan."
>
> "There must be better ways to show the value of our efforts than by circulating results of participant evaluations from classroom sessions. But how is that done with a small staff and tight budget?"

These feelings are pervasive in MD, making the topic of evaluation a perennial favorite for articles and professional presentations.

But just what is evaluation? Why is it important? What barriers stand in the way of performing it successfully? What are the steps in carrying out a program evaluation? This chapter addresses these questions. As a starting point, read over the introductory case study. It dramatizes the high stakes involved in evaluating MD programs and methods.

INTRODUCTORY CASE STUDY

John Terpa is MD director for the Walsh-Healey Company, a multinational conglomerate employing 73,000 people at 908 locations worldwide. Before he was hired, John was employed as a training professional at another conglomerate. He has been in his present job for eight years, having started a comprehensive, centralized MD function from scratch.

John has been very successful in setting up the MD function at Walsh-Healey.

With a modest staff of just ten people at corporate headquarters in Mobile, Alabama, he has been able to offer a dizzying array of MD options to help Walsh-Healey's management employees develop their skills. Through John's function the company offers classroom courses, teleconferences, video-based instruction, computer-based instruction, audiocassettes, and much more.

In the early days of John's employment, managers from company work sites had to crawl on airplanes and take expensive trips to corporate headquarters to participate in planned MD efforts. But over the last few years John eliminated the need for much travel by localizing MD efforts and by using distance learning methods such as teleconferencing. Exhausting travel is no longer a necessity. At present, only executives travel to corporate headquarters for lengthy planned learning experiences, and they do so only because it is preferred by top management.

John has encouraged the appointment of an MD coordinator at each work site. John and his staff work directly with local MD coordinators to identify needs and select appropriate MD methods. John uses corporate staff to help identify and manage vendors for company work sites. John's corporate MD function also serves as a brain trust and troubleshooter, offering expert assistance to MD coordinators at company work sites and sending in helpers to focus on difficult MD-related matters of local concern.

The Walsh-Healey company has recently undertaken a total quality management (TQM) effort. Top managers want to see several direct outcomes from the effort, including:

- Increased quality in the products made and services offered by the Walsh-Healey Company
- Increased involvement of employees in decisions affecting them
- Successful implementation of self-directed work teams
- Fewer layers of management
- Additional employee training in methods of problem solving that may be applied on their jobs
- Improved customer service
- A reduced but more highly trained and highly involved hourly work force of people who find their jobs challenging

John has been directed by the CEO to work directly with an outside TQM consultant to help achieve these goals.

An early step will be to identify the customers of John's own function, to identify world-class MD functions in other organizations against which to compare Walsh-Healey's MD function, to measure customer satisfaction with the products and services offered by the MD function, and to establish efforts for continuous improvement in MD at Walsh-Healey.

While involved in this important effort, which John enthusiastically supports, he received a phone call from Walsh-Healey's budgeting department. That department was recently charged by the company's chairman with the important responsibility of cutting costs and expenses in all nonessential areas in order to make Walsh-Healey more competitive in an increasingly competitive global marketplace.

John is told that he will have to slash his budget by at least 20 percent for the remainder of the year. Management and supervisory training are special targets for reduction. John is asked to cut expenses by 35 percent for those programs. (Recent increases in those programs are directly attributable to the TQM initiative.)

Using information about the contribution of MD to Walsh-Healey's profitability, John wants to show that such a budget cut is ill-advised—particularly during implementation of TQM at Walsh-Healey.

Put yourself in John's situation. How could you demonstrate that a 20 percent budget cut in MD is ill-advised? See the recommended solution to this case in Exhibit 10-7 at the end of this chapter.

What Is Evaluation?

Evaluation is the process of assigning value and making critical judgments. In MD, evaluation answers these questions:

- *What changes* resulted from an MD program or MD methods?
- *How much change* resulted from an MD program or MD methods?
- *What value* can be assigned to those changes?
- *How much value* can be assigned to those changes?

In short, evaluation means assessing how much and how well MD programs or methods contribute to improving organizational, group, or individual performance.

Four Types of Evaluation

In 1960, Donald Kirkpatrick introduced a simple model to distinguish between different types of instructional evaluation.[1] Kirkpatrick's model has been widely adopted, used, modified, and (on occasion) criticized.[2] It provides a useful way to conceptualize the evaluation of MD.

There are four levels to Kirkpatrick's hierarchical model:

1. Participant reaction
2. Participant learning
3. Participant performance
4. Organization results[3]

Each level of Kirkpatrick's hierarchical model has its own purpose, strengths, weaknesses, and guidelines for development.

Participant Reaction

Participant reaction is the first and lowest level of evaluation. It measures participant feelings about one planned learning experience. The most common form of evaluation, it is easy to administer and provides immediate feedback about instructors, facilities, materials, and MD methods. Participant reaction is measured through end-of-course "happiness surveys," informal interviews with participants, and group discussions.

To devise an effective participant reaction, you should:

1. Clarify what issues are to be evaluated.
2. Prepare a questionnaire, interview form, or discussion guide for end-of-course use to evaluate the identified issues.
3. Administer the survey, conduct interviews, or collect information about participant reactions in other ways.
4. Compile the evaluation results.
5. Feed back the evaluation results to stakeholders.

A sample participant evaluation form appears in Exhibit 10-1. Unfortunately, participant reactions are subjective. They do not measure participant learning, participant performance, or organization results.

Participant Learning

Participant learning is the second level of Kirkpatrick's hierarchy of evaluation. It measures how much participants change as a result of a learning experience. Evaluations of participant learning furnish more objective information than do evaluations of participant reactions.

Participant learning is typically measured through paper-and-pencil tests, demonstrations, and role plays, among other methods. To devise effective measures of participant learning, you should:

1. Write test items, or choose other evaluative methods on the basis of performance objectives.
2. Examine test items or other evaluative methods for clarity, validity, and reliability.
3. Administer the evaluation instrument to a small pilot group of individuals to ensure the instrument is clear, valid, and reliable.
4. Administer the test items/evaluative methods to learners before, during, and/or after planned MD experiences.

Measuring participant learning requires special skill in designing tests and other evaluation measures. It thus lies beyond the reach of novices. And it does not provide much useful information about participant performance or organization results.

Participant Performance

The central question underlying the third level of Kirkpatrick's hierarchy of evaluation is this: *How much on-the-job change resulted from MD experiences?* In other words, how much did planned learning experiences help participants improve their job performance?

This form of evaluation is carried out with performance checklists, performance appraisals, critical incidents, self-appraisals, upward appraisals, after-course surveys of participants' immediate organizational superiors or subordinates, and other methods. One way to devise an evaluation of participant performance is to:

1. Draft questions to assess on-the-job change.
2. Administer the survey to participants' immediate organizational superiors and/or subordinates.
3. Compile the evaluation results.
4. Feed back the evaluation results to participants, their immediate organizational superiors, and their immediate subordinates in order to stimulate future development and to improve the planned MD program.

The greatest single barrier to carrying out this form of evaluation is lack of motivation. MD specialists must *want* to collect information about on-the-job change resulting from planned learning experiences. They should also be willing to follow up after long lapses of time. (A sample after-course survey appears in Exhibit 10-2.)

Organization Results

Most decision makers who invest in MD programs would like to know the answer to one simple question: *How much was organizational performance affected or improved by MD experiences?* Yet that is a singularly difficult question to answer.

Common ways of measuring organization results include employee or management suggestions, manufacturing indices, attitude survey results, frequency of union grievances, absenteeism rates, customer complaints, and other measures of organizational results. Unfortu-

text continues on page 273

Exhibit 10-1. Participant evaluation form.

Directions: This evaluation form is intended to gauge your reactions to this course. Place an X above the appropriate space on the line following each question. Then write a narrative in response to questions 10 through 12.

Purpose, Objectives, and Organization:

1. How clearly was the purpose of this course stated?

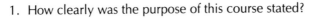

Not at All
   Clearly   Not Sure   Very Clearly

2. How clearly were the objectives of this course stated?

Not at All
   Clearly   Not Sure   Very Clearly

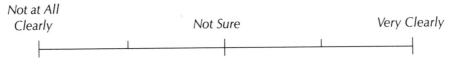

3. How clearly was the organization (structure) of the course described?

Not at All
   Clearly   Not Sure   Very Clearly

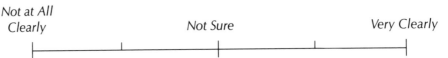

Instructor:

4. How effective was the instructor in presenting the course?

Not at All
   Effective   Not Sure   Very Effective

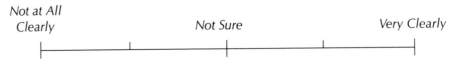

5. How effective was the instructor in making the course interesting?

Not at All
   Effective   Not Sure   Very Effective

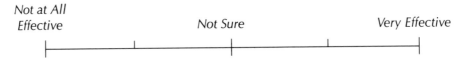

6. Would you recommend this instructor to others?

I would absolutely   I would absolutely
not *recommend* this   recommend this
instructor to others.   Not Sure   instructor to others.

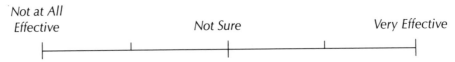
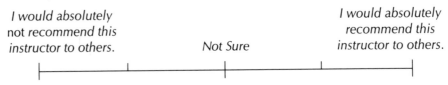

Course Content:

7. How valuable was the course material in helping you perform your job more effectively?

Not at All
Valuable   *Not Sure*   *Very Valuable*

```
├─────────────┴─────────────┼─────────────┴─────────────┤
```

8. How effective was the course material in helping your team, unit, department, or division increase its productivity?

Not at All
Effective   *Not Sure*   *Very Effective*

```
├─────────────┴─────────────┼─────────────┴─────────────┤
```

Facilities:

9. How well did the facilities match up to the requirements of the course, in your opinion?

Not at All
Well   *Not Sure*   *Very Well*

```
├─────────────┴─────────────┼─────────────┴─────────────┤
```

Other Remarks:

10. What did you find *least useful* about the course?

11. What did you find *most useful* about the course?

12. What other remarks do you have to make about the course?

Course title:_____

Location:_____   Date:_____

Exhibit 10-2. Survey for evaluating on-the-job change.

Participant's name: _____

Course participated in: _____Date: _____

Directions: We need *your* help as an immediate organizational superior, or subordinate, of the participant named above. He/she participated in a learning experience, and we would like to have your opinion—in confidence—about how much, if at all, the course has influenced the participant's on-the-job behavior. For each question, provide your frank answers *in complete confidence.* Your responses will *not* be communicated to the participant; rather, they will be helpful to the Management Development program in designing planned learning experiences.

1. Have you noticed any *change* in the participant's on-the-job behavior since he/she returned from the course?
   (Check one response below.)
   ☐ Yes   ☐ No

   > If you checked "No," then skip to question 5; if you *checked* "Yes," then continue on to question 2.

2. What change did you notice? (Describe the situation[s] and your perception of how the participant behaved.)

3. How often has the participant behaved this way?

4. How do you feel about the change in behavior noted in response to question 2?

5. What comments do you wish to make?

PLEASE RETURN THIS TRAINING EVALUATION TO:

Name: _____

Location: _____

Date: _____

---

nately, it is rarely possible to control for so-called *intervening variables* to ensure that organizational changes stem from MD efforts *only*.

To devise an evaluation of participant performance, you should:

1. Identify important measures, on the basis of organizational needs/plans, to be changed as a result of MD experiences.
2. Clarify the degree of change desired.
3. Control for intervening variables to the extent possible.
4. Compare organizational performance *after* planned MD experiences to those existing *before* the experiences.

To measure organization results, MD specialists require much knowledge about the organization and about evaluation methods.

Distinguishing Between Formative and Summative Evaluation

Kirkpatrick's hierarchical model of evaluation focuses on the *results* of learning experiences, chiefly as they affect learners. But another model is needed to evaluate and improve learning materials or methods in MD programs. To that end, MD specialists must turn to *formative* and *summative* evaluation. *Formative evaluation* tests out materials and methods for management training, education, or development before their widespread use; *summative evaluation* assesses changes resulting from management training, education, or development after their widespread use.

Many MD specialists associate formative and summative evaluation with internal group training, since classroom methods were first used as the focus of evaluation. Moreover, classroom methods easily lend themselves to formative and summative evaluation. But other MD methods also lend themselves, though less obviously, to formative and summative evaluation.

The Importance of Evaluation

Evaluation is critically important because it affects the willingness of an organization's decision makers to support a planned MD program. Without evaluation, MD specialists cannot demonstrate that MD has contributed to performance improvement for organizations, work groups, or individuals. That makes MD a ripe target for cost cutting, as dramatically illustrated by the introductory case study in this chapter. After all, decision makers are reluctant to invest precious resources in programs for which payoffs are uncertain or problematic.

Obstacles to Evaluation

Despite the importance of evaluation, few organizations progress beyond participant evaluation or devote substantial resources to assessing the payoffs of MD. The results of one survey study revealed that MD is evaluated primarily by participants alone.[4] Unfortunately, participant reaction measures by themselves are inadequate to demonstrate *what changes* in performance occurred, *how much change* occurred, *what value* resulted from the changes, or *how much value* resulted from the changes.

If MD methods and programs are not evaluated as they should be, then that raises several questions:

- Why aren't they?
- What obstacles block the path of evaluation?
- How can the obstacles be overcome?

The Five Key Obstacles

Five key obstacles block effective evaluation of MD methods and programs.

1. *A reluctance to evaluate.* Some MD specialists see no real or immediate payoff from evaluation, even at a time when dramatic cost cutting and employee slashing in organizations is more the norm than the exception. While top managers pay lip service to evaluation, they reward only highly visible efforts, such as internal group training or flashy new MD programs on trendy topics. Evaluation is seldom visible enough to command real resources or interest.

Moreover, some MD specialists are not sure that MD experiences produce real payoffs because they know few learners are held accountable on their jobs for applying what they learned. This is the *transfer of learning problem.*[5] Examples of this problem are easy to describe:

> Management employees are sent to internal group training. When they return to their jobs, they are asked what they learned. After hearing the responses, their immediate organizational superiors remark that "we don't do things like that around here." That one remark destroys the incentive for participants to apply what they learned and creates enormous frustration for the learners, leading them to believe that the training was a waste.

> Management employees are sent to an expensive external seminar at a prestigious Ivy League university. But they are not told, before they leave, why they are being sent, what they are expected to learn, or why they should care about what they learn. Nor are they later evaluated in any measurable way on how well they applied on their jobs what they learned. (The sponsors of the event claim that transfer of learning is "not important" and, indeed, that transfer of learning is not even appropriate for a "true developmental experience.") Some participants conclude that the seminar is merely a vacation in disguise.

The transfer of learning problem leads to wasted time and resources. One expert estimates that less than 10 percent of what employees learn off the job is actually applied on the job.[6] Since MD specialists cannot control the job environment, they express the results to be achieved by measurable end-of-course performance objectives rather than by more appropriate—but difficult-to-measure—on-the-job results.

2. *Lack of resources.* This is a common obstacle, and a frequent excuse for not evaluating MD. For evaluation to be carried out successfully, adequate time, money, and staff must be budgeted, approved, and used. Not all employers are willing to approve expenditures on evaluation, preferring instead to invest funds where payoffs are more visible, flashy, or trendy. While good evaluation results can help defend MD from the budget cutter's ax, finding the time, money, and people to carry out a worthwhile evaluation effort is not easy when MD specialists struggle to meet the demand for high-priority services with diminishing resources. Nor does evaluation enjoy a large, interested constituency that is breathlessly awaiting results.

3. *Lack of know-how.* Many MD specialists do not have adequate knowledge of research or statistical methods, both of which are critical for carrying out evaluation.[7] Since funding may not be available to hire

outside experts possessing the know-how, in-house evaluation efforts may suffer as a result. Even when appropriate expertise is available, top managers and other stakeholders may not be knowledgeable enough about statistics and research methods to make sense of sophisticated evaluation results that are expressed in social science jargon.

4. *Low credibility.* Few organizations have the luxury—as the world-class benchmark organizations do—of separating evaluation from service delivery. When responsibilities are not separated, MD specialists must deliver services *and* evaluate them. The credibility of that effort is not high. Indeed, it is about as credible as a bank president who heads up a financial audit of her own bank. While the results may be unbiased, skeptical users may worry that they are being fed self-serving or misleading results. That undercuts the credibility of the evaluation effort.

5. *Difficulties in using traditional research methodologies.* The same difficulties plague Organization Development evaluation efforts.[8] These include problems with using control groups, lack of long-term (longitudinal) follow-up, and poor research designs.

Overcoming Obstacles

To overcome the obstacles to evaluating MD, MD specialists should adopt five major strategies. They can:

1. *Overcome reluctance to evaluate by making a commitment.* Take this step first. Go on the record to announce that this commitment has been made. Publicize how evaluation is being carried out, why it is important, and what results from MD activities have been realized by the organization and by individuals. If possible, tie MD results to the organization's strategic plan and/or individual career plans.

2. *Overcome lack of resources.* Use a twofold strategy: Publicize results, and adapt evaluation methods to available resources. Aim to satisfy the information needs of stakeholders. Find out what the stakeholders need to know to make decisions, and then provide it as cost-effectively as possible.

3. *Overcome lack of know-how by stepping up efforts to increase knowledge about evaluation.* Educate stakeholders and MD specialists alike by sending MD staff members and line managers on field trips so they can see how competitors—or organizations renowned for their MD programs—conduct evaluation.

4. *Overcome low credibility by involving stakeholders in the evaluation process.* Use that involvement to increase stakeholder participa-

tion in the program. Above all, avoid jealously controlling evaluation efforts. Remember that quality guru W. Edwards Deming made a significant impact on quality by training frontline employees in how to measure what they do and by involving them in improvement efforts. Take the same approach to evaluating MD by training learners and their immediate organizational superiors in how to measure results. Publicize the results they provide. This approach increases stakeholder involvement in evaluation. (Exhibit 10-3 presents a sample interview protocol to be used with learners.)

5. *Overcome difficulties in using traditional research methodologies by matching methods to stakeholder needs.* Do not pursue evaluation with the rigor needed to satisfy academic purists when that is unnecessary; rather, aim to produce credible results for stakeholders. If possible, work with skeptical stakeholders to identify approaches and results they find convincing. Then work to achieve those results.

Carrying Out Evaluation

When evaluating MD, choose an appropriate blueprint for formative evaluation, summative evaluation, or program evaluation.

Formative Evaluation of MD

Formative evaluation is conducted to improve planned learning experiences *before* learners participate in them on a widespread basis. It masquerades under other names—pilot tests, structured walkthroughs, and previews.

Carrying out a formative evaluation is usually a multistep process of repeated tests and revisions:

1. Assess materials under controlled conditions with one or two randomly selected learners from the targeted population or with several subject matter experts (SMEs).
2. Assess materials with a group of randomly selected learners under controlled conditions.
3. Assess materials with randomly selected learners under field conditions resembling those in which the planned learning experience will actually be carried out.
4. Preview materials with a group of immediate organizational superiors of the targeted learners.

Variations on these steps may be used. Step-by-step procedures for conducting formative evaluations of internal group training are sum-

Exhibit 10-3. Form for collecting information about the results of MD from the users: the success case approach.

Directions: Use this worksheet to collect information from participants in MD experiences, such as internal group training or on-the-job training. Visit with randomly selected learners. Pose the questions below. Record the responses on this worksheet. Later, compile results from several such interviews.

Note: Begin the interview by explaining to the respondent that you are collecting information about the results of MD activities in your organization and that you need his or her help. Then pose the following questions:

---

1. Since participating in [*name of course or other MD experience in which individual participated*] _____
_____ , *describe the worst situation* you have encountered that was directly related to it.

2. What *actions did you take* in this situation?

3. What were the *consequences* or *results* of what you did in this situation?

4. How do you think you would have handled this situation if you had *not* participated in MD? Be truthful, and explain what you think your *probable actions* would have been.

5. What would have been the *negative consequences* of your actions in question 2, in your opinion? In other words, what *bad* results would you or the organization have faced?

6. How could we place a price tag or value on the difference between what you actually did, having participated in the MD experience, and what you would

have done if you had not participated in MD? Is there any way you could *estimate the cost?*

7. If you were an investor, how much would you have been *willing to pay* to avoid making a mistake in this situation?

---

marized in Exhibit 10-4. These procedures may be modified for evaluating other MD methods, such as external group training or on-the-job training.

Summative Evaluation of MD

Summative evaluation measures the results of MD methods. A secondary aim is to reinforce the impetus for change by focusing attention on the results of successful MD applications. This form of evaluation usually occurs after MD methods have been used.

There are various procedures for carrying out summative evaluation. They were first perfected with internal group training but may be modified and applied to after-the-fact evaluation of other MD methods (see Exhibits 10-5 and 10-6). For instance, internal group training may be evaluated at the end of a classroom session by asking learners for their opinions about it. Learners may also be tested for mastery of the subject matter. Their on-the-job behaviors or performance may be evaluated through surveys or interviews directed at them, their immediate organizational superiors, or their immediate subordinates. Organizational results may be evaluated by measuring changes in production or quality, among other factors.

Program Evaluation of MD

A program evaluation assesses the contribution of a planned MD program to the organization it serves. It thus resembles a *program performance audit*, a comprehensive review of an entire governmental program or business function. Such comprehensive reviews are rarely

Exhibit 10-4. Step-by-step procedures for conducting formative evaluation of classroom management training.

Before the test begins, prepare all instructional materials in draft form. Have everything ready to use for Phase 1.

Phase 1: Under controlled conditions, assess the instructional materials with one or two subject-matter experts.

Step 1: Pick a controlled environment, such as a quiet room.

Step 2: Identify subject-matter experts from inside or outside the organization, and ask them to set aside a few hours to go over the instructional materials with you.

Step 3: Explain that the purpose of the test is to obtain expert help in assessing the quality of the instructional materials.

Step 4: Deliver the instructional materials to the expert(s).

Step 5: Ask a colleague to attend the session to take notes on what the experts say about revisions needed in the instructional materials.

Step 6: When you finish, make revisions to the materials in line with the experts' recommendations. If major modifications were recommended, ask the experts to review the instructional materials once you have finished the revisions and before you proceed to Phase 2.

Phase 2: Assess the instructional materials with a handful of people from the population of targeted learners.

Step 1: Pick a controlled environment, such as a quiet room.

Step 2: Identify one or two people from the population of targeted learners.

Step 3: Ask participants to set aside a few hours to go over the course material with you.

Step 4: At the outset, explain the purpose of the test: to determine how well participants are able to understand the instructional materials, to determine how participants feel about the methods used to deliver the instruction, and to identify areas in which the instructional materials may be improved for clarity or delivery.

Step 5: Deliver the instructional materials exactly as you intended them to be delivered.

Step 6: Ask a colleague to attend the session to take notes on what the learners say.

Step 7: Ask learners for their feelings and impressions about the training material as well as about the quality of the content.

Step 8: When you have finished the test with participants, make revisions to the instructional materials in line with the recommendations. If major revisions must be made, ask the participants to review the instructional materials with you before proceeding to Phase 3.

Phase 3: Under field conditions, assess the instructional materials with a small, randomly selected group chosen from the population of targeted learners.

Step 1: Repeat all activities in Phase 2 with a group of people—more than one or two—from the population of targeted learners.

Step 2: When you finish, make revisions to the instructional materials in line with what the learners have recommended. If major modifications must be made, ask the learners to review the instructional materials before proceeding to Phase 4.

Phase 4: Preview the instructional materials with a randomly selected group of the targeted learners' immediate organizational superiors.

Step 1: Schedule the briefing/walk-through in a location resembling that in which the instructional materials are to be used.

Step 2: Identify the participants.

Step 3: Invite the participants to a one-hour overview of the instructional materials and methods.

Step 4: Explain that the test is intended to determine what the participants think of the instructional materials and methods, and brainstorm with them about ways to hold learners accountable on the job for what they learn from the instructional materials.

Step 5: Summarize the instructional materials, describing what you plan to do.

Step 6: Ask a colleague to take notes on what recommendations for improvement are made by the participants.

Step 7: Ask the participants for their impressions of the instructional materials and methods.

Step 8: Ask participants how they can hold the learners accountable for applying on the job what they learn from the instructional materials.

Step 9: When you finish the test, revise the instructional materials and methods in line with the participants' recommendations. If major revisions must be made, ask the participants if they would be willing to review the materials once the revisions have been made.

---

undertaken because they are expensive and time-consuming. Moreover, their payoffs are difficult to assess.

But, much like a comprehensive review of any other organizational system, such as data processing, human resources, financial management, or inventory methods, a program evaluation of MD can provide useful guidance for charting the long-term direction of a planned MD

Exhibit 10-5. Step-by-step procedures for conducting summative evaluation of internal group management training.

Do not wait until the end of a planned learning experience to prepare for summative evaluation; rather, lay the foundation as you design instructional materials and choose instructional methods. While there are many ways to apply summative evaluation to internal group training, here are some suggested steps.

Step 1: Prepare competency tests based on performance objectives. Use the performance criteria appearing in performance objectives as a starting point for writing test items, developing on-the-job performance tests or contriving other methods of measuring learning mastery.

Step 2: Prepare a simple questionnaire to measure how well participants liked an internal group training session. Pose open questions like these:

  ‣ What were the chief strengths of this session?
  ‣ What could be improved most in this session?

  Or pose scaled questions like these:

  1. How much do you feel you learned in this session? *(Mark an X above the space on the line that best indicates your response:)*

	Very			Very	Everything
Nothing	Little	Little	Much	Much	Needed

  ├──── 1 ──────── 2 ──── 3 ──── 4 ──── 5 ──────── 6 ────┤

Step 3: At the end of the session, administer written or oral tests, or ask participants in an internal group training session to demonstrate what they learned.

Step 4: Follow up several weeks or months after the session by sending a questionnaire to participants, their immediate organizational superiors, and /or their immediate subordinates to inquire about any noticeable on-the-job changes. Use open questions or scaled questions.

Step 5: Before delivering the instructional experience, establish control and experimental groups to assess the effects of internal group training on the organization's performance. (Experimental groups consist of those who participated in internal group training; control groups consist of those who did not participate.) Then compare individuals in both groups, promotions occurring to members of both groups, and (if possible) the financial performance of areas led by both groups. Note differences. Do not automatically assume that training leads to improvement, even if significant differences are apparent between control and experimental groups. After all, so-called *intervening variables*—such as individual motivation—may account for differences more than the training does. If all else fails, measure organization performance using the "success case" approach described in Exhibit 10-3.

---

program and for tying the program to the organization's strategic plan. In this respect it is akin to a general assessment of functional operations conducted by professional consulting organizations.

Before undertaking a program evaluation of MD, decision makers should come to grips with several key questions:

‣ *What is the reason for conducting the program evaluation?* Is the aim to assess how much the planned MD program contributes to achieving strategic objectives, personal growth, or some other purpose? Since a program evaluation is expensive to conduct, considerable thought should be devoted to the reason(s) for carrying it out.

‣ *How clear are the desired outcomes of the program evaluation?* Appropriate outcomes may include information on which to base a new MD strategy, improve the linkage between MD and the organization's strategic plan, or refocus a planned MD program after a change of leadership.

‣ *Who should conduct the program evaluation?* Should expertise from inside or outside the organization be used? Each choice has its own advantages and disadvantages. By using internal staff members, the organization can avoid sizable out-of-pocket expenditures because staff salaries and benefits are relatively fixed. Moreover, internal staff members are—or should be—familiar with the organization's culture and traditions in a way external vendors rarely are, so they should require less time to understand the environment in which the planned MD program is functioning. But there are disadvantages to using internal staff members: They may lack credibility and may be perceived as having a stake in the evaluation results. External vendors may enjoy more credibility, may be perceived as unbiased about outcomes, and may be more familiar with state-of-the-art evaluation techniques than internal staff members. But vendors are expensive to employ and are rarely aware of the organization's culture. A third option—the use of both internal staff members and external vendors—is expensive, but it often strikes an ideal balance by capitalizing on the advantages of both groups while minimizing their separate disadvantages.

Exhibit 10-6. Step-by-step procedures for conducting summative evaluation of formal, informal, and special MD methods (excluding internal group training).

It may seem that there is no way to apply summative evaluation to MD methods other than internal group training. But that is not true. It is possible to evaluate participant reactions, participant learning, participant performance, and organization performance for on-the-job training, job rotations, self-study, and other MD methods.

Here are some suggestions:

Step 1: Plan to measure participant reactions by preparing an attitude survey for use at the end of MD experiences, such as on-the-job training, job rotations, or self-study. Administer the survey just as you would at the end of an internal group training session. (In fact, one approach is to modify the participant evaluation questionnaire you use in internal group training so it can be used with other MD methods so that results can be expressed in similar ways.)

Step 2: Plan to measure participant learning by testing. To minimize participant anxiety, call these measures something other than "tests"— such as the more neutral term "learner activity." Although paper-and-pencil tests can be used with some on-the-job training, some facets of job rotations, and external training, you may find it preferable to ask learners to demonstrate what they learned.

Step 3: Plan to measure participant performance by including items on employee performance appraisals that ask how much MD methods—such as on-the-job training, job rotations, self-study, or external education—contributed to the individual's performance.

Step 4: Collect information about organizational performance by asking participants to provide information about "success cases" resulting from what they learned (see Exhibit 10-3).

There are eight basic steps to follow when conducting a program evaluation of MD.

1. *Secure a strong signal of support for the evaluation effort from top management.* Top managers signify their support by providing a mandate for the evaluation, such as a memo to management employees authorizing the program evaluation and setting forth the reason(s) it is being carried out. This mandate should at least:

> ‣ *Establish the evaluation's scope*—how much of the MD program is being examined.

‣ *Set a deadline for completion*—when the program evaluation should be completed.
‣ *Request cooperation from others in seeing the evaluation through to a successful conclusion*—who needs to help, and what help they should provide.

2. *Select or appoint an evaluation administrator to bear project management responsibility and to ensure that the project is carried to completion.* If external consulting help is to be used, the evaluation administrator becomes the organization's chief liaison with the consultant(s). He or she prepares a Request for Proposal (RFP) setting forth the mandate, purpose, scope, deadline, and other key issues for the program evaluation, identifies consulting firms qualified to carry out the evaluation project, encourages them to submit proposals, and oversees the proposal review process.

If internal staff is to be used, the evaluation administrator becomes the project manager. He or she conducts background research on the program evaluation and the planned MD program, finding out as much as possible about what led up to the perceived need for the program evaluation, results desired from it, and the scope of the planned MD program. He or she then forms initial judgments about how the program evaluation should be conducted, determines what information should be collected, decides what analytical methods will be performed, lists project steps, establishes a project time line, and selects a project team whose collective skills are adequate to complete the project successfully.

3. *Set up an entrance meeting with those who authorized the program evaluation.* The meeting's purpose is fourfold:

1. To introduce members of the evaluation team
2. To collect additional background information about the need for evaluation and the results desired from it
3. To explain the flow of project events
4. To clarify the desired "deliverable" (product) stemming from the program evaluation, such as a written or oral report

After this meeting, the evaluation administrator and team members jointly finalize a detailed program evaluation plan to guide the project.

4. *Collect and analyze data.* At this point, the program evaluation team collects information from surveys, interviews, document reviews, or observations. They may also compile results of previous program evaluations. This step is the core of the program evaluation.

text continues on page 288

Exhibit 10-7. Recommended solution to a case study on evaluation in MD.

John will not fend off a budget cut if he has not already estalished a continuing evaluation process for the MD program in his organization.

But he could have headed off the problem had he taken the following steps before he received the call from Budgeting:

Step	Activity	Remarks
1	Establish a Management Development committee in the organization (preferably composed of representatives from more than one organizational level).	This approach builds in employee involvement and creates management "buy-in."
2	Ask committee members for their help in calculating the dollar value return on investments in MD, explaining why that is important to do.	
3	Ask committee members to pick *one* problem that they believe has been addressed effectively by the MD program. (Examples might include reduced turnover in the management ranks, reduced orientation time for supervisors, or some measure of organizational effectiveness such as improved quality or reduced scrap rates).	There should be at least one "success story."
4	Ask committee members to help idenfity two or three individuals who can attest that: —*their* orientation period was reduced due to the MD program. —*they* chose not to quit because of the MD program. —*actual cost savings* or *returns on investments* were realized in their organizational units as a direct result of the MD effort.	By using one or two real people, John develops persuasive circumstantial evidence supporting the value of the MD program.
5	Estimate the value of the savings or return on investment for the actual cases in step 4 above.	While this approach may not convince serious skeptics, it will be emotionally persuasive.

Step	Activity	Remarks
6	Multiply the value of step 5 by the total number of people who participated in the MD experience/course.	Estimate the value added.
7	Estimate the total cost to operate the MD experience (including consultants' fees and staff salaries), and subtract that from the product of step 6.	Estimate the program cost, and subtract from estimated value added.
8	Multiply the total estimated savings or return on investment realized by the one MD experience/course by the number of other courses/experiences administered by the MD program in the organization.	Develop a rough estimate of total value added.
9	Ask committee members to reduce the estimate as they wish.	This step gives skeptics their chance to have their say.
10	Ask committee members to sign off that the cost savings or return on investment accurately reflects the added value provided to the organization by the MD program, in their opinion.	This sign-off indicates management "ownership" and provides independent verification of value added.
11	Publicize the results of steps 1 through 10 periodically.	This step publicizes the value of the MD program.
12	Keep track of any criticism received when using this approach, challenging critics to participate on the committee to come up with more effective approaches to evaluate the dollar value return on investments of the MD program.	This step heads off critics before their skepticism spreads.

While not foolproof, these steps would have helped John to (1) estimate the dollar value return on investments of MD efforts, (2) build management support for the MD effort, and (3) head off the budget cutter's ax—or at least make cost-cutting of the MD program difficult to justify! Try the approach yourself.

5. *Draft the evaluation report.* Having completed data collection and analysis, team members review the fruits of their labors. Team members prepare a written report to describe the background of the program evaluation, the scope of existing MD activities in the organization, the questions addressed during the program evaluation, how the questions were answered, and how the answers were analyzed. They also identify strengths and areas for improvement in the planned MD program and make recommendations for improvements.

6. *Seek response and reaction.* Team members submit a draft report to top managers and to the MD director, the MD coordinator, or MD specialists running the organization's planned MD program. At this time, the representative of the planned MD program is given an opportunity to respond to conclusions reached in the program evaluation. These responses are included in the evaluation report.

7. *Present the results to key stakeholders and decision makers.* They should receive copies of the final report detailing the program evaluation results. They may also attend an oral briefing over the report and its recommendations. Representatives of the planned MD program are invited to attend this briefing.

8. *Implement the recommendations.* Of course, the aim is to improve the planned MD program and establish or maintain a long-term direction for it. The program evaluation should help preserve and strengthen the linkage between the planned MD program and the organization's strategic plan. On the whole, a program evaluation provides a chance to assess the MD program as it contributes to the organization's mission, goals, activities, and results.

While the basic steps of a program evaluation are outlined above, other features may be added. For instance, members of a program evaluation team may:

- Conduct a competitive benchmarking study as part of the program evaluation to determine how much and how well the organization's planned MD program is funded and staffed in comparison to other organizations of the same size or in the same industry.
- Compare the organization's planned MD program to criteria set forth in the Malcolm Baldrige National Quality Award or to the organization's ability to meet those criteria.
- Collect additional information from *external* sources, such as suppliers, distributing wholesalers, retailers, customers, or franchise holders, about MD needs.

‣ Collect information about learning needs from *internal sources* such as exempt and nonexempt employees and assess how well the organization's planned MD program contributes to satisfying those needs.

Summary

This chapter showed how evaluation can provide valuable information for continuously improving a planned MD program. We also defined evaluation, described different types, summarized key obstacles to evaluation, described methods to overcome those obstacles, and provided step-by-step guidance for conducting a program evaluation.

Epilogue
Special Issues in Management Development

Management Development is influenced by some of the same issues that affect other aspects of management practice. We feel that three important related issues deserve special attention as we conclude this book: (1) globalism, (2) downsizing, and (3) team-based management.

Managers in the United States are being forced to think globally. As they do, they find that foreign competitors enjoy a significant advantage over U.S.-based corporations in the areas of labor costs, government policies, government regulations, and labor productivity. This realization has prompted U.S. corporations to reduce operating expenses in order to become more competitive internationally. Downsizing is one way to slash operating expenses dramatically. And downsizing, in turn, has led to a groundswell of interest in team-based management, which makes more efficient use of employees than do traditional approaches to management or job and organization design. By encouraging nonexempt employees to develop their abilities, work cooperatively, and assume additional responsibility, team-based management reduces the need for supervisors, middle managers, and executives. And as nonexempt employees are cross-trained to perform several jobs, fewer workers are needed to cover for absent colleagues.

In this chapter, we define globalism, downsizing, and team-based management and offer suggestions for modifying a planned MD program to take these issues into account.

Globalism

Immediately following World War II, the U.S. market was the largest in the world. American businesses reigned supreme as world-class leaders in their industries. But times have changed. "The global economic arena is no longer exclusively driven by, or designed to favor, the

United States."[1] At present, "of the 500 largest industrial corporations in the United States, at least twenty-five earn more than half of their profits overseas. Today, sixty-eight of the 156 largest multinational organizations are U.S. firms."[2] By 1992, following the unification of the European Economic Community, the U.S. will no longer be the world's largest market.

If we could reduce the world to a village of just 1,000 people, the relationship of North Americans to their fellow villagers would be starkly clear: "Of our 1,000 'neighbors,' 564 would be Asians, 210 would be Europeans, eighty-six would be Africans, eighty would be South Americans and only sixty of that 1,000—a mere 6 percent of the world's population—would be North Americans."[3] The economies of the nations in this global village are interconnected in a transnational economy in which money flows are of key importance.[4] The effects of a transnational economy have prompted increasing interest in *globalism*, "perhaps the hottest business buzzword around."[5] The term connotes a full appreciation of the need to plan, market, and serve customers internationally as well as domestically.

Effects on Businesses

Globalism has affected U.S. businesses in at least two major ways.

First, U.S. business executives can learn valuable lessons from successful foreign competitors, enabling corporations to benefit domestically from their international experience. For example, well-known management guru Peter Drucker has identified six major lessons to be learned from world-class foreign companies:

1. The value of increasing employee responsibility and commitment
2. The importance of careful management of employee benefits
3. The importance of identifying customer priorities and marketing/producing to ensure that the company meets customers' most important needs
4. An emphasis on continuous but long-term improvement, particularly in product or service quality
5. The distinction between short- and long-term initiatives, with care taken to view Management Development as a long-term initiative
6. The transformation from business interests to national interests in foreign economies[6]

Second, U.S. business executives increasingly value international markets as much as—if not more than—domestic ones. Strategic thinkers realize that the U.S. market is no longer necessarily the largest or the most lucrative. But to take full advantage of foreign markets, managers must possess special knowledge and skills, including appreciation of different cultures, legal systems, tariff structures, and exchange rates. The lack of requisite management knowledge and skills poses a significant barrier to U.S. international competitiveness: "An estimated 80 percent of U.S. businesses that could export do not, partly because their managers lack the skills and experience to respond to international competition."[7]

Effects on Management Employees

Successful management employees of the future will possess the knowledge and skills to do business internationally. In fact, "according to a recent Korn/Ferry survey of 1,500 CEOs and senior managers, by the year 2000 the shortage of U.S. managers equipped to run global businesses will be the major concern of human resource management."[8] Experienced managers will have to do more to retool themselves for the international arena than take a college course on international business, learn a foreign language, attend a university-sponsored seminar on international business, or make jaunts to foreign work sites. While those experiences can become important starting points on the road to globalism, they are no substitute for firsthand experience in doing business abroad. Often, that experience can be gained only by lengthy international assignments and international job rotations. Many large organizations have already made such experiences part of their career paths.[9]

To succeed on international assignments and job rotations, management employees must possess special skills. (A description of the prototypical twenty-first-century manager appears in Exhibit E-1.) The same skills will be needed to succeed internationally and domestically; building these skills may become a centerpiece of a Management Development curriculum, a long-term learning plan for an organization's management employees.

Effects on Management Development

How can a planned MD program contribute to an organization's ability to "go global"? How can a planned MD program help equip management employees with the skills they need to succeed internationally?

To answer those questions, MD directors and MD coordinators

Exhibit E-1. The twenty-first-century expatriate manager profile.

Core Skills	Managerial Implications
Multidimensional perspective	Has extensive multiproduct, multi-industry, multifunctional, multicompany, multicountry, and multi-environment experience.
Proficiency in line management	Has an extensive track record in successfully operating a strategic business unit(s) and/or a series of major overseas projects.
Prudent decision-making skills	Is competent, with a proven track record, in making the right strategic decisions.
Resourcefulness	Is skillful in getting himself or herself known and accepted in the host country's political hierarchy.
Cultural adaptability	Adapts quickly and easily to the foreign culture; an individual with as much experience in diverse cultures as possible.
Cultural sensitivity	Has effective skills in dealing with people of various cultures, races, nationalities, genders, religions. Also, sensitive to cultural differences.
Ability as a team builder	Is adept at bringing a culturally diverse working group together to accomplish the major mission and objective of the organization.
Physical fitness and mental maturity	Can endure the rigorous demands of an overseas assignment.
Augmented Skills	**Managerial Implications**
Computer literacy	Is comfortable exchanging strategic information electronically.
Prudent negotiating skills	Has a proven track record in conducting successful strategic business negotiations in multicultural environments.
Ability as a change agent	Has a proven track record in successfully initiating and implementing strategic organizational changes.
Visionary skills	Is quick to recognize and respond to strategic business opportunities and potential political and economic upheavals in the host country.
Effective delegation skills	Has a proven track record in participative management and ability to delegate.

Source: Cecil G. Howard, "Profile of the 21st-Century Expatriate Manager," *HRMagazine,* 437:6 (1992), p. 96. Reprinted with the permission of *HRMagazine* (formerly *Personnel Administrator*), published by the Society for Human Resource Management, Alexandria, Va.

must be willing to facilitate a change in corporate culture. They should start by building top management support—as well as appropriate skills among top management ranks for conducting business internationally. That makes MD the driving force to help an organization "go global" from inside out. In consultation with key decision makers, the MD director or coordinator should:

- Formulate a clear and simple mission statement.
- Have the systems and structures in place to ensure an effective flow of information.
- Create "matrix minds" to facilitate conflict management.
- Develop global career paths.
- Use cultural differences among employees and markets as a resource.
- Implement worldwide management education and team development programs.[10]

A new mission statement will be needed to drive the organization and provide a mandate for a new global MD program. The MD director or coordinator also needs to review pending or existing learning experiences abroad in order to increase communications between international and domestic operations.

When assessing needs, establishing curricula, formulating performance objectives, preparing instructional materials, or selecting MD methods, the MD director or coordinator must take international business needs and other cultures into account. Career paths that include international assignments or job rotation programs must also be established. The organization must use available talent within the organization or hire it from outside so that culturally diverse perspectives are integrated into planned MD efforts. Finally, the MD program as a whole must be reviewed so that its quality is consistent on a worldwide basis even when activities and methods differ by cultural context.

Often, an on-site MD program will have to be established in locations abroad. This decentralizes the effort, making it more responsive to local cultures and business conditions. In large corporations, the corporate-level MD program can serve as troubleshooter, brain trust, and helper. But the knowledge of the culture resides locally.

Downsizing

The term *downsizing* was coined in the 1980s. A more recent euphemism is *rightsizing*. Both terms connote layoffs, voluntary retirement programs, or other reductions in force (RIFs) among full-time employees working for an organization.

In the late 1980s and 1990s, U.S. corporations downsized on a massive scale. Large-scale work force cuts at General Motors and IBM generated national and even international publicity, but similar reductions occurred in other *Fortune* 500 corporations, and many others, as well. Between 1989 and 1991, 2,200 people *per day* lost their jobs through a combination of downsizing, plant closings, and business moves abroad. The U.S. Bureau of Labor Statistics reported a loss of 4.3 million jobs in the United States between 1985 and 1989.[11] Between 1989 and 1992, over 1 million jobs paying over $40,000 per year were eliminated from the U.S. economy.[12]

Causes of Downsizing

Downsizing stems from myriad causes. To cite a few:

- *Tough international competitive conditions* in which foreign firms enjoy a comparative advantage because of lower labor costs
- *Deregulation and industry competition* in which employee reduction efforts in one organization stimulate similar cuts across the industry
- *High employee benefit expenses* (approaching 50 percent on top of employee salary expense) caused primarily by skyrocketing employer health insurance premiums and workers compensation
- *A desire by top managers to increase profits by reducing staff* to mollify sophisticated investors.
- *A belief that reducing staff, particularly at middle and higher levels, will increase efficiency* by pushing decisions down and reducing unnecessary paperwork
- *A desire to increase employee involvement and decision making by enriching jobs,* reducing unnecessary supervisory, middle management, and even top management positions
- *Structural changes in the U.S. economy* in which high-paying manufacturing jobs are being replaced by lower-paying service jobs
- *Automation,* the substitution of technological devices and/or more efficient methods of work processing for human workers
- *Plant shutdowns and business relocations* prompted by lower labor costs abroad

Some industries may also be affected by unique conditions that stimulate downsizing. One example is government agencies that are caught

between inflationary employment costs on one side and declining tax
revenues on the other.

Approaches to Downsizing

Downsizing too frequently conjures up an unpleasant scenario in which
recently hired employees are herded into a room on a Friday and are
unceremoniously handed the dreaded "pink slips"—a *scorched-earth
approach* to downsizing. While this approach is fast and efficient, its
effects can be devastating to organizational productivity and employee
morale. Its aftereffects haunt an organization for years in several ways:

- Increased turnover, an echo of the job insecurity felt by the
  survivors of a downsizing experience
- Reduced corporate ability to fill key positions as the incumbents
  leave, a result of eliminating an entire generation from an organization's work force
- Increased problems in meeting affirmative action goals, since in
  many organizations downsizing particularly affects women, minorities, and the young, all of whom often have less job seniority
  than other employees

However, there are alternatives to the ignominious scorched-earth
approach. For example:

1. *Reduction through attrition.* As employees resign, retire, or
otherwise leave an organization, they are not replaced. This policy
avoids a bloodbath. But a major problem is that not all positions are
equally important to production or service delivery, and the organization may be unable to sustain a naively established but well-inten-
tioned policy of across-the-board staff reduction through attrition. Management may be forced to fill some positions to preserve production or
service levels. Moreover, turnover in different functions or job classes
may occur in a lopsided way, leading to larger reductions in some areas
than in others. A more advisable approach is a *selective* reduction
through attrition, with staffing goals for each function and job class
clearly established in advance.

2. *Reduction through voluntary retirement or termination programs.* Employees are given special incentives to retire early or to quit
voluntarily. To qualify, employees may be required to meet objective
criteria, such as a specified length of service. This approach, like
downsizing through attrition, avoids a bloodbath. But a major problem

is that management may have trouble selectively applying the incentives: Key job incumbents may choose to take advantage of the incentives before the organization has time to prepare replacements, leading to spot talent shortages. Many such shortages have to be handled through external recruitment. A succession planning program, put in place some time before a voluntary retirement or termination effort, can mitigate the loss of key job incumbents.

3. *Layer reduction or delayering.* This policy has become a fad and has been practiced by such large organizations as General Electric, 3M, Firestone Tire & Rubber, Ford, Westinghouse Electric, Hewlett-Packard, and Apple Computer.[13] Advocates tout its value in reducing the "information filters" separating hourly employees and higher-level management, purportedly leading to faster and clearer information flow up and down the organization. As layers are reduced, higher-level managers find they have more—and different kinds—of people to supervise. This broad span of control works as long as the jobs are not highly specialized. But if the jobs are highly specialized, the incumbents require sophisticated attention, which is difficult for managers to provide when they have too many people assigned to them. When the span of control grows too large, employees suffer from too little individualized attention, coaching, and feedback.

4. *Reduction in the number of full-time employees through various methods:*

- Substituting part-time or temporary workers for full-time employees
- Increasing permanent part-time employees in place of full-time employees
- Increasing overtime for full-time employees rather than hiring additional staff

These options, however, are suitable only as short-term measures.

The first, substituting part-time for full-time employees, does hold down labor costs. But it can become expensive, especially when an organization must pay a temporary agency an hourly fee that is much higher than the hourly wage of a full-time employee. Nonetheless, the trend points toward increased use of professional or managerial temps, as well as of clerical temps.[14]

Permanent part-time employees are another option. They can be substituted for full-time employees to hold down employee benefit expenses, since part-time workers are rarely eligible for benefits. Often permanent part-time employees are moonlighters, whose number reached 7.2 million in the U.S. work force in 1991 and 40 percent of whom hold part-time jobs because of economic necessity.[15] While part-time employees can help organizations meet short-term staffing needs, they can be difficult to recruit and retain, especially for daytime employment. Often they are seeking full-time employment and become turnover statistics as soon as they find it.

Overtime is yet another alternative. While it can be used to hold down the employee benefit expenses of full-time workers, it usually works as a short-term solution only. Employees who work overtime for prolonged periods suffer the effects of stress and burnout. Turnover increases. The available evidence already suggests that U.S. employers are using overtime as a strategy for holding down staffing needs—and stress is building among the work force as a result:

> According to recent Bureau of Labor Statistics figures, nearly 25 percent of the 88 million full-time workers in the United States spend forty-nine or more hours on the job each week. That's up from 18 percent just ten years ago. . . . Of those who have supervisory responsibilities, 53 percent [in a recent survey] report their jobs are highly stressful. Nearly half feel more pressure to prove their value to their employers because of the recession.[16]

Thus overtime has decided drawbacks as a long-term strategy for staff reduction.

5. *Reduction by alternative cost-saving measures.* Employers may establish ad hoc cost-saving teams to generate ideas to cut expenses and avoid unpleasant staffing reductions. Such teams may be cross-functional, composed of individuals from many areas of the organization. They operate much like quality circles, a fad in the 1980s. But the primary benefits of such teams are usually realized in the first year. If they continue in operation beyond that, their results rarely equal first-year cost savings.

6. *Work process reengineering.* This is a popular new concept, sometimes linked to a total quality management (TQM) effort. The essence of work process reengineering is "out of box" (creative) thinking. Exempt and nonexempt employees alike are asked to approach what they do and how they do it with a fresh perspective. Work process reengineering is similar to zero-based budgeting—except that a work process rather than a budget is the focus of attention.

Key questions posed by work process reengineering include:

‣ What are the most costly—and most important—work processes performed by the organization?

‣ If the organization were *starting* these functions for the first time, how would they be set up?

‣ What other organizations are especially well-known for these processes? How do those "world-class" organizations perform the processes?

‣ What changes can be made to streamline an organization's work processes to bring them in line with "world-class" organizations, cut needless costs, and reduce superfluous staff?

The answers to these questions can provide valuable guidance for introducing innovation. Useless paperwork is often the first thing eliminated. Employees displaced by changes to work processes are retrained for more organizationally beneficial processes.

7. *Team-based management.* This is discussed later in this chapter.

Downsizing's Effects on Management Employees

Downsizing's effects on management employees depend, to a considerable extent, on the approach used. If a scorched-earth approach is used, downsizing's effects can be profoundly unpleasant. Quality vanishes. Turnover increases. Morale suffers dramatically. Stressed-out people go on overload. These negative feelings affect exempt as well as nonexempt employees, posing a major challenge to management, especially since management also keenly feels downsizing's effects.

The available evidence suggests that wholesale staff reductions of the scorched-earth variety are rarely effective. A survey of 1,005 U.S.-based organizations by the Wyatt Company revealed that downsizing is driven by three key forces: (1) a desire to reduce expenses, (2) a desire for increased profits, and (3) a desire for increased return on investment to shareholders.[17] But "Wyatt found that only 46 percent of the companies met their expense-reduction goals, less than one-third met their profit goals, and only 21 percent increased shareholder ROI."[18] Some companies end up downsizing more than once. They are like undisciplined dieters who gain weight after going off their diets and must later diet again to keep the weight off.

Managing the Effects of Downsizing

At least ten strategies may be used to rethink the way work is performed in the wake of downsizing:

1. *Focus on purpose.* The organization and each work group should clarify its mission and focus solely on it.
2. *Focus on inputs.* Each work group, and the organization as a whole, should look at how the work could be streamlined to reduce staffing needs.
3. *Focus on time and scheduling.* Managers must be acutely aware of the importance of mobilizing resources quickly to cover spot needs when they occur.
4. *Focus on existing work first.* Avoid time-consuming new initiatives that distract management and staff from getting the work out.
5. *Restructure jobs.* Enrich and enlarge jobs.
6. *Restructure work groups.* Reexamine the way work groups are organized, and seek more effective organizational structure.
7. *Contract out.* Shift work outside the work group or organization.
8. *Use part-time assistance.* Rely, as much as is practical and cost-effective, on part-time assistance.
9. *Use overtime.* Ask full-time employees to work overtime in brief spurts to hold down benefit expenses and to meet short-term needs for additional staffing.
10. *Combine methods.* Do not rely on a single method to cope with the aftereffects of downsizing.[19]

Each of these approaches suggests that management employees must cultivate special skills to handle the aftereffects of downsizing. Those skills are a rightful focus of the planned MD program.

Downsizing and Management Development

Downsizing affects management employees in the following ways:

- It changes the responsibilities associated with exempt and nonexempt jobs.
- It creates increasing attitudinal problems resulting from stress, pressure, job insecurity, and increased workload for the same compensation.
- It alters career paths and reduces opportunities for upward mobility.
- It creates increased pressures on management employees to see that the work gets out despite adverse conditions created by having too few people to do the work.
- It creates increasing pressures from higher-level management to

maintain product or service quality and work output despite having fewer people.

In addition, a downsized organization generally creates an environment in which MD programs of all kinds become more difficult to sponsor. For instance, management employees in a downsized organization feel they have less time to participate in *any* planned learning experience. Even when they hunger for these opportunities, they may be unable to get away from the work site during the day and feel too exhausted to take materials home at night. Downsizing is often accompanied by cost reduction efforts, and MD efforts have been hit the hardest during the U.S. recession of the early 1990s.[20]

To cope with these efforts, MD directors and coordinators must be creative. They must come up with ways to ensure that the planned MD program continues despite the tough conditions created by downsizing and cost reduction. To that end, they may:

- Appeal to top management for special support.
- Focus learning activities on "survival skills"—ways to do more with less, cope with stress, and handle overtime.
- Ask for suggestions from steering or advisory committees with which they work.
- Engineer special incentives for management employees who participate in or sponsor MD efforts.
- Build accountability for MD results into management job descriptions, performance appraisals, and other employment decisions.

Use the activity in Exhibit E-2 to structure your thinking about ways to encourage MD efforts in an organization after downsizing.

Team-Based Management

Team-based management is an exciting new philosophy about managing people and organizing work. When defining the concept of *team*, we find it helpful to distinguish variations on a continuum, illustrated in Exhibit E-3. Teams may be project-oriented, semiautonomous, or autonomous. Autonomous teams are usually called *self-directed teams*. Differences between a traditional work group and a team are described in Exhibit E-4.

A *traditional work group* consists of a supervisor and nonexempt employees. The supervisor controls others to ensure that work output and quality are sustained. A traditional work group is responsible for

Exhibit E-2. Activity on encouraging MD efforts in the wake of downsizing.

Directions: Use this worksheet to help structure your thinking—and that of others in your organization—about Management Development in the wake of downsizing. Answer the questions on your own or as part of a small group.

---

1. How was downsizing handled in the organization? (Describe how many employees were affected and over what time period, and what organizational needs led to the downsizing effort.)

2. What have been the effects of downsizing on nonexempt and exempt employees? (Describe how the downsizing has affected work processes, turnover, product or service quality, and other key strategic organizational issues.)

3. What special learning needs have been created by the downsizing?

4. How can the special needs created by downsizing be met through the planned MD program?

5. What should be done by the organization to encourage MD in the wake of downsizing? (*Provide an action plan.*)

---

only one part of a work process. Employees have tightly structured jobs that are akin to "boxes" of tasks governed by job descriptions. As a result of the way the work is organized and divided, cooperation among group members is not necessarily encouraged. Indeed, each employee competes with others for individual merit pay raises, work group

Exhibit E-3. A continuum from traditional work group to autonomous team.

Traditional Work Group	Project or Cross-Functional Team	Semiautonomous Team	Autonomous or Self-Directed Team
‣ Supervisor "controls" ‣ The work performed is part of a larger process ‣ Jobs are specialized ‣ Top-down decision making prevails	‣ Leader is elected or appointed ‣ Coexists with traditional work groups ‣ Spans the gap separating traditional work groups ‣ Exists to perform a special function ‣ Members are chosen on the basis of the team's mission ‣ Member roles are determined by team mission	‣ Team leader "facilitates" ‣ The work performed is part of a larger process, but workers are cross-trained and gradually prepared to do the whole process ‣ Jobs are increasingly general ‣ Combination of top-down and bottom-up decision making	‣ There is no supervisor or team leader ‣ Workers perform the whole task ‣ Jobs are generalized (a team-based job description) ‣ Bottom-up decision making

resources, and the supervisor's attention. If employees are asked to help co-workers, they may object by noting, "That's not in my job description."

A *project, or cross-functional, team* is an effort to bridge the chasm separating activities of work groups, hierarchical levels, geographic locations, and organizational functions. Exempt and/or nonexempt employees work together on special tasks, such as troubleshooting a problem, preparing for a new product line, or discussing ways to streamline production. The project leader is either elected by the project team itself or appointed by a top manager whose authority spans the groups represented. The project leader's authority is limited solely to the project. The project or cross-functional task may endure for some time, and members may rotate on or off the project or cross-functional

Exhibit E-4. Differences between a traditional work group and a team.

Characteristics of Traditional Work Group	Characteristics of a Team
‣ Large—18 to 20 people	‣ Smaller—10–12 people
‣ Less cohesive	‣ More team spirit/cohesiveness
‣ More individual incentives and more credit given to individuals	‣ More group-oriented incentives and credit for group accomplishments
‣ Individual "box" of tasks	‣ "Everybody's tasks"
‣ More "that is not my job" thinking	‣ "I can do that or I want to learn how" thinking
‣ Great emphasis on individual accountability	‣ Greater emphasis on team accountability
‣ Tightly controlled by rules and procedures	‣ More flexible—rules are guidelines that can be broken so long as the underlying principles of the rule are observed

team. On the other hand, the task may have a limited time horizon and the team may disband when the mission is completed.

A *semiautonomous team* is prepared for expanded responsibilities. The supervisor, called a *team leader,* is expected to serve as encourager, coach, on-the-job helper, and group facilitator. Team leaders do not order others around; rather, they help group members interact better among themselves. Members of a semiautonomous team, like a traditional work group, focus their attention on only one part of a work process. However, they may be in training to absorb all the parts of a process. Work responsibilities are not divided up into the "boxes" of individual jobs; rather, the sides of "boxes" are broken out so all work responsibilities are shared by team members. There may be only one or two job descriptions for an entire team, because so many duties are jointly shared.

Cross-training is heavily emphasized in semiautonomous groups, and each team member is expected to master all tasks performed by the team. Employees often react to the introduction of semiautonomous teams with enthusiasm, since teams promote job enrichment and job enlargement. A few, however, may complain that they are being asked to do more without commensurate pay increases. That complaint may create pressure to review, and change, from a traditional compensation program to one that "pays for knowledge."

An *autonomous, or self-directed, work team* "is an intact group of employees responsible for a 'whole' work process or segment that delivers a product or service to an internal or external customer."[21] There is no supervisor or team leader; those duties are dispersed across team members. Employees must therefore exercise self-management and self-control, and cooperation is highly valued. There is a *team job description* that encompasses all team responsibilities. Gone is the bureaucratic view of jobs as "boxes." Team members are expected to master gradually all activities or responsibilities listed on the team job description and are cross-trained to that end. Cooperation, because synonymous with teamwork, is very important and highly valued.

Benefits of Team-Based Management

Team-based management has three major benefits.

1. *It decreases the need for staff.* It reduces dependence on supervisors, managers, and executives in decision making and reduces the need for backup workers to cover for sick, vacationing, or otherwise absent employees. Workers are trained to do all the tasks of a work group and are encouraged to make independent decisions.

2. *It increases the speed and quality of decisions.* Employees do more than participate in decision making. Indeed, they are empowered to act on their own without receiving advance approval from higher-level management. Because decisions rest in the hands of those who do the work and/or interact directly with customers, team-based management is frequently tied to Total Quality Management (TQM) programs. (Nine key requirements for implementing TQM are listed in Exhibit E-5. Note that team-based management is especially linked to point 4, which emphasizes the importance of employee involvement.)

3. *It promotes work-group cohesiveness.* It helps people meet deep human belongingness needs at precisely the time in the United States when social conditions outside the workplace are undermining the satisfaction of those needs. Teams can even, on some occasions, become a substitute for family.

Effects of Team-Based Management

To introduce team-based management successfully in an organization, management employees must accept and live by values different from those corporations have historically embodied. Evidence suggests that management values are indeed changing, with interest in workers increasing faster than self-interest.[22] Against that backdrop, manage-

Exhibit E-5. Key requirements for implementing Total Quality Management.

1. Top managers must set the example and provide full support for making the organization responsive to the needs of its customers.
2. The customer should be the key focus of all organizational efforts, and the customer's definitions of quality is far more important than definitions provided by an organization's management or its employees.
3. The organization should apply benchmarking to uncover the best and most effective methods of serving customers.
4. All employees of the organization should participate fully in the quest for quality.
5. Communication of all kinds, and particularly about quality, should be emphasized throughout the organization.
6. Training, education, and development at all levels must be considered vital to meeting customer needs.
7. Measurement is the only way to assess progress in the quest for a customer-oriented and quality-driven organization. Standards must be established and used, and they should be focused on improving organizational and individual performance.
8. Rewards, incentives, and methods or recognition should be tied to quality measures and customer needs.
9. Organizational improvement should be long-term and continuous rather than short-term and sporadic.

ment roles must change, and management employees must master new skills to enact those roles.

Of course, the values, roles, and skills they need depend on the type of team-based management adopted by the organization. As Exhibit E-3 illustrates, management employees in an organization with cross-functional teams must be comfortable working amid the ambiguity often present in a project-oriented environment. They must be willing to accept matrixed responsibilities in which more than one person is accountable for getting results. Above all, they must prize creativity, since it is creativity that leads to breakthrough thinking and cost savings.

Management employees in an organization with semiautonomous teams must function as group facilitators. They must exude enthusiasm and excitement, serving as workplace cheerleaders for team efforts. More often than not, they must be very knowledgeable about group dynamics, possess strong interpersonal skills, and be capable of handling conflict resolution with expert skill.

Management employees in an organization with self-directed teams are usually limited to middle managers and executives only— since nonexempt employees assume most responsibilities traditionally accorded to supervisors. In such a setting, management employees function as coaches, group facilitators, and trainers. Their aim is to infuse management knowledge, skills, and abilities throughout the organization, spreading self-management to the lowest level possible. This requires a fundamental culture change in most organizational settings, made all the harder because it goes against the grain of the top-down approach to decision making that has been prevalent in the United States since the days of Frederick Taylor and of a changing, more leisure-driven, work ethic among many U.S. workers.

Team-Based Management and Management Development

The introduction of team-based management requires a radical culture change in most organizations. The MD director or coordinator is usually the spearhead or spiritual leader of this change. Frequently, it means that exempt and nonexempt employees alike must discard notions they have acquired over years of experience about the best or the most appropriate approaches to management practice. Some can't or won't make the change. They may prefer alternatives, such as early retirement, transfer, or departure from the organization. Such moves, when motivated by what is best for the organization and the individual, should be permitted or even encouraged.

The introduction of team-based management should be handled in a way that reflects the high value placed on employee involvement in decision making. Involvement is one important goal of such an effort. To that end, many organizations begin with one or more management retreats at the highest levels. Facilitated by the MD director or coordinator—perhaps with the valuable assistance of an outside vendor who has experience in introducing such changes in other organizations—the retreat(s) first reviews the competitive and business needs driving the change. From there, the participants formulate their own definitions of teams, clarify desired roles of nonexempt employees in a team setting, clarify desired roles of management employees *at each level* after the change, pinpoint key issues affecting implementation, and devise a unified action plan. High-level retreats should be followed up by retreats for employees at lower levels in the organizational hierarchy. Once participants understand the reasons to make changes and have been involved through *action learning* in the changes that are to be made, they should receive detailed training to build the skills they need to make the culture change successful.

Typically, the introduction of team-based management necessitates a review of the responsibilities at each level in the organization. One way to do that is to form task forces to rewrite executive, management, supervisory, and nonexempt job descriptions as they should appear after the successful introduction of teams. These job descriptions then provide a useful starting point for subsequent changes in the planned MD program, leading to new efforts to assess needs, formulate performance objectives, identify or prepare instructional materials, select and deliver appropriate MD methods to meet identified learning needs, and evaluate results. Another, related way is to conduct DACUM sessions at each level to formulate desired job responsibilities. (For a brief description of the DACUM method, see Exhibit 3-2.)

Team-based management is still a very new approach to management and to job/organization design. It is unclear whether the long-term results will match up to the short-term successes that have been reported. But it does appear to offer a valid and fascinating alternative to traditional views about management and methods of management. If it does succeed, all employees—not just exempt workers—will become eligible to participate in planned MD programs. And that is truly an exciting prospect!

Summary

This chapter focused on three important topical issues that are influencing planned MD programs in the United States: (1) globalism, (2) downsizing, and (3) team-based management. The three issues are related. In the chapter we defined what they are, how organizations can approach them, how they affect management employees, and how a planned MD program can take them into account.

Notes

Chapter 1

1. A. Mumford, "Myth and Realities in Developing Directors," *Personnel Management*, 19:2 (1987), p. 29.
2. Leonard Nadler and Zeace Nadler, *Developing Human Resources*, 3rd ed. (San Francisco: Jossey-Bass, 1989), p. 4.
3. Ibid.
4. Ibid., p. 74.
5. John Lawrie, "Differentiate Between Training, Education, and Development," *Personnel Journal*, 69:10 (1990), p. 44.
6. Lester Bittel and John Newstrom, *What Every Supervisor Should Know*, 6th ed. (New York: McGraw-Hill, 1990), p. 7.
7. Richard Wellins, William Byham, and Jeanne Wilson, *Empowered Teams: Creating Self-Directed Work Groups That Improve Quality, Productivity, and Participation* (San Francisco: Jossey-Bass, 1991), p. 9.
8. Victor Vroom, *Work and Motivation* (New York: Wiley, 1964).
9. "What the Recession Means for HR," *Issues in HR* (January 1992), p. 3.
10. Michelle Martinez, "Glass Walls Must Tumble Before Ceiling Breaks," *HR News*, 11:4 (1992), p. A3.
11. Anthony Carnevale and Leila Gainer, *The Learning Enterprise* (Alexandria, Va.: American Society for Training and Development and U.S. Department of Labor, Employment and Training Administration, 1989), pp. 23, 25, 28.
12. Allen Kraut, Patricia Pedigo, Douglas McKenna, and Marvin Dunnette, "The Role of the Manager: What's Really Important in Different Management Jobs," *Academy of Management Executive*, 3:4 (1989), p. 287.
13. Ibid., p. 290.
14. Bittel and Newstrom, op. cit., p. 7.
15. Carnevale and Gainer, op. cit., p. 28.
16. Ibid., p. 30.
17. "The Training Gap," *Training and Development Journal*, 45:3 (1991), pp. 9–10.
18. Jack Gordon, "Training Budgets: Recession Takes a Bite 1991," *Training*, 28:10 (1991), p. 38.
19. Kraut et al., op. cit., p. 287.
20. Max Wortman, Jr., and JoAnn Sperling, *Defining the Manager's Job*, 2nd ed. (New York: AMACOM, 1975).
21. Chris Lee, "Who Gets Trained in What 1991," *Training*, 28:10 (1991), p. 55.
22. Carnevale and Gainer, op. cit., p. 26.
23. Lee, op. cit., p. 48.
24. Gordon, op. cit., p. 38.
25. *Reinventing the CEO* (New York: Korn/Ferry International and Columbia University Graduate School of Business, 1989).

26. Carnevale and Gainer, op. cit., p. 25.
27. Ibid.
28. John Burgoyne, "Management Development for the Individual and the Organization," *Personnel Management* (June 1988), p. 41.
29. Ibid.

Chapter 2

1. Jan de Jong, "Final Word: The Future of On-Site Training," *Human Resource
Development Quarterly*, 2:4 (1991), p. 331.
2. Manuel London, *Developing Managers: A Guide to Motivating and Preparing People
for Successful Managerial Careers* (San Francisco: Jossey-Bass, 1985), pp. 119–136.
3. George Morrisey, *Management By Objectives and Results in the Public Sector*
(Reading, Mass.: Addison-Wesley, 1976), p. 25.
4. R. Frizell and William Gellerman, "Integrating the Human and Business Dimen-
sions of Management and Organization Development," in Sidney Mailick, Solomon
Hoberman, and Steven J. Wall, eds., *The Practice of Management Development* (New
York: Praeger, 1988), pp. 27–38.
5. Wendell French and Cecil H. Bell, Jr., *Organization Development: Behavioral
Science Interventions for Organization Improvement*, 4th ed. (Englewood Cliffs, N.J.:
Prentice-Hall, 1990).
6. William J. Rothwell and H. C. Kazanas, "Participation: Key to Integrating Plan-
ning and Training?" *Performance and Instruction*, 26:9,10 (1987), pp. 27–31;
William J. Rothwell and H. C. Kazanas, "Training: Key to Strategic Management,"
Performance Improvement Quarterly, 3:1 (1990), pp. 42–56.
7. William J. Rothwell and H. C. Kazanas, "Results of a 1992 Survey on Management
Development Practices in the U.S." (Urbana, Ill.: Department of Vocational and
Technical Education, 1992, unpublished).
8. William J. Rothwell and H. C. Kazanas, *Strategic Human Resource Development*
(Englewood Cliffs, N.J.: Prentice-Hall, 1989).
9. Anthony J. Fresina and Associates, *The Identification and Development of High
Potential Managers* (Palatine, Ill.: Executive Knowledgeworks, 1987).
10. A. Spector, "The Human Resource Development Policy Study: Identification and
Analysis of Human Resource Development Policy in Selected U.S. Corporations,"
doctoral dissertation, George Washington University, 1985.
11. Lise Saari, Terry Johnson, Steven McLaughlin, and Denise Zimmerle, "A Survey of
Management Training and Education Practices in U.S. Companies," *Personnel
Psychology*, 41 (1988), pp. 739–740.
12. Morrisey, op. cit., p. 25.

Chapter 3

1. William J. Rothwell and H. C. Kazanas, *Mastering the Instructional Design Process:
A Systematic Approach* (San Francisco: Jossey-Bass, 1992).
2. W. McGehee and P. Thayer, *Training in Business and Industry* (New York: Wiley,
1961).
3. Milan Kubr and Joseph Prokopenko, *Diagnosing Management Training and Development Needs: Concepts and Techniques* (Geneva: International Labour Office,
1989).
4. Lise Saari, Terry Johnson, Steven McLaughlin, and Denise Zimmerle, "A Survey of
Management Training and Education Practices in U.S. Companies," *Personnel
Psychology,* 41 (1988), p. 734.
5. Robert Camp, *Benchmarking: The Search for Industry Best Practices That Lead to*

Superior Performance (Milwaukee: Quality Press; White Plains, N.Y.: Quality Resources, 1989).

6. *Management Development Survey Report* (Alexandria, Va.: American Society for Training and Development, 1992), p. 3.

7. Dugan Laird, *Approaches to Training and Development*, 2nd ed. (Reading, Mass.: Addison-Wesley, 1985), pp. 49–50.

8. Ibid.

9. William J. Rothwell, "HRD and the Americans with Disabilities Act," *Training and Development*, 45:8 (1991), pp. 45–47.

10. Thomas L. Quick, *Training Managers So They Can Really Manage: Confessions of a Frustrated Trainer* (San Francisco: Jossey-Bass, 1991).

11. William J. Rothwell and H. J. Sredl, *The ASTD Reference Guide to Professional HRD Roles and Competencies*, 2nd ed. (Amherst, Mass.: Human Resource Development Press, 1992).

12. Tim R. V. Davis, "Whose Job Is Management Development?—Comparing the Choices," *Journal of Management Development*, 9:1 (1990), pp. 58–70.

Chapter 4

1. K. Egan, "What Is Curriculum?" *Curriculum Inquiry*, 8:1 (1978), pp. 65–72.

2. Julia R. Galosy, "Curriculum Design for Management Training," *Training and Development Journal*, 37:1 (1983), p. 48.

3. William J. Rothwell, "Strategic Curriculum Design for Management Training," *Journal of Management Development*, 3:3 (1984), pp. 39–52.

4. Ibid.

5. Ibid.

6. Ibid.

7. Ibid.

8. William J. Rothwell and H. C. Kazanas, "Curriculum Planning for Training: The State of the Art," *Performance Improvement Quarterly*, 1:3 (1988), pp. 2–16.

Chapter 5

1. Ron Zemke, "In Search of a Training Philosophy," *Training*, 22:10 (1985), pp. 93–94, 96, 98.

2. Melville Dalton, "Conflicts Between Staff and Line Managerial Officers," *American Sociological Review*, 15 (1950), pp. 342–351.

3. Frederick Hills, *Compensation Decision Making* (Chicago: Dryden Press, 1987).

4. Dale Feuer, "Paying for Knowledge," *Training*, 24:5 (1987), pp. 57–58, 60, 61–66.

5. Hills, op. cit.

6. Chris Lee, "Who Gets Trained in What 1991," *Training*, 28:10 (1991), p. 55.

7. Chris Lee, "Trainers' Careers," *Training*, 22:10 (1985), pp. 75–81.

8. Robert Fulmer, "Corporate Management Development and Education: The State of the Art," *Journal of Management Development*, 7:2 (1988), p. 65.

Chapter 6

1. "New Survey on Senior-Level and Executive Training," *The Business of Training: News and Trends for Training Executives*, January 1990, p. 2.

2. *Management Development Survey Report* (Alexandria, Va.: American Society for Training and Development, 1992), p. 2.

3. Ibid.

4. Lise Saari et al., "A Survey of Management Training and Education Practices in U.S. Companies," *Personnel Psychology,* 41 (1988), pp. 731–743.
5. Ibid., p. 735.
6. Thomas L. Quick, *Training Managers So They Can Really Manage: Confessions of a Frustrated Trainer* (San Francisco: Jossey-Bass, 1991).
7. Dugan Laird, *Approaches to Training and Development,* 2nd ed. (Reading, Mass.: Addison-Wesley, 1985), pp. 49–50.
8. Robert Gagne and Leslie Briggs, *Principles of Instructional Design,* 2nd ed. (New York: Holt, Rinehart and Winston, 1979).

Chapter 7

1. Arthur Deegan, *Succession Planning: Key to Corporate Excellence* (New York: Wiley, 1986).
2. Anthony J. Fresina and Associates, *The Identification and Development of High Potential Managers* (Palatine, Ill.: Executive Knowledgeworks, 1987).
3. William J. Rothwell and H. J. Sredl, *The ASTD Reference Guide to Professional HRD Roles and Competencies,* 2nd ed. (Amherst, Mass.: Human Resource Development Press, 1992).
4. Zandy Leibowitz, Caela Farren, and Beverly Kaye, *Designing Career Development Systems* (San Francisco: Jossey-Bass, 1986).
5. Kathleen Christensen, *Flexible Staffing and Scheduling in U.S. Corporations* (New York: The Conference Board, 1989).
6. Leibowitz, Farren, and Kaye, op. cit.
7. Stephen Merman and Zandy Leibowitz, *Career Development Systems: Questions Worth Asking and Answers Worth Questioning* (Alexandria, Va.: American Society for Training and Development, 1987).
8. Barbara Moses and B. J. Chakiris, "The Manager as Career Counselor," *Training and Development Journal,* 43:7 (1989), pp. 60–65.
9. Ibid.
10. Donald Kanter and Philip H. Mirvis, *The Cynical Americans: Living and Working in an Age of Discontent and Disillusion* (San Francisco: Jossey-Bass, 1989).
11. Anthony Carnevale and Leila Gainer, *The Learning Enterprise* (Alexandria, Va.: American Society for Training and Development and U.S. Department of Labor, Employment and Training Administration, 1989), p. 25.
12. Chris Lee, "Who Gets Trained in What 1991," *Training,* 28:10 (1991), p. 55.
13. Ibid.
14. Ibid.
15. Thomas L. Quick, *Training Managers So They Can Really Manage: Confessions of a Frustrated Trainer* (San Francisco: Jossey-Bass, 1991).
16. Wesley Foshay, Kenneth Silber, and Odin Westgaard, *Instructional Design Competencies: The Standards* (Iowa City, Iowa: International Board of Standards for Training, Performance and Instruction, 1986).
17. Ibid.
18. Walter Dick and Lou Carey, *The Systematic Design of Instruction,* 2nd ed. (Glenview, Ill.: Scott-Foresman, 1985).
19. A. Huczynski, *Encyclopedia of Management Development Methods* (London: Gower, 1983).
20. Chris Lee, "Who Gets Trained in What 1991," *Training,* 28:10 (1991), p. 55.
21. Susan Butruille and Lee Allen, *Lesson Design and Development* (Alexandria, Va.: American Society for Training and Development, 1989).
22. Donald Kirkpatrick, *Evaluating Training Programs* (Madison, Wis.: American Society for Training and Development, 1975).
23. *Management Development Survey Report* (Alexandria, Va.: American Society for Training and Development, 1992).

24. William J. Rothwell and H. C. Kazanas, *Strategic Human Resource Development* (Englewood Cliffs, N.J.: Prentice-Hall, 1989).
25. Howard Shenson, *How to Develop and Promote Successful Seminars and Workshops: The Definitive Guide to Creating and Marketing Seminars, Workshops, Classes, and Conferences* (New York: Wiley, 1990).
26. Lise Saari, Terry Johnson, Steven McLaughlin, and Denise Zimmerle, "A Survey of Management Training and Education Practices in U.S. Companies," *Personnel Psychology*, 41 (1988), p. 735.
27. J. Naisbitt and P. Auburdene, *Reinventing the Corporation: Transforming Your Job and Your Company for the New Information Society* (New York: Warner, 1985), p. 51.
28. J. Kouzes and B. Posner, *The Leadership Challenge: How to Get Extraordinary Things Done in Organizations* (San Francisco: Jossey-Bass, 1989), p. 285.
29. Leonard Nadler and Zeace Nadler, *Developing Human Resources*, 3rd ed. (San Francisco: Jossey-Bass, 1989), pp. 65–66.
30. William J. Rothwell and H. C. Kazanas, "Issues and Practices in Management Job Rotation Programs as Perceived by HRD Professionals," *Performance Improvement Quarterly*, 5:1 (1992), pp. 49–69.
31. Ibid.
32. Ibid.
33. Ibid.
34. Ibid.
35. Malcolm Knowles, *Using Learning Contracts: Practical Approaches to Individualizing and Structuring Learning* (San Francisco: Jossey-Bass, 1986).
36. William J. Rothwell and H. C. Kazanas, "Issues and Practices in Management Job Rotation Programs as Perceived by HRD Professionals," *Performance Improvement Quarterly*, 5:1 (1992), pp. 49–69.
37. T. Gilmore, *Making a Leadership Change: How Organizations and Leaders Can Handle Leadership Transitions Successfully* (San Francisco: Jossey-Bass, 1988).
38. William J. Rothwell and H. C. Kazanas, "Issues and Practices in Management Job Rotation Programs as Perceived by HRD Professionals," *Performance Improvement Quarterly*, 5:1 (1992), pp. 49–69.
39. M. Lombardo and R. Eichinger, *Eighty-Eight Assignments for Development in Place: Enhancing the Developmental Challenge of Existing Jobs* (Greensboro, N.C.: Center for Creative Leadership, 1989).

Chapter 8

1. Charles Watson, *Management Development Through Training* (Reading, Mass.: Addison-Wesley, 1979).
2. Anthony Carnevale and Leila Gainer, *The Learning Enterprise* (Alexandria, Va.: American Society for Training and Development and U.S. Department of Labor, Employment and Training Administration, 1989), p. 25.
3. William J. Rothwell and H. C. Kazanas, "Structured On-The-Job Training (SOJT) as Perceived by HRD Professionals," *Performance Improvement Quarterly*, 3:3 (1990), p. 21.
4. Ibid.
5. M. Wichman, "On the Job Training: Formalizing Informality OR Shouldn't Supervisors Do the Training?" *Performance and Instruction*, 28:1 (1989), pp. 31–32.
6. Ibid.
7. William J. Rothwell and H. J. Sredl, *The ASTD Reference Guide to Professional HRD Roles and Competencies*, 2nd ed. (Amherst, Mass.: Human Resource Development Press, 1992).
8. *American Heritage Dictionary*, 2nd college ed., p. 285.
9. See, for instance, S. Cunningham, "Coaching Today's Executive," *Public Utilities*

Fortnightly, 128:2 (1991), pp. 22–25; Steven J. Stowell and Matt Starcevich, _The Coach: Creating Partnerships for a Competitive Edge_ (Salt Lake City, Utah: Center for Management and Organization Effectiveness, 1987).

10. K. Blanchard and S. Johnson, _The One Minute Manager: The Quickest Way to Increase Your Productivity_ (New York: Berkeley, 1981).

11. Elizabeth Alleman and William A. Gray, _Design Productive Mentoring Programs_ (Alexandria, Va.: American Society for Training and Development, 1986); K. Kram, _Mentoring at Work_ (Glenview, Ill.: Scott-Foresman, 1985).

12. Mary Cunningham, _Powerplay—What Really Happened at Bendix_ (New York: Ballantine, 1989); Belle Rose Ragins, "Barriers to Mentoring: The Female Manager's Dilemma," _Human Relations,_ 42:1 (1989), pp. 1–22.

13. Cyril O. Houle, _The Inquiring Mind_ (Madison, Wis.: University of Wisconsin Press, 1961).

14. Allen Tough, _The Adult's Learning Projects_, 2nd ed. (Toronto: Ontario Institute for Studies in Education, 1979), p. 6.

15. Ibid., p. 1.

16. David A. Kolb, _Experiential Learning: Experience as a Source of Learning and Development_ (Englewood Cliffs, N.J.: Prentice-Hall, 1984).

Chapter 9

1. Paul F. Buller, John R. Cragun, and Glenn M. McEvoy, "Getting the Most Out of Outdoor Training," _Training and Development Journal,_ 45:3 (1991), p. 58.

2. Judy Springer and Jack Thomas, "An Experiment in Individual Leadership Development," _Performance and Instruction_, 31:2 (1992), pp. 44–48.

3. Mark Lipton, "New Age Organizational Training: Tapping Employee Potential or Creating New Problems?" _Human Resources Professional_, 3:2 (1991), pp. 72–76.

4. John Storey, "Management Development: A Literature Review and Implications for Future Research," _Personnel Review_, 18:6 (1989), pp. 13–19.

5. Wendell L. French, "Organization Development: Objectives, Assumptions, and Strategies," _California Management Review_, 12:2 (1969), p. 26.

6. A. Van Gundy, _Techniques of Structured Problem Solving_ (New York: Van Nostrand Reinhold, 1981).

Chapter 10

1. Donald Kirkpatrick, "Techniques for Evaluating Training Programs," _Journal of the American Society for Training and Development_ [now _Training and Development_], 14:1 (1960), pp. 13–18.

2. Martin Smith and Dale Brandenburg, "Summative Evaluation," _Performance Improvement Quarterly_, 4:2 (1991), pp. 35–58.

3. Kirkpatrick, op. cit., pp. 13–18.

4. _Management Development Survey Report_ (Alexandria, Va.: American Society for Training and Development, 1992), p. 2.

5. Dennis R. Laker, "Dual Dimensionality of Training Transfer," _Human Resource Development Quarterly_, 1:3 (1990), pp. 209–224.

6. D. Georgenson, "The Problem of Transfer Calls for Partnership," _Training and Development_, 36:10 (1982), pp. 75–78.

7. Patricia McLagan, _Models for HRD Practice_ (Alexandria, Va.: American Society for Training and Development, 1989).

8. Chris Argyris, "Some Unintended Consequences of Rigorous Research," _Psychological Bulletin_, 70 (1968), pp. 185–197; A. Armenakis, A. Bedeian, and S. Pond III, "Research Issues in OD Evaluation: Past, Present, and Future," _Academy of Management Review_, 8 (1983), pp. 320–328.

Epilogue

1. Cecil G. Howard, "Profile of the 21st-Century Expatriate Manager," *HR Magazine*, 37:6 (1992), p. 94.
2. David Ricks and Vijay Mahajan, "Blunders in International Marketing: Fact or Fiction," *Long-Range Planning* (February 1984), p. 78.
3. Patricia Howard, "Worldshrink," *HRMagazine*, 36:1 (1991), pp. 42–43.
4. Peter F. Drucker, *The New Realities in Government and Politics/In Economics and Business/In Society and World View* (New York: Harper & Row, 1989).
5. Beverly Geber, "The Care and Breeding of Global Managers," *Training*, 29:7 (1992), p. 32.
6. Peter F. Drucker, "Learning From Foreign Management," *The Wall Street Journal*, June 4, 1980, p. 1.
7. Patricia Howard, op. cit., p. 43.
8. Ibid.
9. Geber, op. cit., p. 32.
10. Stephen H. Rhinesmith, "Going Global From the Inside Out," *Training and Development*, 45:11 (1991), p. 46. Used by permission of *Training and Development* and the American Society for Training and Development.
11. Chris Lee, "After the Cuts," *Training*, 29:7 (1992), p. 18.
12. S. Overman, "The Layoff Legacy," *HRMagazine*, 36:8 (1991), p. 29.
13. Reed E. Nelson, "Common Sense Staff Reduction," *Personnel Journal*, 67:8 (1988), p. 50.
14. Max Messmer, "Right-Sizing Reshapes Staffing Strategies," *HRMagazine*, 36:10 (1991), p. 60.
15. "Moonlighting Madness," *Personnel Journal*, 71:6 (1992), p. 18.
16. Lee, op. cit., p. 19.
17. Ibid., p. 20.
18. Ibid.
19. William J. Rothwell, "Ten Strategies for Rethinking How Work Is Performed After Downsizing," *Performance and Instruction*, in press.
20. Jack Gordon, "Training Budgets: Recession Takes a Bite 1991," *Training*, 28:10 (1991), p. 38.
21. Richard S. Wellins, William C. Byham, and Jeanne M. Wilson, *Empowered Teams: Creating Self-Directed Work Groups That Improve Quality, Productivity, and Participation* (San Francisco: Jossey-Bass, 1991), p. 3.
22. Beverly Geber, "Managers Are A Changin'," *Training*, 29:7 (1992), p. 73.

Index